The "Man" Question in International Relations

The "Man" Question in International Relations

edited by

Marysia Zalewski
University of Wales, Aberystwyth

Jane Parpart
Dalhousie University

 WestviewPress
A Division of HarperCollins*Publishers*

Copyright © 1998 by Westview Press, A Division of HarperCollins Publishers, Inc.

Published in 1998 in the United States of America by Westview Press, 5500 Central Avenue, Boulder, Colorado 80301-2877, and in the United Kingdom by Westview Press, 12 Hid's Copse Road, Cumnor Hill, Oxford OX2 9JJ

Library of Congress Cataloging-in-Publication Data
The "man" question in international relations / edited by Marysia Zalewski and Jane Parpart.
    p.   cm.
Includes bibliographical references and index.
ISBN 0-8133-2395-9 (cloth). — ISBN 0-8133-2396-7 (pbk.).
1. International relations—Psychological aspects.
2. Masculinity—Political aspects.   3. Feminism.   4. Feminist theory.   I. Zalewski, Marysia.   II. Parpart, Jane L.
JZ1253.2.M36   1998
327.1'01—dc21   97-25242
                                                                        CIP

The paper used in this publication meets the requirements of the American National Standard for Permanence of Paper for Printed Library Materials Z39.48-1984.

10   9   8   7   6   5   4   3   2   1

Contents

Acknowledgments

It can be very difficult coediting a book across continents; perhaps our first thanks should go to email! However, we do have humans to thank as well—first our contributors for their patience as well as their chapters. A special thanks to some who stretched their imaginations to incorporate "the personal is political" in new ways. We also want to thank the editors who have variously overseen this project: Jennifer Knerr, Brenda Hadenfeld, and Adina Popescu. They have been patient and supportive throughout. Both of us are very grateful for the presence of the Feminist Theory and Gender Section of the International Studies Association. The support of the people in this group is an absolute necessity, and it has enriched both of us personally and professionally.

Marysia would also like to thank the gender working group of the British International Studies Association and the individuals who have been very important over the years in which this book has developed: Cynthia Enloe, Jill Steans, Marianne Marchand, Spike Peterson, Jan Jindy Pettman, J. Ann Tickner, Gillian Youngs, and Cynthia Weber. Marysia would also like to thank Jane Parpart for getting this project started, for her support and friendship (and patience!), and for being the diplomatic one. Jane would like to thank all of the above (excluding herself), particularly Marysia for carrying the load on this book when Jane was preoccupied with other work. She would also like to thank the Postcolonial/Postmodern Reading Group at Dalhousie for agreeing to discuss masculinity(ies) for endless sessions; Blye Frank for his collection and insights; and Dorothy Hodgson, Lily Ling, and Rob Morrell, whose work on masculinity has inspired some of her own thinking. Finally, but definitely not least, Marysia would like to thank her children, Tessa and Laura, for just accepting what she does, and Cindy Weber for being Cindy. Jane would like to thank her husband, Tim Shaw, and her children, Laura, Lee, Ben, and Amanda, for putting up with her preoccupation with this and other projects. They make life worth living.

Marysia Zalewski
Jane Parpart

Introduction: From the "Woman" Question to the "Man" Question in International Relations

Marysia Zalewski

A man and a woman are talking over dinner in a restaurant. The man tells the woman about his life and finally says, "OK, that's enough about me. Let's talk about you. What do you think about me?"

This is *not* a book simply about men in international relations. This is a book about masculinities in international relations.

This is a book that is informed and inspired by feminist questions. And it is a book that has moved from asking the "woman" question to asking the "man" question. We do not assume that women are a problem to be solved. Instead we want to problematize masculinities, the hegemony of men, and the subject of man within the theories and practices of international relations.

International Relations as a Man's World

It seems obvious, even natural, to think about international relations as a man's world. The world's militaries are mostly populated by men, especially in the combat and senior ranks. The majority of state decisionmakers are men. Women appear to be largely absent from these arenas of "high politics." And with regard to one of the most central topics in international relations—war—one general's view is that

> war is a man's work. Biological convergence on the battlefield [women serving in combat] would not only be dissatisfying in terms of what women could do, but it would be an enormous psychological distraction for the male, who wants to think that he's fighting for that woman somewhere behind, not up there in the same foxhole with him. It tramples the male ego. When you get right down to it, you have to protect the manhood of war.[1]

Beliefs about gender, what it means to be a "real" man or a "real" woman are clearly evident in the general's words. Such beliefs are commonplace in international relations and find their way in through images, metaphors, and symbols of masculinity, femininity, and sexuality. "Weak" states and statesmen are often defined as feminine. For example, during the Carter administration, it was said that "under Jimmy Carter the United States is spreading its legs for the Soviet Union."[2] How are we to think about these evocations and representations of men, women, gender, and sexuality? What are their effects on international relations as a field of study and practice?

One way that we, the editors of this volume and academics interested in gender, sought to tackle these evocations and representations was to join in the efforts to engender the field of international relations. Inspired by feminist analysis, we initially tried to highlight the absence of women in the field as well as the power and dominance of men. However, we began to question those traditional feminist methods; the result of that questioning has led to this volume, which represents an attempt to problematize the subjectivities of men, the subject of man, and the effects of masculinities in international relations. It also led to a series of questions about the effects and implications of apparently opposing feminist strategies to engender the field. This introduction explores what all of this means and how we got from the "woman" question to the "man" question.

The Personal Is Political—Or Is It?

Uncomfortable questions surround the phenomenon of men "doing feminism" in international relations. The idea for this book was partly sparked at the 1992 International Studies Association (ISA) conference in a panel on feminism. The questions following the panel revolved around the politics of men doing feminism and the relationship of men and masculinity to the theory and practice of international relations. One male panelist puzzled over the abilities and motivations of male scholars participating on such a panel; a male audience member commented that although he was committed to feminist politics in his personal life, he could not see the connection with his work as an international relations scholar. Is the personal so unconnected to the professional? Why are men asking these questions of themselves? What are the implications for our understanding of the gendered character of international relations?

We asked several men and women to write papers for a panel tentatively titled "Masculinity, Feminism and Power in International Relations" to be presented at the 1993 ISA conference. As editors we were plagued with still more questions. Should we be suspicious of men's desires to get involved in feminist analysis? What were their motivations? Conversely, could we persuade men to take feminist work seriously by involving them in it? Might this involvement lead them to realize that *their* personal is political? How would we go about exposing the overwhelming masculinity and maleness of the discipline and practice of international relations in a way that encouraged insights into the effects of this domination, especially with regard to power and privilege? In what way would such exposure work to assist feminist projects?

What's in a Title?

What's in a title? The short answer is "a lot." This volume has had several titles since its genesis, and the changes reflect some of the shifts in our thinking.

There are many ways of doing feminism or being a feminist, and heated debates have recently marked Western feminist discourse. To simplify, the debates in the 1960s and 1970s coalesced around the question of which theory was the most adequate or appropriate to deliver women's equality and liberation.[3] In the 1980s and 1990s the debate shifted focus somewhat to one centering on the value of modernist versus postmodernist feminisms, the latter emphasizing culture and language. A crucial point of difference between the two revolved around the centrality of the traditional subject of feminism—woman—leading many modernist feminists to accuse postmodernist feminisms of being incapable of politics. Simply put, the postmodernist deconstruction of the subject woman was deemed to annihilate the basis for feminist political action:

> The postmodernist project, if seriously adopted by feminists, would make any semblance of feminist politics impossible. To the extent that feminist politics is bound up with a specific constituency or subject, namely, women, the postmodernist prohibition against subject-centred inquiry and theory undermines the legitimacy of a broad-based organized movement dedicated to articulating and implementing the goals of such a constituency.[4]

This debate raises many of the same questions and issues that occur in some of the debates about how to engender international relations. Does engendering international relations simply mean incorporating women? Or does it involve revealing that women are already part of the field of study and thus extending the agenda to highlight the activities of women?

Engendering the study and practice of international relations is often linked by feminists to the modernist feminist project of eventually achieving the equality and liberation of women. But does the deconstruction of woman and the postmodern suspicion about modernist, emancipatory projects imply that incorporating and exposing women's activities is a doomed enterprise? And more pertinent, surely the analysis of gender demands that attention be paid to men and masculinity as well as to women and femininity. What is the best way to engender international relations?

In an early discussion about the relationship between feminist theories and international relations, Barrie Thorne, a sociologist, posed a similar question:

> Will the relatively "late" acknowledgement of feminist scholarship in international relations permit it to "leap-frog" the tortuous phases and proceed from current feminist insights? Or does the progression from "add women and stir," to "including women as objects," to recognizing the theoretical implications of "including women as subjects" have to be replayed in every discipline? Perhaps even by each practitioner?[5]

Whether we can consider the move from "adding women and stirring" to "including women as objects" to recognizing the implications of "including women as subjects" as evidence of progression is a moot point and is considered later. Various feminist strategies have been replayed in the development of this volume, perhaps alongside a certain amount of leap-frogging with regard to engendering international relations. The original title of this volume was *Women, Men, and Power: Engendering International Relations*. One might argue that problematizing men and masculinity in the form of the "man" question signifies a theoretical journey or process paralleling the feminist modernist versus feminist postmodernist debate. I will briefly discuss the metamorphosing titles of this volume in order to explain what I mean.

Women, Men, and Power: Engendering International Relations

In this first title we were intent on placing women center stage, believing that women had been consistently marginalized. We also wanted to expose the fact that men had power in the discipline and practice of international relations both personally and institutionally—and we wanted men to address this issue. We wanted to insist that the field was in need of engendering—taking gender seriously, examining sexist bias within the discipline, and exposing male power, especially in the form of "academic machismo." We were explicitly drawing upon that classic feminist principle "the personal is political," particularly with regard to the power of men. We did not want to analyze masculinity just at an abstract or purely theoretical level but at micropersonal levels.

We were unprepared for the difficulties some of the male contributors initially had writing their chapters. This had less to do with the usual academic pressures and more to do with epistemological angst and personal reluctance. Perhaps we were asking too much of the male scholars, expecting them to delve deeply into their personal behaviors or to think about how being a man had anything to do with the theories and practices of international relations. Exposing the constructed, but effective, character of masculine hegemony in international relations proved for some to be very uncomfortable.

We assumed that because men predominated in international relations they automatically had power (in a pre-Foucaultian sense of possessing power) and that they could or would confront this power in more than superficial or defensive ways. We thought that one way to assist the achievement of the project of women's equality and liberation would be to expose this power and at the same time try to find out what sort of patriarchal mechanisms were being employed to limit women's participation and visibility in the field of international relations. It's not that we thought each individual man was plotting to "keep women down." Rather, we wanted men to ask Arthur Brittan's questions: "As a man, am I responsible for patriarchy? Am I responsible for all men? As an author of a text on masculinity am I merely trying to assuage my own guilt?"[6] So if we were looking for (radical) mechanisms for feminist interventions to facilitate a gendered transformation of international relations, we assumed these would be rather traditional feminist ones whereby women's visibility was raised and men's collusion (intended or not) in the patriarchal order was exposed and confronted.

Women, Masculinity, and Power in International Relations

This second title retained the centrality of women, but we moved away from men as a category to masculinity. Why? Partly because of questions such as Which men? All men? Is it *men* or *masculinity* that is "the problem"? We could not include all men or even use the category—though we clearly wanted to retain the category of "women"—but we still wanted to address masculinity in all its variations and its relationship with power in the context of international relations. As such, our underlying views about what it would take to engender international relations were the same as with the first title, but we now had a more nuanced approach to male power.

Feminism, Masculinity, and Power in International Relations: Theory and Practice

Here we dropped the category of "women" but insisted on signifying the *feminist* impulse of the book. The addition of the qualifying words *theory* and *practice* indicated a connection between the theory of international relations and the practice of it—the latter including the practice of the discipline (conferences, seminars, teaching) and the practices of world politics.

Masculinity and Power in
International Relations: Theories and Practices

We moved from wanting to explicitly highlight the "categories" of women and feminism to accepting that their presence is implicit in any perusal of the gendered category of masculinity.

The "Man" Question in International Relations

The final title of the book was inspired by Kathy Ferguson's *The Man Question: Visions of Subjectivity in Feminist Theory.* As Ferguson suggests, asking the "woman" question reinforces the framework of woman as problem and male as norm. One of the ironies of the "woman" question is that women tend to disappear from the center to become troublesome mysteries, exemplified by Freud's question "What do women want?"[7] Renaming the book *The "Man" Question* signaled our desire not to construct woman as a problem but to highlight the ways in which masculinities are implicated in international relations theories and practices.

Feminist Strategies to
Engender International Relations

In moving from *Women, Men, and Power: Engendering International Relations* to *The "Man" Question in International Relations,* we had decided on a change in strategies to engender, or rather expose gender, in international relations (IR). One of our initial strategies—drawing men into the field of gender and international relations to confront their own masculinities—had proved difficult if not always completely insurmountable. But this strategy continued to generate questions. What are the implications of men doing feminism? The motives of individual men are, of course, different. One man suggested that it was very pleasurable to be working with women because it was so subversive—it made the male establishment feel uncomfortable.[8] As for the implications, often they may be at odds with the stated motives. For example, when Robert Keohane wrote about the utility of the feminist standpoint for international relations versus the inadequacies of feminist empiricism and feminist postmodernism, did he really believe he was "joining in the feminist conversation"? Cynthia Weber suggests that he was instead "mutilating the feminist body."[9]

Why is it that men need a special reason to study gender and IR? The reasons women do feminism or even do not do feminism are clearly varied, but at some level the need for these explanations seems less crucial than for those men who do feminism. Some of the suggested reasons for men "doing gender and international relations" are that they feel guilty,[10] are actual or latent homosexuals,[11] are using a phallocentric counterstrategy,[12] are paranoid,[13] or have a feminist wife or partner.[14] Drawing men into the engendering of international relations has resulted in the discovery of certain gendered implications about the different ways work (especially work that is seen to be overtly ideological) is received and perceived, implications that are dependent on the gender of the individual doing the work.[15]

The reformulated title might prompt readers to ask the question Tania Modleski poses in *Feminism Without Women*: "What's in this for feminism and women"?[16] Modleski argues that the focus on masculinity represents an unwanted move away from the "feminist project and the aid it can give us in illuminating the causes, effects, scope and limits of male dominance."[17] She labels books such as Alice Jardine and Paul Smith's *Men in Feminism* "postfeminist" because they return men to center stage while tacitly assuming and promoting the liberal notion that men and women are equal and their viewpoints are structurally accorded equal weight. The Modleski position that focusing on masculinity is detrimental to the feminist project and the Ferguson position that focusing on women promotes the perception of woman as problem represent two rather different ways of interpreting feminist politics and (though I don't want to push the comparison too far) mirror the project's underlying intellectual debates.

The project's starting point revealed a faith in the modernist commitment to the political importance of bringing women into the position of subjecthood. We implicitly accepted that women's subjecthood could be exposed and revealed in the study and practice of international relations, hoping that this would also reveal the nature of male dominance and power. Posing the "man" question instead reflects our diminishing belief that the exclusion of women can be remedied by converting them into subjects. As Susan Hekman articulates this view, "Postmodernist feminists may well agree that with the ascendancy of the Cartesian subject women have been systematically excluded from the realm of subjectivity: this exclusion cannot be remedied by converting women into Cartesian subjects, but, rather, this definition of the subject must be rejected."[18]

Of course the issues are never quite so clear cut. The feminist modernist project of focusing on women, placing women at the center, can paradoxically highlight the fluidity of the subject of woman rather than revealing the solidity of her position, however illusory. The presence of female state leaders can expose both the centrality of women in international relations and the uneasiness and ambiguity surrounding issues of gender. Margaret Thatcher was often represented both as a man in drag and as a woman using her "feminine charms" to flirt with male world leaders. But highlighting the presumed subjectivity of women in international relations has not appeared to destabilize the field. International relations is still very much a man's world. So instead of trying to assert an illusory Cartesian subject position for women, this volume questions and problematizes the sub-jecthood of man. If the subject of international relations is constructed around men and masculinity, then perhaps destabilizing the subject of "man" will help to destabilize the whole field in ways that "adding women and stirring" has not seemed to. Asking the "man" question problematizes men's subject position in international relations. This leads us to ask questions about the roles of masculinity in the conduct of international relations and to question the accepted naturalness of the abundance of men in the theory and practice of international relations.

In order to start this conversation about men and masculinities in international relations, Spike Peterson and Jacqui True suggest in Chapter 1 that our current global context is one of new times that demand new thinking. Peterson and True argue that the radical feminist insight that the personal is political transgresses *the* definitive political boundary highlighting the fact that our understanding of power is mystified because of the perceived divide between public and private. Claiming that this entrenched divide is supported by hegemonic masculinity, Peterson and True outline the mascu-line/feminine dichotomy as a fundamental structural feature of social life.

In Chapter 2, Charlotte Hooper delves deeper into masculinist practices in international relations, pointing out that writing about men may reinforce the marginalization of women. If the overall balance of feminist scholarship is women-centered, however, this effect can be mitigated. Hooper suggests that international relations is a primary site for the production of masculinities, the masculinized spheres of war and diplomacy being situated at the furthest extreme from the private sphere of families, women, and reproduction. She traverses between an analysis that resists attempts to fix the meanings around masculinity and a recognition that there are collective inequalities between men and women. She suggests that using the concepts of hegemonic and subordinate masculinities is a useful device, allowing for the recognition of fluidity in the construction of masculinities without causing us to lose our sense of the relationship between masculinity, power, and women's subordination.

Steve Smith discusses in Chapter 3 the reaction to feminist and gender work in the discipline of international relations, analyzing two aspects of the "man" question in international relations and the kinds of men and masculinities produced within the discipline and practice of the subject of international relations. The male position of privilege, he claims, does not necessarily provide an epistemological advantage for males reflecting on masculinity and international relations. He argues that important feminist contributions have either been ignored or incorporated with minimal understanding, suggesting that for many male academics, feminist work poses a threat. He also suggests a probable deep incompatibility between feminist work and international relations. One of Smith's conclusions is that a focus on masculinity is likely to prove even more threatening than work that seemingly concentrates only on women.

Lucian Ashworth and Larry Swatuk open Chapter 4 with a news story of a woman severing her husband's penis. They link the loss of such a potent symbol of masculinity with fears of emasculation in mainstream international relations theory. They suggest that although realism and liberalism define themselves in opposition to each other, they have a mutual disdain of dominant Western conceptions of femininity. For realists, to be "idealist" is to be irrational (and therefore feminine). Liberals respond to the Western conception of femininity with masculinized appeals to science, rational analysis, and technological advance. Ashworth and Swatuk assert that the realist/liberal dispute, rather than being a logical argument between objective paradigms, can be seen as a dispute between two different conceptions of the masculine world. Both sides present the other as not "properly" masculine—realism's *hypermasculinity* standing in defiance of liberal *rational masculinity*.

In Chapter 5, Craig Murphy asks why most male scholars are consumers rather than producers of gendered research programs. Murphy looks at six masculine roles in world politics that are drawn not from conventional social science data but from his own experiences growing up as the son of a career serviceman in the U.S. Air Force during the Cold War. He identifies these roles as the good soldier, the civilian strategist, the military son, the good comrade, the Sisyphean peacemaker, and the fashionable pacifist, tentatively concluding that the men in the field of international relations who identify with the Sisyphean peacemaker's role more than with the civilian strategist's role are more likely to be sympathetic to reflections on gender simply because the threat to their masculinity is not as great. But there is still a threat for the least "masculinized male" in international relations partly because, Murphy suggests, of a "deep fear of looking too closely at the microstructuring of masculinity." The assault on masculine identity implied by feminist analysis may be one explanation—if not an excuse—for the reluctance of many men to consider gender as central to their own understanding of international relations.

Chapters 6, 7, and 8 move to an analysis of masculinities in the practical realm. Although these chapters are collectively limited in their shared focus on the U.S. military, each chapter serves as a distinct example of how to ask the "man" question in an empirical context. Steve Niva explicitly asks the "man" question in the context of the Gulf War and the new world order. He remarks that it may seem redundant to emphasize that the Gulf War was largely a man's war and that it is exceedingly difficult to recognize men as gendered subjects in international politics. This difficulty, he argues, is symptomatic of a broader impoverishment of political discourse about international politics and warfare. Redressing this impoverishment, Niva looks at both the Vietnam War and the Gulf War, claiming that the American defeat in the former generated a crisis that made explicit the links between foreign policy and particular conceptions of masculinity that in turn significantly assaulted dominant paradigms of American manhood. In an attempt to heal the wounds of damaged masculinity, American culture remasculinized itself into a situation in which the slogan "no more Vietnams" was transformed from its "feminized" meaning of opposition to military involvement to an aggressively "masculinized" and Ramboesque position epitomized by the question Do we get to win it this time? Illustrating the changing form of masculinities, Niva suggests that perhaps the most important element of "new-world-order masculinity" is its slight feminization through the construction of a tough and aggressive yet tenderhearted masculinity. Pitted against the construction of a hypermacho Saddam Hussein, the new U.S. hegemonic masculinity combines toughness, in the form of a resolve to "win this time," but also tenderness, especially in the form of representing the United States as civilized in comparison to the barbaric Iraqis.

In Chapter 7, Carol Cohn looks at the furor surrounding attempts to lift the ban on gays in the U.S. military. One of her central arguments is that the possibility that the military could appear as anything other than a masculine heterosexual institution is fundamentally upsetting. If the military functions as a central guarantor and producer of masculinity in society, then any threat to the military's masculinity will be resisted. Cohn suggests that having "out" male homosexuals in the military is seen to severely dent its masculine character. Why is there so much emotional intensity about this issue? Who or what is being protected by having closeted gays in the military? She argues that it is not gays who are being protected but the appearance of the heterosexual masculinity of the institution itself.

In Chapter 8, Cynthia Weber offers a symptomatic reading of the U.S. invasion of Panama. In "Something's Missing," Weber reads two of the major actors in the Panama invasion—General Manuel Noriega and President George Bush—first as hysterical males (men uncoded as men) and then as feminized males (men recoded as women). Weber claims that both the recoding of these actors and the Bush administration's invasion strategy invite a deconstruction of two ubiquitous dichotomies in international relations discourse—domestic politics/international politics and domestic = feminine/international = masculine. Aware that her readings of the U.S. presidency and military intervention might be interpreted as profane, Weber argues that she focuses on aspects of the invasion that are analytically neglected and that enable atrocities to occur.

Ralph Pettman, in Chapter 9, asks, "Why do players try so hard to win?"—a question that occurs to him in the context of a "private" discussion about a soccer match. This is a deliberate attempt to include something—a personal anecdote—that is deemed unacceptable by positivist ana-lysts. But for Pettman, such stories are necessary to account for world affairs. Musing on the connections among masculinity, positivist objectiv-ity, and manipulation of readers, Pettman questions the notion that there are only two sexes. He argues that there are at least five sexes despite attempts to enforce a conformity to one or the other of the preferred forms. He concludes that a combinant sexuality such as the hermaphrodite might be advantageous to the human species. But the constant attempt to elimi-nate hermaphrodites shows how much of an imposition gender is—from sexing bodies to controlling people's behavior. International politicians, Pettman asserts, are also involved in the "gendering game" in perpetuating a particularly assertive form of masculinism. Most international politicians, he claims, are highly assertive males who take for granted the global desir-ability of assertive masculinism. Pettman suggests less assertive or non-assertive possibilities—the grail of positive collaboration. Admitting that the grail may be impossible to attain, he claims that what is achieved in the process of trying to attain such a grail is what matters.

In Chapter 10, Christine Sylvester takes us on a poetic and eclectic jour-ney through the discourses surrounding "masculinity" and "femininity" in international relations. Following Judith Butler, Sylvester asserts that gen-der is performance and that international relations has been in the business of acting out the masculinizing and remasculinizing of certain relations for seventy-five years. The masculinities within international relations may be sometimes strutting, sometimes limpid, but they are always stalking. Sylvester quotes feminist writers in international relations who unequivo-cally want to "find the place" of men and women in the field—Enloe, Tickner. But Sylvester tangentially cautions against such sure positions. Gender is confusing rather than certain for Sylvester. Greenham women, Kennedy women, men and women who "go to the moon," are all used to show the slipperiness of what gender is and is not.

Conclusion: Theoretical Progression?

Does the move from the "woman" question to the "man" question imply a progression? The comments made by Barrie Thorne in 1989, mentioned earlier, indicate that the move from "adding women and stirring" to "including women as objects" to considering the theoretical implications of including "women as subjects" was a form of progression. Is moving to the "man" question the fourth stage in this typology? Some feminist postmod-ern approaches would (paradoxically) imply that the move is evidence of progression.[19] But feminist approaches that remain loyal to an emancipa-tory feminism based on the subject of woman would stress the importance of keeping men out of the center of feminist analysis and insist on the insertion of women as subjects and objects. The move to the "man" question, for them, is full of regressive tendencies, as Tania Modleski has suggested. In this introduction I have tried to set out what is at stake for these two approaches in the specific context of engendering international relations. Clearly, in our decision to call the book *The "Man" Question,* we believed that we could air these issues in rather different ways than placing women center stage allows. But I would hesitate before assuming that the move is evidence of progression if progression means the previous strategies are mostly useless or outdated. Such an assumption would reduce the signifi- cance of the varied and necessary array of feminist strategies that in differ- ent ways confront the masculinity of the discipline of international rela- tions. For me, moving from the "woman" question to the "man" question represents not a progression but a change in tactics.

In the specific context of the discipline of international relations, the sta- sis created by its masculinist and neopositivist epistemological and onto- logical commitments has confounded many attempts to expose the gen- dered character of the subject of man and the subject of international relations. Questioning the unquestionable—the stable subject position of man in international relations—provides another strategy of resisting and breaking through that stasis.

Notes

1. Comments made by General Robert H. Barrow, commander of the U.S. Marines until 1983. Quoted in Nancy C. Hartsock, "Masculinity, Heroism and War," in A. Harris and Y. King, eds., *Rocking the Ship of State* (Boulder and Lon- don: Westview Press, 1989), p. 134.

2. Quoted in Carol Cohn, "Wars, Wimps and Women," in M. Cooke and A. Wolla- cott, eds., *Gendering War Talk* (Princeton: Princeton University Press, 1993), p. 236.

3. A classic example of this approach is Alison M. Jaggar, *Feminist Politics and Human Nature* (Brighton: Harvester Wheatsheaf, 1983). Jaggar makes the claim that "socialist feminism is the most adequate of the feminist theories formulated to date" (p. 9).

4. Christine Di Stefano, "Dilemmas of Difference," in Linda J. Nicholson, ed., *Feminism/Postmodernism* (London: Routledge, 1990), p. 76.

5. Barrie Thorne's comments were made at a conference exploring the integra- tions of feminist theory and international relations theory held at the Center for International Studies, University of Southern California, April 28 and 29, 1989. The quote is from V. Spike Peterson's report on the conference entitled "Woman, The State and War: What Difference Does Gender Make?" unpublished manuscript, Los Angeles, 1989, p. 20.

6. Arthur Brittan, *Masculinity and Power* (Oxford: Basil Blackwell, 1989), p. 200.

7. Ibid., p. 7.

8. Alice Jardine and Paul Smith, "A Conversation," in Jardine and Smith, *Men in Feminism* (London: Routledge, 1987), p. 262.

9. Cynthia Weber, "Good Girls, Little Girls and Bad Girls: Male Paranoia in Robert Keohane's Critique of Feminist International Relations," *Millennium* 23, 2 (1994), pp. 337–349.

10. Caroline Ramazanoglu, "What Can You Do with a Man?" *Women's Studies International Forum* 15, 3 (1992), p. 339.

11. Collinson and Hearn, "Naming Men as Men: Implications for Work, Organization and Management," *Gender, Work and Organisation* 1, 1 (1994), pp. 2–22.

12. Elizabeth Gross, "What Is Feminist Theory," in C. Pateman and E. Gross, *Feminist Challenges* (Sydney: Allen and Unwin, 1986), p 197. Gross was not specifically talking about IR, but the point is relevant.

13. Weber, "Good Girls, Little Girls and Bad Girls," pp. 337–349.

14. Ulterior motives are often suggested for men doing feminism in international relations. Mark Neufeld told a revealing anecdote about his journey to the 1995 ISA conference in Chicago. On the bus from the airport he was asked by a senior male professor (he wouldn't reveal the name!) what he was doing at the conference. When Mark said his first appearance was as discussant on a feminist panel, he was asked, "What's in it for you?" Apparently the senior male professor could not understand that there might be intellectual reasons for Mark's interest in this work. Some other motive was implicated.

15. See also Cary Nelson, "Men, Feminism: The Materiality of Discourse," in Jardine and Smith, *Men in Feminism*, p. 170.

16. Tania Modleski, *Feminism Without Women: Culture and Criticism in a "Postfeminist" Age* (London: Routledge, 1991), p. 5.

17. Ibid., p. 5.

18. Susan Hekman, *Gender and Knowledge: Elements of a Postmodern Feminism* (London: Polity Press, 1990), p. 79.

19. I say "paradoxically" because postmodern approaches tend toward incredulity at stories of linear progression. However, such implications exist in the work of some feminist postmodernists (though they deny they are telling a story of progression), but they do comment on the contemporary virtual uselessness of liberal, radical, and socialist feminisms (see the introduction and the chapter by Moira Gatens in Michele Barrett and Anne Phillips, eds., *Destabilizing Theory: Contemporary Feminist Debates* [Oxford, Polity Press, 1992]).

1

"New Times" and New Conversations

V. Spike Peterson and Jacqui True

Theory is always for someone and for some purpose. All theories have a perspective. Perspectives derive from a position in time and space, specifically social and political time and space.[1]

Many perspectives frame theoretical debates in international relations (IR): realism, neorealism, critiques of these mainstream IR theories, and feminism. These perspectives, as the above quotation from Robert Cox reminds us, derive from particular social contexts and relations of power. Our current global context is one of "new times": interacting and simultaneous sociocultural, economic, and political transformations that demand new perspectives, not least in how we theorize international relations.[2]

To talk of new times is not to suggest that we are living in a qualitatively different world undergoing swift and total transformation. It is, however, to speak of the dimensions of change that we are currently experiencing that cannot be understood through "old" theoretical paradigms such as Marxism, liberalism, positivism, or (neo)realism. It is to rethink the relations between individuals and contemporary economic, political, and sociocultural structures in terms of their multilevel, multisource variables and their dynamics of change.

With the authors of *New Times*, we acknowledge that looking for the new amid old and unsolved problems and contradictions is a contestable endeavor. Nevertheless, *New Times* is also an invitation to join in conversation concerns that are all too often dealt with individually. By situating various international relations perspectives in the context of new times, we hope to facilitate old conversations—conversations that include many voices[3] and permit more illumination of today's relationships and realities.

In particular, the purpose of this chapter is to broaden the conversation of international relations to include its simultaneous reliance on and refusal to theorize hegemonic masculinities. Contemporary international relations theory must address not only how power politics shapes the world we live in but also how masculinist subjectivities, symbols, and structures shape power politics. By focusing on feminist contributions to and interventions in the field of international relations, we expose some of the dichotomous processes through which hegemonic masculinities operate in the field as well as introduce new dialogues into the field for these new times.

Feminist Contributions and Transformations

Feminists have offered important critiques of IR theories. However, there is no one feminism, no single approach to the construction of feminist theory. Contemporary feminisms analyze not only patterns of difference constituted by the dichotomies of maleness and femaleness but also patterns of differences among women. In Catherine Stimpson's words, "Every woman is more than a woman. She belongs, as well, to a class, a race, a nation, a family, a tribe, a time, a place."[4] This diversity among women poses tremendous challenges to feminist praxis, understood as interactive theory and practice oriented toward the objective of ending gender and related oppressions. Although there is no one feminism, feminist commitments to the transformation of structural oppressions generate a commonality of concerns or questions without specifying universal or totalizing solutions.

Initially, feminists worked within existing classification systems and explanatory frameworks. In discipline after discipline, their research exposed how truth claims were systemically distorted by androcentric (male as norm) bias.[5] This scholarship revealed both how actual women—and their ways of being and knowing—were excluded from conventional accounts and also how symbolic "woman" was constructed as deviant from or deficient in respect to male-as-norm criteria. Feminist scholars attempted to correct these accounts by "adding women"—by rendering them visible and by challenging the trivialization of symbolic "women." These studies were significant for documenting the extent and tenacity of androcentric bias and for expanding our range of inquiry through the inclusion of domestic activities and everyday practices.

But these studies also revealed that women could not simply be added to categories that are literally defined by their man-ness.[6] For example, the public sphere, economic power, and citizenship are not gender neutral. They presuppose categorically masculine traits (rationality, productivity, autonomy, agency) that are defined by their *exclusion* of feminine traits (irrationality, reproductivity, dependence, passivity). Insofar as adding women introduces the feminine, it contradicts the conventional meaning of these terms. Gender is thus not only a variable that can sometimes be "added" but also an analytic category with profound consequences for how we categorize, think about, and "know" the world.

Hence contemporary feminisms are not simply about adding women to conventional accounts in order to improve their accuracy by exposing and rectifying traditional male biases. Although this corrective project is valuable and necessary, feminist scholarship now extends well beyond this "add women and stir" approach. Wendy Brown captures the contemporary feminist perspective when she states, "Everything in the human world is a gendered construction."[7] By recognizing gender as an analytical category "within which humans think about and organize their social activity,"[8] feminists challenge structures of thought as well as structured practices. They argue that gender is not simply a dimension of individual subjectivity but a structural feature of social life.

Sandra Harding identifies three processes through which gendered social life is structured and (re)produced. Gender identity is "a form of socially constructed individual identity only imperfectly correlated with either the 'reality' or the perception of sex differences." Gender symbolism is "the result of assigning dualistic gender metaphors to various perceived dichotomies that rarely have anything to do with sex differences." Gender structure is "the consequence of appealing to these gender dualisms to organize social activity."[9] Although the particular referents for these aspects of gender vary cross-culturally, they are interrelated within any particular culture.

By reference to these three aspects, we gender not only our subjective but also our intersubjective and objective worlds. Thus Harding's interrelated aspects reveal the pervasiveness and potency of gender in structuring our world(s) and confirm the importance of "taking gender seriously" in our study of "reality." But if gender is so present and powerful, how has it been so effectively hidden in our study of social relations generally and international relations specifically? How have these multiple effects been rendered so invisible? We do not attempt a comprehensive answer in this chapter.[10] Rather, we focus specifically on how gender identities and dualisms interact to impede our willingness and ability to "see" gender and take its oppressive effects seriously.

In terms of individual identities, we are all truly "subjected" to gender-specific socialization. As a consequence, we do not act in or think about the world as abstract humans but as embodied, acculturated, therefore gendered, beings. Whatever other identities we simultaneously embrace and deem in particular situations to be most salient, gender is never wholly absent.[11] Gender infuses all of our identities so that race, age, class, ethnicity, ability, and nationality are also gender-specific identities: They have different meanings and typically constitute different experiences for those who see themselves as women or men. Moreover, gender identity is so entangled with sexual preference, presentation, and performance—all heavily freighted in contemporary culture—that issues of self-esteem come to the surface when issues of gender come to the table. In other words, as specific individuals, our sense of self-identity and security may seem disproportionately threatened by societal challenges to gender ordering.

Given our (conscious or otherwise) subjective investments in gender identity, we are more likely than not to resist critiques of gender hierarchy that implicitly destabilize our sense of self. In the absence of motivating forces (which take a variety of forms but under conditions of patriarchy are the exception, not the norm), it seems easier to ignore than to interrogate gender realities. After all, a great deal is at stake (e.g., conventional self-esteem, the naturalization of heterosexuality, emotional and cognitive maps of "reality"). Many people seem to sense how high the stakes are even as they avoid any conscious articulation of their own and societal dis-ease with the status quo.

At the same time, a smaller but not insignificant number of people *do* (presumably, in the presence of motivating forces) take action to expose and transform gender hierarchy. Yet even when motivation is in place, our understandable investment in gender identity constrains feminist movements. It is one kind of struggle to write letters in support of human rights, to recycle plastic in support of sustainable ecology, to organize voters in support of participatory democracy, or to engage in civil disobedience in support of pacifism. (And these are important activities!) But it is another kind of struggle to take responsibility for feminist politics in the bathroom, bedroom, nursery, and kitchen; to take responsibility for one's subjectivity and sexuality as well as one's public sphere activities. Later chapters in this book suggest multiple ways in which buried assumptions, gender dichotomies, and unquestioned stereotypes render this "other kind of struggle" very difficult indeed.

The radical feminist insight that the personal is political transgresses *the* definitive political boundary: the one that divides public from private and excludes the latter from what counts as politics. The concept of power is central to this division. By identifying the public with politics and politics with power relations, the division of public and private mystifies our understanding of power in several ways. First, hierarchical relations and exploitative labor within the household are associated with "natural" familial functions and thereby deemed nonpolitical and not power-laden. Second, focusing on the public sphere as specifically the domain of power relations constructs abuse of power within the family and household (incest, domestic violence, patriarchal control) as personal and therefore as not public or political. Third, the division masks the fact that public sphere power—manifested as economic productivity, military efficacy, or governmental potency—is not independent from but *depends upon* and *reinforces* the "proper" functioning of private sphere activities. In each case, the masculinity of the public sphere is privileged *at the expense* of feminine activities in the private sphere.

Broaching this fictitious but entrenched divide is intimidating enough from the vantage point of our investments in gender identity. Hegemonic masculinity especially is dependent on maintaining this separation insofar as masculine power in the public sphere is defined by the exclusion of feminine agents and values. But the more telling (though less frequently told) challenge emerges from the deeper implications of recognizing how this divide implicates numerous "others." To flesh out this claim, we take a critical look at the gender dichotomy of masculine-feminine and how it shapes a litany of dualisms—and oppressions—that are key to Western thought and practice.

Traditionally, politics has been a definitively masculine domain. Classical Athenian texts (and practice) reserved the public sphere for propertied men, a tradition continued well into the twentieth century.[12] In the modern era, the division of public and private spheres marked politics as an exclusively male activity requiring masculine characteristics of freedom, reason, autonomy, and disinterested objectivity. By contrast, women were relegated to the inferior private sphere of necessity, affect, dependence, and embodied subjectivity. This dichotomy of public and private, in Carol Pateman's words, "is, ultimately, what the feminist movement is about."[13]

As noted earlier, women cannot simply be "added" to categories (e.g., the public sphere) that are constituted by their masculinity because such categories are defined by the exclusion of femininity. Either women as feminine cannot be added (i.e., women must become men) or the category must be transformed to accommodate the inclusion of women and femininity. Doing so transforms not only the meaning of the category but also the meaning of masculinity (because masculinity and the public sphere are defined in terms of each other and masculinity and femininity are a mutually constituted dichotomy). In this sense, the "empirical gesture" of adding women has theoretical implications: Changing the terms and their relation changes the implicit framework of those relations, and theory must address such changes.[14]

Feminists argue that the dichotomy of masculine-feminine is a structural feature of social life, rendering gender an analytical category with systemic implications for advancing our understanding of social relations. To appreciate the implications requires a familiarity with issues raised by critiques of positivism. IR's "third debate" ostensibly addresses these issues—though with regrettably little evidence of dialogue.[15] The mainstream of IR continues to marginalize this debate and resist taking seriously the challenges it poses. One consequence is an inability to appreciate the force of feminist critiques. For it is the rejection of positivist dichotomies—categorically separating subject and object, fact and value, theory and practice—that is crucial to appreciating the extent of feminist challenges and their transformative implications.[16]

Feminists join postpositivists, poststructuralists, postmodernists, and deconstructionists in criticizing binary logocentrism. But they go beyond these nonfeminist critiques to argue that dichotomized (either-or) thought cannot be adequately understood and therefore effectively transformed without attention to gender. They argue instead that dichotomies acquire the status and authority of givens in part because they so readily "map onto" the dichotomy of gender.[17] And the gender dichotomy gains its "givenness" by (mistaken) association with biological ("natural") sex difference. Because of this interaction, gender dualisms have political significance far beyond their role in male-female relations: Gender informs multiple dichotomies that structure how we think about and act within world politics—how we *make* yet tend to reify our world(s). We clarify these claims by examining the structure, status, and androcentrism of dichotomies.[18]

Binary logocentrism engenders a "structuring of paired opposites" that "at once differentiates one term from another, prefers one to the other, and arranges them hierarchically, displacing the subordinate term beyond the boundary of what is significant and desirable."[19] This oppositional structure constrains our thought and therefore action by presenting only two mutually exclusive choices, as if these exhausted the possibilities. Locked into polarities, we lose sight of alternative, nonoppositional constructions. Oppositional meanings also appear fixed, as if they are givens of logic and language rather than social conventions; in this sense they resist critical reflection by presenting what appears to be "necessary" or inevitable categories. In addition, the oppositional form of dichotomies denies any overlap or commonalities between terms: It puts difference in focus at the expense of viewing terms *relationally and dynamically*. But social reality is complex and conditioned by multiple variables. Categorical oppositions misrepresent (distort) social relations by eliminating this complexity and interdependence. In sum, the structure of dichotomies promotes patterns of thought and action that are stunted (unable to envision alternatives), static (unable to acknowledge or address change), and dangerously oversimplified (unable to accommodate the complexities of social reality).

The *structure* of dichotomies makes gender stereotypes harder to "see," critique, and alter; the *status* of dichotomies in Western thought and science poses additional problems. Although all cultures employ categories of comparison, Western metaphysics and positivism employ a binary logic that fuels dichotomization. The dichotomies institutionalized by positivist perspectives are not, however, gender-neutral. As a now extensive feminist scholarship documents, science's claims of rationality and objectivity are masculinist, and the dichotomies made familiar by scientific thought—subject-object, abstract-concrete, fact-value, mind-body, culture-nature, objective-subjective—are inextricable from a naturalized, asymmetrical dichotomy of masculine-feminine.[20] Because dichotomies are so pervasive and privileged in Western culture, they lend authority to the particular dichotomy of gender. And the dichotomy of gender is so taken as "given" that it lends authority to the "natural" separation of other categories into oppositional pairs. This reciprocal interaction means that gender dichotomies have social-structural effects, and these effects in turn reproduce subjects, intersubjective meanings, and objective conditions that are gendered.

Finally, these dichotomies are not only hierarchical (privileging the first term over the second) but also *androcentric*: The first term is associated with masculinity or assumes a male-as-norm point of view. This androcentrism has three interacting effects. First, it privileges that which is associated with masculinity (reason, autonomy, culture) over that which is associated with femininity (affect, interdependence, nature). In IR, neorealism privileges state sovereignty and autonomy over interdependence and intergovernmental cooperation; wielding "power over," not mutually enabling "power to," is paramount. Second and closely related, this androcentrism denigrates or dismisses the qualities associated with the second term; that which is associated with women and femininity is given less attention and typically disparaged. In IR, the categorically masculinist "power politics" of militarism and state power are favored over the "soft politics" of pacifism, refugee issues, development, and environmentalism.

Third, this androcentrism assumes that activities associated with men and masculinity (war, diplomacy, global finance) constitute the "main story"; the realities of women, nonelite men, children, and nature are merely background that is not important enough to warrant being spotlighted.[21] This selective attention leaves us ignorant of the background itself (we make assumptions but do not systematically study the background) and dangerously ignorant of its relationship to the main story (we do not know to what extent and in what ways the main story *depends on* the background). The on-stage actors may be our focal point, but attending only to their behavior explains nothing of why they are there, how they got there, or what their behaviors signify in the bigger picture.

In sum, dichotomies are pervasive in our thought and practice. Their structure promotes stunted, static, and oversimplified thinking (though it is "efficient"). Their "scientific" status protects them from both commonsense and foundational critiques. Their androcentrism privileges what are in fact partial and particular understandings. Thus if gender identity fuels an *unwillingness* to analyze the power and pervasiveness of gender, the symbolic order of dualistic thinking (which is also gendered) naturalizes an *inability* to "see" how the dichotomy of masculine-feminine structures our thought and action. By conflating masculine-feminine with dichotomies generally, we reinforce gender hierarchy in our use of dichotomies by our assumption of natural sex difference. By doing so, we extend the effects of "gendering" but render them invisible by *naturalizing* them. What is natural is not political and presumably not problematic: It warrants little analytical attention. The combination of gender identity and gender dualisms then serves to hide the extent to which masculinism is a structural feature of social life. The structural power of masculinism, moreover, naturalizes the everyday practices of gendered identities and the potency of related gender dualisms.

Until recently, gender was hidden in the study of IR.[22] Christine Sylvester diagnosed the status of gender studies in *International Studies Notes*, pointing out that IR specialists

> have avoided thinking of men and women *qua* embodied and socially constituted subject categories in three ways: by subsuming them in the "more relevant" categories . . . ; by too readily accepting into scientific analyses the common social assumption that women are located inside the separate sphere of domestic life . . . [having] nothing to do with the usual activities IR chronicles and theorizes . . . ; and by retreating to abstractions (the state) that mask a masculine identity (as competitive, rational, egoistic, power-seeking).[23]

Paralleling our own analysis, Sylvester's diagnosis suggests that IR specialists have avoided taking their own and others' embodiment seriously, have been unwilling to reflect critically on positivist dichotomies and their gendered politics, and have favored "disembedded" abstractions that obscure the power and pervasiveness of gender. This denial of gendered bodies fuels a denial of gender privilege[24] and, as subsequent chapters illustrate, promotes an acritical reproduction of masculine hegemony.

Given the resistance to gender-sensitive research, the recent growth spurt in IR scholarship that addresses women's issues, gender, and feminism is impressive.[25] These studies explore both how international processes have gender-differentiated patterns and how gender shapes the ways in which we think about, study, and practice IR. Some of this research amends and expands our understanding of world politics by adding women as an empirical category. Other scholarship implicitly, and sometimes explicitly, challenges the field's foundational givens, raising questions about agents (rational, competitive, self-interested men and states), dichotomies (war-peace, protector-protected, developed-developing, self-other, public-private, domestic-international, inside-outside, order-anarchy, autonomy-dependence, politics-economics, core-periphery), and problematics (anarchy, self-help, security dilemma) that constitute the discipline as such.

As noted earlier (and in the context of so much resistance!), studies that add women to existing frameworks are pathbreaking and make important contributions. World politics looks (because it is) different when women's activities, understandings, and struggles are taken seriously. Men's activities—and their powers—are no longer seen as exclusively rational, autonomous, and competitive. The public sphere is no longer seen as constituting the whole picture. If, however, we acknowledge gender as an analytical category, feminist theory not only adds to but transforms our understanding and knowledge. The reference to transformation is central. In the context of "new times," problem-solving research that focuses on the world "as it is" can only illuminate part of the picture. Conventional accounts that favor the study of "objective conditions" at the expense of subjectivity and intersubjective systems are less satisfactory than ever. On the one hand, we require more adequate understanding of the processes of continuity and change: In what historical conditions do concepts, practices, and institutions emerge, and how are they reproduced—or transformed—through time? On the other hand, we need alternative understandings that permit alternative visions to come into focus: How can we address the complex challenges posed by simultaneous processes of integration and disintegration? Rather than simply "reacting" against crises and constraints, how can we move constructively forward to chart "new *futures*"?

Feminisms offer valuable insights on and resources for responding to these questions. Critical reflection is familiar terrain for feminists. Contemporary critiques of positivism expose the nexus of power and knowledge; the categorical separation of subject and object, fact and value, and theory and practice can no longer be sustained. Because all research and knowledge claims are embedded in social context, we must critically examine not whether but in what ways politics and normative commitments affect knowledge production.[26] Feminists have exposed the masculinisms in positivist constructions of science, rationality, and objectivity. They are currently exposing the masculinisms in neorealist constructions of the state, sovereignty, and power politics (see Chapter 3).

Challenges to positivism entail understanding subject and object, fact and value, and theory and practice not oppositionally but in relation. This is important for contemporary efforts to address how (gendered) subjectivity and normative commitments shape the world(s) we live in and the changes we are caught up in. Rather than relegating affect, subjectivity, and ideological commitments to supplemental or "superstructural" status, feminists have studied these dynamics *in relation* to reason, objectivity, and embodied practices. In this sense, feminist scholarship has long been exploring the implications of postpositivism and illuminating the interactive *processes* of changing reality.

Finally, feminisms do not simply amend and expand but also transform our understanding. They go beyond critique by envisioning alternatives (see the conclusion to this volume). Transformation is in part a dimension of all critiques: Specifying problems, tensions, and contradictions illuminates potential corrections or resolutions. But it is also a dimension specific to today's multiple feminisms. The historical conditions of contemporary feminisms include the challenges posed by postpositivist understanding and the dilemma of diversity (differences among women) in the face of demands for women's solidarity (enabling effective political action). In this context, feminists can ill afford to ignore critiques of positivism, the danger of totalizing moves, or the structural violence attending most women's lives. In an important sense, the escape route of disembodied abstraction and academic theorizing is cut off and feminists are forced to address "the big picture"—with its complexity, confusion, and contradictions intact.

Conclusion

Feminists and some IR theorists have been struggling to expand our conversational spaces. In this chapter, we reviewed recent feminist perspectives on topics at the heart of IR conduct and inquiry. We also drew attention to the multiple dimensions of and challenges posed by "new times." In the face of rapid change and the interaction of local, national, and global processes, it is appropriate to rethink our perspectives and the theories they inform. It is not only "objective" conditions—the world "as it is"—that we must analyze and reflect upon. Political, economic, and sociocultural developments compel us to recognize that gendered subjective identities, intersubjective meaning systems, and objective conditions are codetermined and irreducible elements of social reality: They constitute the world "as we make it." Theorizing that is adequate for the 1990s cannot rely on problem-solving approaches that take the world as given. Rather, we must adopt what Robert Cox calls critical theories that understand the world as one we make, indeed continue to make (and can therefore remake) through dynamic interaction of multiple variables.

Turbulence and transformation in IR have encouraged a rethinking of mainstream theory and practice. Attention to voices within the "third debate" offers the hope of new theoretical directions and more critical conversations. Yet mainstream "problem-solvers" appear impervious to these developments.

Feminist theories begin with a different perspective and lead to further rethinking. They distinguish "reality" from the world as *men* know it. They not only add women but also ask how gender—a structural feature of social life—has been rendered invisible. We considered how gender identity and subjectivity and the symbolic order of gendered dichotomies interact, rendering us unwilling and unable to "see" gender's pervasive effects. But gender *is* pervasive and powerfully shapes the world(s) we make. As noted in our epigraph, "all theories have a perspective" that derives "from a position in time and space." Because of their locations within the world and commitments to social transformation, we suggest how feminist perspectives offer valuable insights on and resources for addressing the challenges posed by new times.

Empirically, feminist IR documents "other" (local and global) realities and reveals pervasive insecurities imposed by the structural violence of state and global systems. It demonstrates how international processes have gender-differentiated consequences and how gender lenses filter our thought and practice. In regard to theorizing, feminists have been charting new directions in response to critiques of positivism and the deconstruction of dichotomies. Attentive to everyday realities and reproductive activities, feminists are able to illuminate the complex processes of continuity and change. Normatively, feminists challenge the luxury and pretension of theorizing the world in abstraction, "as it is." Without dismissing systemic inquiry *or* critiques of positivism, feminists get on with studying complexity and identifying strategies for change in the world(s) we make.

As a result of these efforts, feminists bring new perspectives to conventional and critical IR conversations. New times challenge all of us to rethink our givens, to critically address the codetermination of subjective, intersubjective and objective conditions. In these daunting and exciting times, we are all better served by good conversation and may benefit enormously from it as we move toward new futures.

Notes

1. Robert W. Cox, "Social Forces, States and World Orders: Beyond International Relations Theory," in Robert O. Keohane, ed., *Neorealism and Its Critics* (New York: Columbia University Press, 1986), p. 207.

2. Stuart Hall and Martine Jacques, eds., *New Times: Changing Conceptions of Politics in the 1990s* (London: Lawrence and Wishhart, 1989).

3. Although we advocate the inclusion of more voices, this edited volume reflects (and reproduces) the Eurocentric and elitist hegemony of IR theory. A more global perspective is required before theorizing about masculinities and IR can achieve a much-needed global balance.

4. Catherine Stimpson, "Feminism and Feminist Criticism," *Massachusetts Review* 24 (1983), p. 286. We acknowledge that universalizing tendencies have been and remain a problem in feminism insofar as the category "woman/women" is employed acritically. However, the recognition that there are multiple feminisms has arisen out of the feminist movement itself. Women of color and lesbians challenged totalizing presentations of "woman" that suppressed differences among women, notably the different modes of oppression women face in racism, imperialism, ageism, heterosexism, classism, ableism, and so on. Contemporary feminists respond to this internal critique by attempting to recognize, respect, and theorize differences among women without renouncing feminist objectives and the solidarity that is an element of working toward those objectives. See Gloria Anzaldúa,

Creative and Critical Perspectives by Women of Color (San Francisco: Aunt Lute Books, 1990); Chandra Talpade Mohanty, Anne Russo, and Lourdes Torres, eds., *Third World Women and the Politics of Feminism* (Bloomington: Indiana University Press, 1991); Flora Anthias and Niro Yuval-Davis, eds., *Women-Nation-State* (London: Macmillan Press, 1989); Zillah Eisenstein, *The Color of Gender* (Stanford: University of California Press, 1994).

5. See Sandra Harding and Merrill B. Hintikka, *Discovering Reality: Feminist Perspectives on Epistemology, Metaphysics, Methodology and the Philosophy of Science* (Dordrecht, Netherlands: D. Reidel, 1983); Dale Spender, *Men's Studies Modified* (New York: Pergamon Press, 1981).

6. See Carole Pateman and Elizabeth Gross, *Feminist Challenges: Social and Political Theory* (Sydney: Allen and Unwin, 1986); V. Spike Peterson, "Introduction," in V. Spike Peterson, ed., *Gendered States: Feminist (Re)Visions of International Relations Theory* (Boulder, CO: Lynne Rienner, 1992); Zillah Eisenstein, *The Radical Future of Liberal Feminism* (New York: Longman, 1981).

7. Wendy Brown, *Manhood and Politics: A Feminist Reading in Political Theory* (Totowa, NJ: Rowman and Littlefield, 1988); also Barbara Nelson, "Women and Knowledge in Political Science," *Women and Politics* 9, 2 (1989), pp. 1–25.

8. Sandra Harding, *The Science Question in Feminism* (Ithaca: Cornell University Press, 1986), p. 17.

9. Ibid., pp. 17–18.

10. For discussions of how gender is hidden in IR, see J. Ann Tickner, *Gender and International Relations: Feminist Perspectives on Achieving Global Security* (New York: Columbia University Press, 1992); V. Spike Peterson, "Transgressing Boundaries: Theories of Knowledge, Gender and International Relations," *Millennium* 21, 2 (Summer 1992); V. Spike Peterson and Anne Sisson Runyan, *Global Gender Issues* (Boulder, CO: Westview Press, 1993); Jan Jindy Pettman, "Gendering International Relations," *Australian Journal of International Affairs* 47, 1 (1993), pp. 47–61; and Marysia Zalewski, "Feminist Theory and International Relations," in M. Bowker and R. Brown, eds., *From Cold War to Collapse: Changes in World Politics in the 1980's* (Cambridge: Cambridge University Press, 1993).

11. Our focus here on gender is not to suggest its separability from differences of, for example, race and class. Whereas gender is not always the most salient or oppressive dimension at work in a particular context, we believe gender always shapes the expression of other dimensions (e.g., racist policies are also gendered); and insofar as gender identities are integral to our sense of self and personal security, it often profoundly shapes our commitments to particular lenses.

12. See Rebecca Grant, "The Sources of Gender Bias in International Relations Theory," in Grant and Newland, eds., *Gender and International Relations* (Buckingham: Open University Press, 1991); Philip Windsor, "Women and International Relations," *Millennium* 17, 3 (1988); S. Peterson, "Security and Sovereign States: What Is at Stake in Taking Feminism Seriously?" in Peterson, *Gendered States*.

13. Carole Pateman, *The Disorder of Women* (Stanford: University of California Press, 1989), p. 118.

14. Peterson, "Introduction," in *Gendered States*.

15. The postpositivist and postmodernist critiques of transcendental foundations and universal objectives have forced the discipline of international relations into a phase of metatheoretical debate—of theorizing about theories of international politics. The debate has provoked strong and disparate responses without stimulating much dialogue. For an introduction see Yosef Lapid, "The Third Debate: On the Prospects of International Theory in a Post-Positivist Era," and related articles in *International Studies Quarterly* 33, 2 (1989); also the special issue of *International Relations Quarterly* 34, 3 (September 1990). For critiques of the lack of critical reflexive and gender-sensitive thinking in the "third debate" see Mark Neufeld, "Reflexivity and International Relations Theory," *Millennium* 22, 1 (Spring 1993); and Sandra Whitworth, "Gender in the Inter-Paradigm Debate," *Millennium* 18, 2 (Summer 1989), pp. 265–292. For a "bridge-building" attempt to bring the "opposing camps" into dialogue, see Peterson, "Transgressing Boundaries." Also see Sandra Whitworth, *Feminism and International Relations* (London: Macmillan, 1994).

16. Peterson, "Transgressing Boundaries."

17. Susan Hekman, "The Feminization of Epistemology," in *Women and Politics* 7 (1987), pp. 65–83; Genevieve Lloyd, *The Man of Reason: "Male" and "Female" in Western Philosophy* (Minneapolis: University of Minneapolis Press, 1984); Susan Bordo, "Feminist Scepticism and the Maleness of Philosophy," *Journal of Philosophy* 86, 11 (1994), pp. 619–626.

18. This material is adapted from Peterson and Runyan, *Global Gender Issues,* pp. 21–29.

19. Donna Gregory, "Foreword," in *International/Intertextual Relations,* ed. James Der Derian and Michael J. Shapiro (Lexington: Lexington Books, 1989), p. xvi.

20. See Sandra Harding and Merrill B. Hintikka, *Discovering Reality* (Dordrecht: Reidel, 1983); Sandra Harding, *The Science Question* and *Whose Science? Whose Knowledge?* (Ithaca: Cornell University Press, 1991); Evelyn Fox Keller, *Reflections on Gender and Science* (New Haven, CT: Yale University Press, 1985); Donna Haraway, *Simmons, Cyborgs, and Women: The Reinvention of Knowledge* (New York: Routledge, 1991); Susan Hekman, *Gender and Knowledge: Elements of a Postmodern Feminism* (Cambridge: Polity Press, 1990); and Lloyd, *The Man of Reason.*

21. See Simona Sharoni, "Gender and the Israeli-Palestinian Accord," *Review of Middle East Studies* (Winter 1994).

22. Fred Halliday, "Hidden from International Relations: Women and the International Arena," *Millennium* 17, 3 (1988), pp. 419–428.

23. Christine Sylvester, "Feminist Theory and Gender Studies in International Relations," *International Studies Notes* 16/17, 3/1 (Fall-Winter 1992), p. 32.

24. Peggy McIntosh, "White Privilege and Male Privilege," in Margaret L. Anderson and Patricia Hill, eds., *Race, Class and Gender* (Belmont, CA: Wadsworth, 1992).

25. Kenneth Boutin's extensive bibliography (145 pages) on gender and international relations is available from the Centre for International and Strategic Studies, York University, 4700 Keele Street, North York, Ontario, Canada M3J 1P3. This includes the most recent feminist IR books, such as Christine Sylvester, *Feminist Theory and International Relations in a Post-Modern Era* (Cambridge: Cambridge

University Press, 1994); Peterson and Runyan, *Global Gender Issues*; Peterson, *Gendered States*; Mary-Ann Tetrault, ed., *Women and Revolution in Africa, Asia and the New World* (Columbia: University of South Carolina Press, 1994); Ralph Pettman, *International Politics: Balance of Power, Balance of Productivity, Balance of Ideologies* (Boulder, CO: Lynne Rienner, 1991); Francine D'Amico and Peter Beckman, eds., *Women and World Politics* (New York: Bergin and Garvey, 1995); Grant and Newland, *Gender and International Relations*; Cynthia Enloe, *Bananas, Beaches and Bases: Making Feminist Sense of International Politics* (London: Pandora, 1990), and *The Morning After: Sexual Politics After the Cold War* (Stanford: University of California Press, 1993). Special Issues: "Women and International Relations," *Millennium* 17, 3 (Winter 1988); "Feminists Write International Relations," *Alternatives* 18, 1 (Winter 1993), edited by Christine Sylvester; and "Gender and International Relations," *Fletcher Forum of World Affairs* 17, 2 (Summer 1993).

26. Contemporary critiques of positivism do not entail absolute relativism in the sense of "anything goes." Equating the postpositivist rejection of transcendental foundations with the impossibility of any comparative criteria for evaluating knowledge claims presupposes an opposition between absolute and relative that is repudiated by postpositivism. Postpositivism denies only that our mapping and comparing of social constructions can be "grounded" by reference to ahistorical, decontextualized claims. See Peterson, "Transgressing Boundaries,"; Susan Hekman, *Gender and Knowledge*; Ann Yeatman, ed., "Postmodern Critical Theorising," special issue of *Social Analysis* 30 (December 1991).

2

Masculinist Practices and Gender Politics: The Operation of Multiple Masculinities in International Relations

Charlotte Hooper

Feminists have criticized the inherent masculinism of both the discipline of international relations (IR) and the practice of international politics. They have convincingly demonstrated how completely women and "the feminine" are marginalized and excluded from "malestream" analysis.[1] As Chapter 1 illustrates, such critiques have paved the way for a feminist reconstruction of the scope and content of IR in which the task has been not merely to add women but rather to critically examine the gendered and gendering practices of IR within the wider context of a global politics and global political economy.[2] This reconstruction has provided new horizons and new tools for an important expansion of women-centered scholarship in the field. However, it is also worth remembering that the very masculinism of international politics makes it a particularly fertile ground for the study of men and masculinities. Indeed, as one of a few powerful but virtually all-male spheres, it is likely to be a primary site for the cultural and social production of masculinities.

Although any feminist who writes predominantly about men risks replicating and hence further reinforcing the marginalization of women, if the balance of feminist scholarship as a whole remains women-centered, this effect can be mitigated. And if we fail to take it upon ourselves to scrutinize men and masculinity in depth, in tandem with our more sophisticated and nuanced understandings of women and "the feminine," then we shall severely restrict our own critical analysis and understanding of the gender order, as "gender is not a synonym for women."[3] We shall leave an intellectual and academic vacuum for others, with different agendas, to fill.[4]

The first section of this chapter furthers the development of feminist theory regarding men and masculinities by synthesizing the strengths of three (often discrete) literatures: postmodern feminist debates on fluidity and difference in gender identity, feminist critiques of masculinism in IR, and the rapidly expanding literature on masculinities. I treat the politics of masculinity as a contested field of power moves and resistances rather than as a fixed set of power relations, and I explore the relationships among different masculinities without losing sight of men's overall position of power and privilege over women. In the second section, I discuss how such a perspective improves our understanding of the gendering processes at work in IR with a view to further questioning and challenging the practices that support such processes.

Theorizing Masculinities: Masculinism and Difference

Postmodern Feminists and the Question of Difference

Over the past decade, feminist theorists have turned their attention to the differences between women. The recognition that earlier feminist theory was often middle-class, heterosexist, and Eurocentric has forced the issue of these differences to the center of feminist debates.[5] Initially issues of heterosexism, racism, class position, and homophobia were treated as added burdens that some women carry, but now they are considered to intersect in the way gender identities are constructed in the first place so that, for example, gender identities are always already racialized and racial identities are always already gendered.[6]

Postmodern feminists have pushed the question of difference one step further and argue that the privileged and powerful may have experienced their identities as unitary and coherent in the past, but marginalized peoples have rarely had such a luxury; and no identity is truly coherent. Any one individual is constituted by an ensemble of "subject positions" that is always contingent and precarious.[7] Postmodern feminism is interested in the problematic of "otherness," new forms of subjectivity, and new theories and practices of speaking as subjects. These new subjectivities and possibilities for political practice are a feminist response not only to the limitations of modernity but also to contemporary globalization: the introduction of new technologies, capitalist restructuring, changing relations of production, and emerging social relations of postmodernity (see Chapter 1).[8]

Although postmodern feminism is not just about difference, the recognition of difference, fluidity, and multiplicity in gender identities remains one of its dominant themes: "Postmodern feminist theory would dispense with the idea of a subject of history. It would replace unitary notions of woman and feminine gender identity with plural and complexly constructed conceptions of social identity, treating gender as one relevant strand among others, attending also to class, race, ethnicity, age, and sexual orientation."[9]

For postmodern and postcolonial feminists, the normative embracing of contradictory multiple or mobile identities and weaving them into new kinds of life stories represents an opportunity to bring the marginalized into the center and move away from fixed identity politics whose divisions threaten our increasingly complex multicultural societies.[10]

The logical conclusion of this tendency to deconstruct the (female) subject is to view the category of "women" as the problem rather than as the point of departure for women's liberation.[11] But too much emphasis on difference and fluidity can obscure women's common oppression on the basis of their sex and can suggest a voluntarism that is unrealistic, for we cannot "vault over the stubborn harshness of lived gender."[12] Fluidity and multiplicity are always limited by context and location, so a balance needs to be struck between making generalizations about women and focusing on differences. As Susan Bordo argues, "Generalizations about gender can obscure and exclude. Of course this is true. I would suggest, however, that such determinations cannot be made by methodological fiat but must be decided from context to context. The same is true of the representation of heterogeneity and complexity. There are dangers in too wholesale a commitment to either dual or multiple grids."[13]

Bordo urges us to steer a middle course between focusing exclusively on the dual grid of gender and losing sight of it in a never-ending examination of difference. Whereas the context for this discussion has been differences among women, her argument is about analyses of *gender*, and her warnings should apply equally to both discussions of the relationships among men, masculinity, and power and discussions of women, femininity, and oppression. However, with a few exceptions, feminists have tended to pay much less (if any) attention to the differences between men.[14] Perhaps this is because if emphasis on multiplicity and difference threatens to undermine the feminist project by dissolving the category of women as an oppressed group, then examination of the differences between men could be used to dissolve, or obscure our view of, the oppressor. Examining the differences between men and masculinities must not involve losing sight of the collective inequalities between men and women.

Masculinism and Masculinity

There can be a tension between these postmodern insights into the nonfixed and nonfoundational construction of gender, on the one hand, and the accounts of masculinity provided in feminist critiques of the inherent masculinism of IR, on the other.[15] Briefly, masculinism is "the ideology that justifies and naturalizes gender hierarchy by not questioning the elevation of ways of being and knowing associated with men and masculinity over those associated with women and femininity."[16] Masculinity is defined in opposition to femininity in the dichotomous pair masculine/feminine. There are connections between this pair and other modern dichotomies such as rational/emotional, active/passive, war/peace, culture/nature, objective/subjective, competitive/caring, and order/anarchy. In each pair the first, masculine, term is generally valued over the second, feminine, term. Some feminists argue that the masculine/feminine dichotomy is the primary one through which other dichotomies receive their status by association, because they are so readily "mapped onto" gender.[17] The centrality of "masculine" qualities as rationality, autonomy, strength, power, logic, boundary setting, control, and competitiveness in the disciplinary values and practices of science and politics helps to reinforce the links between masculinity and the disciplines themselves. "Feminine" qualities such as intuition, empathy, vulnerability, and cooperation are downgraded or distrusted, and women are excluded by such practices; so science and politics remain thoroughly masculinist. Explanations of this masculinism range from the argument that it represents the experience of elite males writ large through object relations and Lacanian psychoanalytic explanations to Derrida's account of the binary logic of Western metaphysics.[18]

However, this kind of analysis is too heavily weighted toward dual grids and not enough toward multiple ones. It can inadvertently reinforce the very dualism it seeks to expose, especially when masculinity is repeatedly associated with men and femininity (or feminist standpoints) with women.[19] Nor is such a criticism intended to deny the very real and enduring effects of the masculine/feminine dichotomy on social life. The power of this dichotomy is clear, for example, in the gendered division of employment into overwhelmingly male and predominantly female occupations in Britain, which are deemed to require masculine and feminine qualities, respectively.[20] In IR the division of labor is no less stark; men overwhelmingly dominate political, diplomatic, entrepreneurial, advisory, technical, management, and military combat roles, and women provide largely "invisible" domestic, administrative, and medical support; cheap factory and agricultural labor; and sexual, welfare, and hostessing services.[21]

As well as helping to construct and naturalize gender differences and inequalities in their image, gendered dichotomies also obscure more complex relationships, commonalities, overlaps, and intermediate positions.[22] For example, the job of soldiering has been traditionally characterized as a manly activity requiring the "masculine" traits of physical strength, action, toughness, and capacity for violence. Officers must evidence resolve; technical skills; and logical, tactical, and strategic thinking. But such jobs could equally be characterized as requiring the traditionally "feminine" qualities of total obedience and submission to authority, attention to dress detail, and endless repetition of mundane tasks (at least in the case of the lower ranks). Military combat also offers opportunities for open displays of mutual concern, tears, and other "feminine" demonstrative emotional gestures.[23] One only has to scratch the surface of social life to see that men routinely engage in practices and exhibit characteristics that could be interpreted as feminine. Often similar activities are labeled masculine or feminine depending on context or even the choice of descriptive words; in employment, for example, what counts as acquired skills (culture) in men gets described as mere natural ability (nature) in women, with pay and status to follow.[24]

The insight that gendered dichotomies construct masculinity and femininity as opposites, treat masculinity as active and femininity as passive, and valorize the masculine is important because it illuminates the close associations between masculinity and power. To be fair, masculinity is not always portrayed in a monolithic way in critiques of masculinism. Ann Tickner, for example, discusses a number of different models of masculinity, but the direction and logic of her overall argument (focused on the systematic exclusion of women) tends to obscure rather than highlight the differences between them.[25] Such a strategy may have been necessary for feminists to get an initial grip on IR, but perhaps now we need to pay more attention to these relatively unexamined differences. One way to reconcile critiques of masculinism with postmodern notions of fluidity in gender constructions is to argue for analysis that is both relational and contextualized. This would specify how the ingredients of masculinity and femininity get to be defined in relation to each other in the particular context under examination.[26] Masculinity, then, is a fluid construction rather than a fixed set of traits. Rather than men generally displaying a stable set of masculine qualities that are then more highly valued (an inherently essentialist position because of the presumed stability of the "masculine" qualities), it is more likely that qualities that are valued as power-enhancing get defined as masculine and hence are associated with men. Masculinism produces and reinforces such claims, whereas what counts as masculine may itself be subject to change according to the requirements of power in different circumstances. Strategies of masculinization and feminization are likely to play an important part in the direction and consolidation of such changes by upgrading or downgrading various activities, practices, and groups of people in the struggle for recognition and power. In addition, although all men gain to some extent from the associations between masculinity and power, not all men have equal access to these associations. Thus we return to the question of differences among men and how such differences might themselves form part of the gender order.

Multiple Masculinities

A brief examination of contributions to the history of Western masculinity suggests that we have inherited at least four different models or ideal types of dominant masculinities from different periods of our cultural and social history: the Greek citizen-warrior model; the patriarchal Judeo-Christian model; the honor-patronage model; and a Protestant bourgeois rationalist model.[27] The Greek model combined militarism with rationalism and equated manliness with citizenship in a masculine arena of free speech and politics. In contrast, the Judeo-Christian ideal of manliness emphasized a more domesticated ideal of responsibility, ownership, and the authority of the father. The honor-patronage model was an aristocratic ideal in which personal bonds between men, military heroism, and risk-taking were highly valued with the duel as the ultimate test of masculinity. The bourgeois rationalist model idealized competitive individualism, reason, and self-control or self-denial, combining respectability as breadwinner and head of household with calculative rationality in public life. These types overlap to some extent: The honor-patronage model is heavily indebted to the Judeo-Christian legacy, and the bourgeois rationalist model is to some extent the result of a fusion of the Greek citizen-warrior with Judeo-Christian ideals. Modern Western masculinities can be seen to have descended from these types, whose elements have been combined and recombined in different ways. Previous layers of reformulations, combinations, and manifestations lend an air of continuity and timelessness to today's construction, so that although the term "masculinity" is unstable, this instability is masked and the masculine/feminine dichotomy remains dominant.

Within these broad types there are also more specific formulations. Dominant styles of masculinity in Britain and the United States also appear to be subject to a great deal of flux and change in relatively short time spans, almost from one decade to the next. Examples from the literature include the change from the men of letters in Britain in the middle of the nineteenth century to the flight from domesticity of the new colonialism in the 1890s; the twentieth-century withering of martial masculinities and splitting of Victorian hegemonic masculinity into varieties based on expertise and domination; the emergence of working-class masculinity; the rigid domestication of men in the breadwinner role in the United States in the 1950s combined with a period of "angry young men" in the United Kingdom; and a general softening of masculinities in both countries from the 1960s onward.[28] The term "masculinities" seems more adequate to characterize this confusing plurality and fluidity than does the concept of "masculinity" in the singular.

A useful way of understanding this multiplicity of masculinities is proposed by Harry Brod, who applies Wittgenstein's philosophical concept of "family resemblances": "Just as members of a family may be said to resemble each other without necessarily all having any single feature in common, so masculinities may form common patterns without sharing any single universal characteristic."[29] If this model is adopted, it can be seen that masculinities need have no ultimate common basis. By sharing some common characteristics with a number of other masculinities, each variety remains recognizably masculine. New elements can be introduced to accommodate change, and no two images or manifestations of masculinity need be exactly alike. However, although the historicization of masculinities dispels the belief that masculinity is fixed and stable, there is a problem with this kind of account when it contains no analysis of the relationship among masculinities, power, and subordination. There can be a tendency toward a bland pluralism in which relations with women drop out of the picture altogether.[30]

A Synthetic Approach: Introducing Hegemonic and Subordinate Masculinities

Having summarized these three approaches, I want to begin to synthesize their strengths: the attention to difference and fluidity, albeit contextualized; the exposure of masculinist practices; and the empirical identification of multiple masculinities. It is helpful to use Bob Connell's notion of "hegemonic" and "subordinate" masculinities.[31] Whereas there may be many masculinities and femininities in existence at the same time, hegemonic patterns of masculinity operate at the level of the whole society, shoring up male power and advantage. Hegemonic masculinity is constructed in relation to a range of subordinate masculinities as well as in opposition to femininity. There exists a hierarchy of masculinities in which gender intersects with other factors such as class and sexuality. Hegemonic masculinity is constitutive of and embodied in numerous institutional practices such as enforced competitive sport for schoolboys. Individual men are therefore forced to negotiate their identities in relation to practices and relationships informed by hegemonic masculinity and the alternative gender models offered. When men publicly identify with hegemonic masculinity or otherwise collaborate with such public images, they boost their own position; any degree of compliance, however grudging or unconscious, will help to shore up existing inequalities.

Connell's model employs a Gramscian approach to hegemony but one stripped of its class-based analysis. Hegemony is achieved largely through an ideological ascendancy over a cultural mix—moral persuasion and consent rather than brute force (although such ascendancy may be backed up by force). As Raymond Williams has argued, cultural hegemony need not rely on the employment of conscious or deliberate strategies of domination by elites. Elites are just as likely to be implicated in the dissemination of cultural hegemony through their participation in a system of meaningful practices that reproduce and confirm their own identities.[32]

The concept of hegemonic and subordinate masculinities is an extremely useful heuristic device that allows for the recognition of multiplicity, fluidity, and change in the construction of masculinities, but without threatening to obscure the relationships among masculinity, power, and women's subordination that are analyzed by feminists.[33] The concept of hegemonic masculinity has no female equivalent. All varieties of femininity are subordinate; whereas there are also subordinate varieties of masculinity, the overall dominance of masculinities and men is clearly signaled. Once the perspective of hegemonic and subordinate masculinities is adopted, masculinist practices (including strategies of masculinization and feminization) can be seen to police male behavior and allow some varieties of masculinity and the men associated with them to gain ascendancy over others at the same time that men's overall position of privilege in the gender order is sustained.

Policing Hegemonic Masculinities and Marginalizing Subordinate Men

One of the ways in which male conformity to hegemonic ideals is policed is through the threat of feminization. It has been argued that the creation of the homosexual as a distinct type in the late nineteenth century served this purpose. Before this, the emphasis was on prohibited behavior such as sodomy, but there was no concept of a special type of person with distinctive desires or aptitudes who indulged in it. Once the homosexual had been defined as a deviant and effeminate personality type, the norm could be established as heterosexual. The threat of effeminacy would then police conformity to this norm among the majority of men.[34]

The subsequent effectiveness of this threat can be seen particularly clearly in the post–World War II United States. Barbara Ehrenreich shows that in the late 1940s and 1950s, hegemonic masculinity was policed by the threat of "latent homosexuality" as propounded by a host of psychological, medical, and sociological experts.[35] At this time women were being coerced back into the home after the war, and femininity was being redefined in domestic terms. Masculinity was equated with adulthood, marriage, and the breadwinning role in an era of production and reproduction organized around currency stability, Keynesian welfarism, and the family wage.[36] Any apparently heterosexual man who failed to live up to this role in full might be suffering from "latent" or "pseudo" homosexuality and had to be on his guard against such possibilities. Only in the 1970s were heterosexual men allowed much more freedom to indulge in formerly suspect behavior without losing their citizenship privileges. Ironically, this was because of the increasing visibility of gay men:

Where the notion of latency had established a secret continuum between the heterosexual and the homosexual, there was now a sharp divide. . . . Homosexuality might still be feared and stigmatised, but it could no longer be used as the null point in a hypothetical scale of masculinity. With the old equations between homosexuality and effeminacy broken, "straight" men were free to "soften" themselves indefinitely without losing their status as heterosexuals.[37]

Of course, the feminization of homosexuals as deviants not only had helped to keep the heterosexual majority in the hegemonic fold but also was part and parcel of their own stigmatization and subordination in the hierarchy of masculinities, thus demonstrating that masculinist practices not only marginalize women but also subordinate groups of men.

The first truly global gender order was developed in the context of European colonialism, and another example of the feminization of subordinate masculinities can be seen in the context of British imperial rule in the nineteenth century. A global, racialized (and racist) hierarchy of masculinities was created as part of the institutionalization of a complex set of race and gender identities; this hierarchy helped to sustain and justify British imperialism itself and still has a cultural legacy today. Broadly speaking, British imperialists imagined the "Orient" as an exotic, sensual, and feminized world, a kind of halfway stage between "Europe's enlightenment" and "African savagery." "Oriental" men were positioned as effeminate (and "Oriental" women as exotic); black Africans of both sexes were deemed uncivilized and, in a projection of European sexual fantasies, saturated with monstrous lust. In Britain, sex was seen as both natural (uncivilized) and a threat to the moral order. White women were regarded as lust-free symbols of this moral order and were always in danger of being raped by black male "savages" if they were not protected. The English gentleman positioned himself at the top of this hierarchy as a self-disciplined, naturally legitimate ruler and protector of morals. He regarded his sexuality as overlaid and tempered by civilization. He became the embodiment of imperial power, seeming to rule effortlessly and justifying his colonial mission as a civilizing one.[38] As a type, then, the Victorian English gentleman was at least as much a product of imperial politics as of domestic understandings of Englishness, aristocracy, and masculinity.

Within these broad stereotypes were more nuanced and shifting positions. In British India, for example, Bengali men were deemed more effeminate than Punjabis and as a result had fewer political and civil rights.[39] Meanwhile, turn-of-the-century Chinese immigrants to the United States were condemned as effeminate for doing "women's work" such as laundry and cooking, but the Japanese were demonized as ruthless and intent on "infiltration," a "yellow peril" whose effeminate characteristics were supposedly restricted to manipulative tendencies and general untrustworthiness.[40] Nuanced differences were also ascribed to various African peoples and to different classes and ethnic groups within the white population.

The nineteenth-century pathologizing of African masculinities has echoes in contemporary changes to hegemonic masculinity in the United States. Some argue that hegemonic masculinity is being reconstituted in the "new man" image so that middle-class men can enjoy the emotional fruits of parenting without losing their class and gender privileges and can simultaneously deflect feminist criticism (see Chapter 6). But the ideological image of the new man needs a counterimage to stand against. Hence,

> those aspects of traditional hegemonic masculinity that the New Man has rejected—overt physical and verbal displays of domination, stoicism and emotional inexpressivity, overt misogyny in the workplace and at home—are now increasingly projected onto less privileged groups of men: working class men, gay bodybuilders, black athletes, Latinos and immigrant men.[41]

In practice the family life of immigrant Mexicans, for example, with its high rate of female employment and shared domestic chores, may be more egalitarian than the family life of "new men," who often pay only lip service to domestic responsibilities.

It is important to recognize that such representations are no more a mirror of the actual social experiences of men in subordinate groups than the masculine/feminine dichotomy is a mirror of male and female experience. The relationships between the cultural projections of dominant groups and patterns of internalization and resistance within subordinate groups are complex and disputed. For example, some groups of black and Latino men do undoubtedly subscribe to so-called hypermasculine street styles based on honor codes of masculinity. This has been interpreted variously as a reflection of their own distinct cultural heritage, as a form of internalized oppression, and as a strategy of resistance to the relative powerlessness and associated feminization of their social position.[42] What is clear is that although white Euramericans have access to a heterogeneous body of masculinities from which hegemonic masculinities get fashioned and refashioned, subordinate groups of men have far less choice: "Contrary to the historically variable and shifting range of hegemonic masculinities, the representation of the identity of racially subordinated groups stands out for its monologic and homogeneous economy, resting virtually on the negative side of the masculine equation."[43]

Perhaps this difference in the range of choices, more than any other factor, distinguishes the construction of restricted and restricting subordinate masculinities from enabling and powerful hegemonic ones. Such changes as the softening of hegemonic masculinities should not necessarily be seen as a sign of the imminent demise of male power. Indeed, taking the space previously reserved for "the feminine" and thereby dealing with female power by incorporating it may well be a frequently used strategy when masculinity is in crisis.[44] As Arthur Brittan points out, "While styles of masculinity may alter in relatively short time spans, the substance of male power does not."[45] There may be a window of opportunity for radically undermining the gender order in what Connell refers to as the "contemporary multilateral struggle for hegemony in gender relations,"[46] but the historical record is hardly a cause for optimism.

Multiple Masculinities and International Relations

What light can this analysis of masculinities throw on IR? As the study of multiple masculinities in IR is in its infancy, the intention here is to paint in very broad strokes and to offer some initial provocations as starting points for further discussion. To start with, it is worth considering the proposition that international politics is itself a primary site for the production of masculinities and masculine identities. The traditional conceptualization of IR as a wholly masculine sphere of war and diplomacy, at the furthest extreme from the "private" sphere of families, women, and reproduction in the private/public/international divide of modernity, is instructive. The cultural and social production of gender differences and gendered character traits segregates the sexes in various ways to construct and make visible the lines of difference between them. Generating gendered constructions is an integral part of any such segregational practice. If the boundaries of international politics inscribe it as a virtually all-male sphere, it follows that the content and qualities of IR will inform the definition and production of masculinities. The emphasis on power politics, then, reinforces the associations between such masculinities and power itself, associations that are crucial to masculinism.

This traditional framework is not a natural reflection of external events, and the political/international divide has quite rightly been challenged from within the discipline. However, as long as the private/public divide remains unchallenged, other relationships are obscured, such as the supporting, reproductive, and economic roles of women in international affairs.[47] The production of masculinities is also rendered invisible by the failure to recognize the interconnections between the international and the private world of personhood. The private/public/international division not only inscribes an all-male sphere that helps to produce masculine identities but then obscures these processes by rooting questions of identity in the private realm, far from the reach of IR's focus of analysis.

The Production of Masculinities
and the Practices of International Politics

One practical implication of taking multiple masculinities seriously would be for contributors to IR to examine how the cultural production and interpretation of masculine identities as a political process informs other, more conventionally defined political and international struggles. In strategic analysis, for example, it may be worth investigating whether the degree to which hegemonic masculinities are constructed through military or heroic ideals affects belligerence. Ignoring cultural and psychological factors has led to poor risk perception in the past.[48] Similarly, discussions on cultural identity and societal security[49] would be enriched by considering different constructions of masculinity (and femininity) as relevant variables of cultural and political identities. However, adding masculinities onto strategic analysis as variables would be the least radical way of thinking about masculinities in IR, as the epistemological limitations of such analysis would obscure the politics of masculinities: the relational and power-laden processes of their construction. In addition, while paying attention to how masculinities might affect international politics, it ignores how international politics might construct masculinities. Masculinities are not just domestic cultural variables but are to some extent formed by international politics itself, as "it is not only men that make wars, it is wars that make men."[50] Political events and masculine identities are both the products of men's participation in "international" practices, as in the case of the previously discussed masculinities produced by nineteenth-century British colonialism.

The question of the construction of identities through international politics has recently been addressed by David Campbell. He argues that an explicit goal of U.S. foreign policy has been the construction and maintenance of an American identity.[51] For example, a major component of Cold War politics was the creation of a "society of security"[52] in which a vigorous loyalty and security program sought to define Americans in terms of excluding the communist "other" both externally and internally. Campbell notes the gendered nature of such exclusionary practices; for example, Communists and other undesirables were linked through feminization. But he stops short of recognizing that the construction and maintenance of American identity corresponds to the construction and maintenance of hegemonic masculinity during this period. Vigilance against the possibility that unsuspecting liberals might unwittingly help the Communist cause paralleled and intersected with the vigilance needed to ward off the threat of "latent homosexuality" mentioned previously, as indicated by the abusive term "pinko." Ehrenreich argues that "communism kept masculine toughness in style long after it became obsolete in the corporate world and the consumer marketplace."[53] Eventually, it was not only the increasing visibility of gay men but also the Vietnam War and its aftermath that engendered a crisis in this hegemonic masculinity of anti-Communist machismo. Not only did the enemy turn out to be women, old men, and children but U.S. masculinity was shown nightly on television in a pathological, brutal light.[54] The "emasculation" of American men following the defeat in Vietnam and the desire to reverse this helped to provide support for both the politics of the Reagan era and the Gulf War (see Chapter 6).[55]

Just as Campbell's work could form a starting point for further investigations into the construction of masculinities through international politics, so might Cynthia Enloe's discussion of the varied relationships among women, degrees and types of militarization, constructions of masculinity, and international political practices in different locations and at different times.[56] That the links between masculinity and militarism are contingent is highlighted in this account. For example, going back to British imperial practices, apparently the construction of imperial armies was no mean feat, as colonized groups of men often took some persuading that soldiering was in any way a manly pursuit. Complex bargains over conditions of service had to be struck depending on differing local requirements of manly respectability.[57] Enloe's discussion of the different constructions of masculinity is in effect an account of masculinities with a focus on how differing relations between men and women influenced their production. This kind of analysis could be extended by examining the relationships among the different masculinities themselves. Similarly, recent research on the gender constructions associated with nationalist discourses could usefully form the basis for an exploration of the relationships among international politics, nationalism, and the construction of masculinities.[58] Discussions of cultural imperialism in IR might also be enhanced by drawing on accounts of internalized oppression and resistance in the literature on hegemonic and subordinate masculinities. There are many ways in which the scope of gender-sensitive analysis can be enhanced by paying attention to masculinities, their construction, and the relationships among them.[59]

The Global Context

Another question worth investigating might be What is the relationship between the construction of masculinities and long-term global or systemic change? Different eras may be associated with different kinds of hegemonic masculinity. One can see, for example, that militarized masculinities, prominent in Greece and Rome, lost status in the Middle Ages. Under the papal unification of Europe, power was in the hands of clerics, and mainstream masculinities tended to be agricultural or monastic; military life was on the whole relegated to a soldier caste. The revival of military service as an important feature of masculinity and citizenship, central to the identity of men, was associated with the rise of city-states and then nation-states[60] and was exported from Europe to the rest of the world through colonialism and its aftermath.

Contemporary changes in hegemonic masculinities also need to be set in the context of systemic change, this time the changes associated with the processes of globalization and capitalist restructuring.[61] The introduction of new technologies, global capital mobility, the new international division of labor, and new forms of regionalism have set in motion a complex set of economic, political, and social changes, all of which are changing the terms of gender oppression. The gradual softening of hegemonic masculinities in metropolitan countries, noted previously, coincided with the start of the recent round of global capitalist restructuring, which began after the collapse of the Bretton Woods currency system.[62] Other indicators also support the idea that this softening of hegemonic masculinities is linked to or is even integral to the processes of globalization. First, the ties between hegemonic masculinity and the military are currently loosening in Western Europe and North America. There has been a decline in conscription and an increase in civilian influences on military life. Recent developments such as the increasing visibility of women and gay men in European and American forces (together with improved promotional prospects for black men in the U.S. forces) and the 1990s emphasis on the caring, humanitarian side of military duties lend support to the idea that the military is indeed becoming more detached from hegemonic masculinity in an era when the nation-state is losing ground to world cities and new forms of regionalization (see Chapters 5–7).[63]

Second, activities and qualities that were previously defined as feminine or effeminate are being increasingly integrated into hegemonic masculinity as the global economy is restructured: Men in the developed world are now positioned as consumers, a traditionally feminine role; U.S. mainstream culture is becoming increasingly, if subtly, homoerotic; and business and managerial strategies are changing to emphasize the formerly feminine qualities of flexibility, interpersonal skills, and teamwork.[64] Although the feminization of the workforce at first meant casualization at the lower end of the job market as a strategy to reduce labor costs, as global restructuring has gathered pace, such phenomena as delayering, outsourcing, and the casualization of employment practices has started to hit professional and managerial staff. There is some evidence that this phase of the feminization of working practices and managerial strategies, which might on the face of it offer improved career prospects for professional women, is being accompanied by redefinitions of hegemonic masculinity so that professional men can stay ahead of the employment game, albeit under less secure conditions. Within the pages of such magazines as the *Economist*, flexibility in job descriptions and career paths is being reinterpreted as "masculine" risk-taking and entrepreneurialism, and computers have lost their feminine associations with keyboard skills and are now marketed as macho power machines.[65] Meanwhile, the techniques of alternative therapy forged in the 1960s counterculture, which were originally used by antisexist men and feminist sympathizers to discover their so-called feminine side, are now widely used in management-training seminars designed to cultivate interpersonal skills and group work and in mythopoetic men's movement workshops that claim to develop the emotional "wild man" within.[66] Such activities are not only socializing white, middle-class men into feminized working practices but are crucially redefining these practices as masculine. As Connell argues, "The larger consequence of the popular forms of masculinity therapy is an adaptation of patriarchal structures through the *modernization* of masculinity."[67]

In the struggle to transform hegemonic masculinity there is also rivalry between "new men" and a backlash masculinity, which is supported by disaffected blue-collar males who have lost both their job security and their patriarchal positions in the family. In the United States these "angry white males" have disciplined Bill Clinton, the "new style" president, forcing him to reinvent himself as an "all American man's man" who will keep Hillary, "the wicked witch of the West," out of the public eye.[68] There is also a complex relationship of rivalry, accommodation, and even synthesis between Western models of hegemonic masculinity and those presented by the rising powers of Asia. Whereas the Japanese have been demonized as a threat to both the U.S. economy and, Campbell argues, American identity,[69] the so-called feminization of corporate practices in the West has been heavily influenced by Japanese production and management methods. Meanwhile, as some of the fallout from global economic restructuring begins to hit Japan's domestic arrangements in adverse ways, some Japanese men are trying to foster a more entrepreneurial and individualistic culture in Japan.[70] In these struggles, each variety of would-be hegemonic masculinity, and the interest groups it represents, are modifying themselves in response to the perceived successes of the others. At stake in these struggles between different styles of hegemonic masculinity are the pace and direction of global restructuring itself and the composition of the masculine elite within that process.

Multiple Masculinities and Interparadigm Debates

Just as there are competing masculinities on the ground, so there are in IR theory. Realism can be seen to embody hegemonic masculinity, the perspective of elite white men wherein the ideal of the glorified male warrior has been projected onto the behavior of states.[71] However, even within a realist perspective, there are a number of different and contradictory archetypes and formulations of hegemonic masculinity in play. Machiavelli, for example, revised the Greek archetype of the warrior-citizen for modern times; Hobbes uneasily combined elements from the patriarchal model with an individualism associated with the emerging bourgeois rationalist model.[72] In spite of their incompatibility, both are considered founding fathers of contemporary realism. Indeed, the credibility and durability of the realist approach may partly lie with the fact that it does appear to combine and embody traits that have been associated with male power and dominant masculinity under different historical conditions, providing a manly trait for every occasion. This credibility has been bolstered by the post–World War II importation of scientific methods and economistic assumptions derived more wholeheartedly from the bourgeois rationalist tradition but overlaying rather than obscuring the warrior-citizen and patriarchal elements. In contrast, rival liberal and pluralist perspectives have depended more singularly on the bourgeois rationalist model. Given that realism and neorealism have dominated international relations, it is worth recalling the previous argument that masculinities that are hegemonic have a broader range of traits to draw from than others (they also compete for hegemonic status; see Chapter 4).

These different archetypes of masculinity imply different relationships to women and feminism. The heroic warrior-citizen model tends toward overt misogyny, as it "involves a notion of manliness which is tied to the conquest of women. In Machiavelli's own words, 'Fortune is a woman, and it is necessary if you wish to master her, to conquer her by force.'"[73]

Meanwhile, the patriarchal model ignores women. Where were the women in Hobbes's state of nature?[74] They were presumably in a state of nurture (producing the next generation), or life would have been nonexistent rather than merely "nasty, brutish and short." The bourgeois rationalist model is softer, more egalitarian and democratic. Its philosophers have championed women's rights, and feminism itself has its roots in bourgeois rationalist thought.[75] The affinities between early feminism and bourgeois rationalism might explain some of the similarities between some feminist and liberal critiques of realism, critiques that have encouraged liberals such as Robert Keohane to take an interest in feminist perspectives.[76] Although the concept of cooperation (often promoted in feminist-standpoint approaches) may be a dangerous sign of feminine weakness for realists, bourgeois rationalist masculinity can accommodate it when it is deemed to be in one's rational self-interest to do so. Whether a given quality counts as feminine depends on one's model of masculinity. However, in spite of considerable overlap between liberal and feminist-standpoint critiques of realism, bourgeois rationalism remains problematic for all but liberal feminists for a number of reasons, not least its paternalism.[77]

It is interesting to speculate that gendered rivalries among different models of masculinity may have had a hidden and unacknowledged influence on the interparadigm debate. For example, realism, largely developed in a Cold War climate, has an affinity with the type of Cold War masculinity discussed previously, the masculinity of tough-talking presidents and of John Wayne and James Bond (in his earlier, less parodic appearances). But by 1972, Robert Rothstein was able to argue that realism was outdated and dangerous, remaining popular only because it suited statesmen.[78] This kind of argument resonates with new-man arguments about pathological varieties of masculinity embodying outdated traits. In contrast, if we read between the lines of Kenneth Waltz's counterattack and defense of realist parsimony, the implication is that pluralists and liberals of the 1960s and 1970s were intent on domesticating international relations by examining irrelevant "low" politics and confused matters through theoretical over-complication.[79] Both domesticity and lack of mental clarity have feminine connotations, and one could argue that Waltz and others strove to reinforce their rehabilitation of realism by subtly feminizing "the other" of pluralism.

The convergence of neorealist and neoliberal institutionalism and increased interest in international political economy in the 1980s coincided with the deregulation of international finance. But at the same time there was a transformation of masculinities associated with international banking and finance.[80] Just as academic realism was starting to take political economy more seriously, so new financial forces in the global economy were being clothed in the Cold War imagery of masculinity, images redolent of the diplomat and spy and complete with high-tech gadgetry.[81] Taken together, these developments might reflect the interplay between the processes of globalization, academic developments, and the reorientation of hegemonic masculinities. Moreover, if the latest big debate in IR theory is one between positivist neoliberal and neorealist institutionalists on the one hand and postpositivists on the other,[82] then it is worth considering the relationship between changing constructions of hegemonic masculinity and the development of postpositivist approaches to IR.

Postpositivists, Dissidence, and Hegemonic Masculinities

Some feminists have expressed concern over the continued absence of sustained gender analysis in the majority of postpositivist approaches to international relations despite the obvious compatibilities and epistemological affinities (such as deconstructing dualisms and identities, abolishing the international/political divide, exploring exclusionary strategies, and transforming the agenda) between these and feminist approaches to international relations.[83] Christine Sylvester discusses the claim of some postpositivist dissidents to write from the margins and to bring into view that which has been excluded from modern perspectives. Although such contributors acknowledge that both woman as the "other" of man and femininity as the "other" of masculinity fall into the category of exclusion, they have so far failed to follow this observation up by drawing on feminist scholarship in their own work or including feminist contributions in their edited collections. In this respect they have ended up mimicking the masculinism they might elsewhere undermine.[84]

Acknowledging multiple masculinities would also enrich the arguments made by postpositivists. Richard Ashley, for example, has exposed and deconstructed the paradigm of "sovereign man" that lies behind the concepts of sovereignty, anarchy, and states as rational actors. He argues that the practice of combining atomistic conceptions of man and state sovereignty with systemic arguments about the logic of anarchy is inherently contradictory. To expose these contradictions is to see that

> a paradigm of sovereign man, far from being a pure and autonomous source of history's meaning, is never more than an effect of indeterminate practical struggles in history. It is to see the figure of man as an effect that is always resisted, always an effect that might not happen, and therefore, always an effect in the process of being imposed, resisted, and reimposed, often in transformed form.[85]

Ashley does not explore even the more obvious gendered dimensions of his discourse: the exclusion of women in this paradigm. But whereas at one level this is a discussion of rhetorical strategies in the production of academic knowledge, Ashley is also in effect discussing the ongoing construction of hegemonic masculinities. The conclusion that "modern statecraft is modern mancraft"[86] applies not only to the production of modern theories of IR but also to the production of hegemonic masculine subjectivities through practical participation in modern forms of politics. The "other(s)" of such a paradigm include not only "woman" but also subordinate masculinities and marginalized groups of men.[87]

Ashley is heavily influenced by both Foucault and Derrida, neither of whom address the question of male power directly in spite of their preoccupations with the power/knowledge nexus.[88] The failure to take on board feminist scholarship is not confined to postpositivists in international relations. One could argue that such perspectives are therefore masculinist: Challenging enlightenment dualisms allows the "pimps of postmodernism" to get "a bit of the Other" by indulging in academic cross-dressing. Just like "new men," they enjoy playing with the previously forbidden fruits of femininity (and other exotic cultures) without surrendering their gender privileges.[89]

In spite of such accusations, in challenging the assumptions of modern theory, academic postpositivists have clearly opened up a conceptual space for change with possible gender implications. Peterson has noted that "to the extent that masculinism is privileged, forms of knowledge—including post-positivism—associated with the 'subjective' and the 'feminine' are devalued and resisted as inferior to 'hard science' with its claims to objectivity, certainty and control."[90]

Postpositivist approaches remain marginal to the bulk of IR scholarship.[91] Under these circumstances incorporating feminist scholarship might expose such perspectives, and the male academics who pursue them, to further marginalization.[92] But continuing to recuperate "the other" in conceptual terms alone will not necessarily mean progress as far as women and subordinate men are concerned: "We deceive ourselves if we believe that postmodern theory is attending to the 'problem of difference' so long as so many concrete others are excluded from the conversation."[93]

The moves of postpositivists must be examined against the backdrop of flux and change in hegemonic masculinities, discussed previously. Academic postpositivists open up conceptual spaces for change, but without a clear commitment to dismantling the gender order, such spaces may merely facilitate the further transformation of hegemonic masculinities to serve a new era of globalization. Dissident discussions on such topics as simulation, surveillance, and new technologies may unwittingly mark out the new agendas for hegemonic masculinities to colonize.[94] The struggle between institutionalist and postpositivist approaches can easily become one between competing masculinist futures.

Intellectual rigor notwithstanding, the academic discipline of IR is not exempt from the general observation that the more men align themselves with hegemonic masculinities, the more they boost their own credibility and perpetuate that hegemony.[95] The further away from hegemonic masculinities their perspectives roam, the more easily such perspectives are marginalized. Most female academics are already on the margins, professionally speaking,[96] and as such have less to lose by endorsing feminist approaches. Postpositivists open up an intellectual space that can be used either to undermine the gender order or to reconstitute hegemonic masculinities. If they take on board feminist scholarship in a sustained fashion, they risk further marginalization; if they keep quiet, they find their work recuperated for masculinist purposes.

Conclusion

Multiple masculinities can be examined without losing sight of feminist insights into masculinist power strategies. The perspective outlined here demonstrates that as well as divisions between men and women, the relationships among different masculinities play a part in the gender order. This is not to endorse the elevation of gender as the primary source of oppression over all others or to argue that the gendered dimensions of political processes are always to be prioritized.[97] In hierarchies of masculinities, gender is unlikely to be the only or even the most salient division. However, it is important to pay attention to the gendered aspects of such hierarchies because they demonstrate how the gender order itself curtails the identity choices of subordinate groups of men; they allow us to think more clearly about the complex gendered relationships between differently positioned women and different groups of men,[98] and they also illustrate the pervasiveness of masculinist strategies and gendered metaphors in struggles for power. Theorizing multiple masculinities offers a more rounded, historicized, and contextualized view of gender differences; it provides a theoretical basis for analyzing changes and developments within the gender order; it deals with the complex links between race, gender, class, and other divisions in a more integrated fashion; it offers feminists and their male sympathizers the prospect that some masculinities are more progressive (or at least less regressive) than others; and last, it further denaturalizes the dichotomy of masculinity/femininity by moving away from dualistic grids of analysis.

In terms of IR, an awareness of multiple masculinities raises new questions about the relationships among different masculinities and international practices both for gender-sensitive analyses of specific topics and in connection to overall systemic changes.[99] It also reinforces feminist criticisms of the boundaries of the discipline, because one effect of traditional conceptualizations of IR is that it is constructed as a primary site for the production of masculinities at the same time that this production process is obscured by eliminating personal life and questions of identity from the scope of analysis. Meanwhile, the discipline itself both reflects and (re)produces the dynamics of competing masculinities in the struggle for hegemony. Under such circumstances, challenging the gender order is clearly in the interests of all marginalized perspectives in IR, not just in the interests of avowed feminists.

Notes

I would like to thank the Economic and Social Science Research Council for supporting me during the production of this chapter. Thanks also to Judith Squires, Eric Herring, Richard Little, Richard Shapcott, and my editors, Marysia Zalewski and Jane Parpart, for their helpful comments. The arguments put forward here are being further developed in my Ph.D. thesis, provisionally entitled "Masculinity, Identity and World Politics."

1. See Cynthia Enloe, *Bananas, Beaches and Bases: Making Feminist Sense of International Relations* (London: Pandora, 1990); Rebecca Grant and Kathleen Newland, eds., *Gender and International Relations* (Milton Keynes, England: Open University Press, 1991); J. Ann Tickner, *Gender in International Relations* (Oxford: Columbia University Press, 1992).

2. V. Spike Peterson, "Introduction," in V. Spike Peterson, ed., *Gendered States: Feminist (Re)Visions of International Relations Theory* (Boulder, CO: Lynne Rienner, 1992), p. 8. See also V. Spike Peterson and Anne Sisson Runyan, *Global Gender Issues* (Oxford: Westview Press, 1993); Cynthia Enloe, *The Morning After: Sexual Politics at the End of the Cold War* (Berkeley: University of California Press, 1993); Christine Sylvester, *Feminist Theory and International Relations in a Postmodern Era* (Cambridge: Cambridge University Press, 1994).

3. Terrell Carver, "Introduction," in *Feminist Theory/Political Theory: Perspectives on Gender* (Boulder, CO: Lynne Rienner, 1995).

4. Not all men's studies and men's movement literature is informed by either feminist sympathies or feminist analysis. Even contributors who do see themselves as feminist sympathizers often have woefully inadequate understandings of the workings of the gender order. See Lynne Segal, *Slow Motion: Changing Masculinities, Changing Men* (London: Virago, 1990); and Harry Brod and Michael Kaufman, eds., *Theorizing Masculinities* (London: Sage, 1994).

5. The intervention of black and other postcolonial feminists helped to raise the issue of difference. Their experiences and voices have contributed to the development of postmodern feminism. See bell hooks, *Ain't I a Woman* (Boston: Southend, 1981), and *Feminist Theory: From Margin to Center* (Boston: Southend, 1984); Chandra Talpade Mohanty, "Under Western Eyes: Feminist Scholarship and Colonial Discourses," in Mohanty, Ann Russo, and Lourdes Torres, eds., *Third World Women and the Politics of Feminism* (Bloomington: Indiana University Press, 1991), pp. 51–80; Gayatri Spivak, "Three Women's Texts and a Critique of Imperialism," *Critical Enquiry* 12, 1 (1985); T. Minh-ha Trinh, *Woman, Native, Other: Writing Postcoloniality and Feminism* (Bloomington: Indiana University Press, 1989).

6. Vron Ware, *Beyond the Pale* (London: Verso, 1992).

7. Chantal Mouffe, "For a Politics of Nomadic Identity," in George Robertson, Melinda Mash, Lisa Tickner, Jon Bird, Barry Curtis, and Tim Putnam, eds., *Traveller's Tales: Narratives of Home and Displacement* (London: Routledge, 1994), p. 110.

8. Andreas Huyssen, "Mapping the Postmodern," in Linda J. Nicholson, ed., *Feminism/Postmodernism* (London: Routledge, 1990). Postmodern feminism shares some preoccupations with other varieties of postmodernism and poststructuralism but is a specifically feminist articulation of these preoccupations. For a summary of debates over postmodernity see Barry Smart, *Modern Conditions, Postmodern Controversies* (London: Routledge, 1992).

9. Nancy Fraser and Linda J. Nicholson, "Social Criticism Without Philosophy: An Encounter Between Feminism and Postmodernism," in Nicholson, *Feminism/Postmodernism*, pp. 34–35.

10. Gloria Andalzúa, *Borderlands/La Frontera* (San Francisco: Spinsters/Aunt Lute, 1987); Donna Haraway, *Simians, Cyborgs and Women: The Reinvention of Nature* (London: Free Association Books, 1991); Kathy E. Ferguson, *The Man Question: Visions of Subjectivity in Feminist Theory* (Berkeley: University of California Press, 1993); Mouffe, "For a Politics of Nomadic Identity."

11. This is the position taken by Judith Butler. See Judith Butler, "Gender Trouble, Feminist Theory, and Psychoanalytic Discourse," in Nicholson, *Feminism/Postmodernism*.

12. Denise Riley, *Am I That Name? Feminism and the Category of "Women" in History* (Minneapolis: University of Minnesota Press, 1988), p. 3.

13. Susan Bordo, "Feminism, Postmodernism and Gender-Scepticism," in Nicholson, *Feminism/Postmodernism*, p. 149.

14. Exceptions include Segal, *Slow Motion*; Andrea Cornwall and Nancy Lindisfarne, eds., *Dislocating Masculinity: Comparative Ethnographies* (London: Routledge, 1994); and, to a lesser extent, Enloe, *The Morning After.*

15. Although both stem from the feminist critique of the "universal subject" of science, critiques of masculinism stop short of deconstructing it altogether and rather view it as an exclusively masculine subject. See Sandra Harding, *The Science Question in Feminism* (Milton Keynes, England: Open University Press, 1986).

16. Peterson and Runyan, *Global Gender Issues*, p. 191.

17. Ibid., p. 23.

18. V. Spike Peterson, "Introduction," in Peterson, *Gendered States.* Binary logic is the logic of thinking and ordering knowledge in asymmetrical oppositions, rooted in linguistic practices that distinguish sharply between "self" and "other."

19. Sandra Whitworth, "Gender in the Inter-Paradigm Debate," *Millennium* 18 (Summer 1989); Marysia Zalewski, "Feminist Theory and International Relations," in M. Bowker and R. Brown, eds., *From Cold War to Collapse: Theory and World Politics in the 1980's* (Cambridge: Cambridge University Press, 1993).

20. Harriet Bradley, *Men's Work, Women's Work* (Cambridge: Polity Press, 1989).

21. Enloe, *Bananas, Beaches and Bases.*

22. Peterson and Runyan, *Global Gender Issues*, pp. 24–25.

23. Lynne Segal, *Slow Motion*; David Morgan, "Theatre of War: Combat, the Military and Masculinities," in Brod and Kaufman, *Theorizing Masculinities.*

24. Bradley, *Men's Work, Women's Work.*

25. See Tickner, *Gender in IR.*

26. V. Spike Peterson, "Transgressing Boundaries: Theories of Knowledge, Gender and International Relations," *Millennium* 21 (Summer 1992).

27. Peter N. Stearns, *Be a Man: Males in Modern Society* (London: Holmes and Meier, 1979); Jean Bethke Elshtain, *Public Man, Private Woman* (Princeton: Princeton University Press, 1981); Joan Cocks, *The Oppositional Imagination: Feminism, Critique and Political Theory* (London: Routledge, 1989); Victor J. Seidler, *Rediscovering Masculinity: Reason, Language and Sexuality* (London: Routledge, 1989); David Morgan, *Discovering Men* (London: Routledge, 1992); R. W. Connell, "The Big Picture: Masculinities in Recent World History," *Theory and Society* 22 (1993).

28. Michael Roper and John Tosh, eds., *Masculinities in Britain Since 1800* (London: Routledge, 1991); J. A. Mangan and James Walvin, eds., *Manliness and Morality: Middle Class Masculinity in Britain and America 1800–1940* (Manchester: Manchester University Press, 1987); Stearns, *Be a Man*; Connell, *The Big Picture*; Arthur Brittan, *Masculinity and Power* (Oxford: Blackwell, 1989); Barbara Ehrenreich, *The Hearts of Men: American Dreams and the Flight from Commitment* (London: Pluto Press, 1983); Segal, *Slow Motion.*

29. Harry Brod, "A Case for Men's Studies," in Michael S. Kimmel, ed., *Changing Men: New Directions in Research on Men and Masculinities* (London: Sage Focus, 1987), pp. 275–256.

30. Harry Brod, "Some Thoughts on Some Histories of Some Masculinities: Jews and Other Others," in Brod and Kaufman, *Theorizing Masculinities*, p. 86.

31. R. W. Connell, *Gender and Power* (Cambridge: Polity Press, 1987), pp. 183–188.

32. Raymond Williams, *Marxism and Literature* (Oxford: Oxford University Press, 1977), p. 10.

33. Andrea Cornwall and Nancy Lindisfarne, "Dislocating Masculinity: Gender, Power and Anthropology," in Cornwall and Lindisfarne, *Dislocating Masculinity*.

34. Jeffrey Weeks, "Questions of Identity," in Pat Caplan, ed., *The Cultural Construction of Sexuality* (London: Tavistock, 1987).

35. Ehrenreich, *Hearts of Men*.

36. Although men have a long history of supporting the family wage system, Ehrenreich documents a growing dissatisfaction with domestic life among middle-class men in this period. Ibid.

37. Ibid., p. 130.

38. Kobena Mercer and Isaac Julien, "Race, Sexual Politics and Black Masculinity: A Dossier," in Rowena Chapman and Johnathan Rutherford, eds., *Male Order: Unwrapping Masculinity* (London: Lawrence and Wishart, 1988); Chandra Talpade Mohanty, "Introduction," in Chandra Talpade Mohanty, Ann Russo, and Lourdes Torres, eds., *Third World Women and the Politics of Feminism* (Bloomington and Indianapolis: Indiana University Press, 1991); Karen Hansen, *Distant Companions* (Ithaca: Cornell University Press, 1989).

39. Mrinalini Sinha, "Gender and Imperialism: Colonial Policy and the Ideology of Moral Imperialism in Late Nineteenth Century Bengal," in Kimmel, *Changing Men*. See also Mrinalini Sinha, *Colonial Masculinity: The "Manly Englishman" and the "Effeminate Bengali" in the Late 19th Century* (Manchester: Manchester University Press, 1995).

40. For a discussion of American portrayals of the Japanese as feminine see David Campbell, *Writing Security: United States Foreign Policy and the Politics of Identity* (Manchester: Manchester University Press, 1992), p. 238.

41. Pierrette Hondagneau-Sotelo and Michael A. Messner, "Gender Displays and Men's Power: The 'New Man' and the Mexican Immigrant Man," in Brod and Kaufman, *Theorizing Masculinities*, p. 207. See also Ehrenreich, *Hearts of Men*.

42. See Mercer and Julien, "Race, Sexual Politics"; and Segal, *Slow Motion*.

43. Rosa Linda Fregoso, "The Representation of Cultural Identity in Zoot Suit," *Theory and Society* 22 (1993), p. 661.

44. Tania Modleski, *Feminism Without Women: Culture and Criticism in a "Postfeminist" Age* (London: Routledge, 1991), p. 7.

45. Brittan, *Masculinity and Power*, p. 2.

46. Connell, "The Big Picture," p. 613.

47. R.B.J. Walker challenges both the international-political divide, in *Inside/Outside: International Relations as Political Theory* (Cambridge: Cambridge University Press, 1993), and the private-public divide, in "Gender and Critique in the Theory of International Relations," in Peterson, ed., *Gendered States*. Cynthia Enloe coined the phrase "the personal is international" in Enloe, *Bananas, Beaches and Bases*, p. 195.

48. Ken Booth, *Strategy and Ethnocentrism* (London: Croom Helm, 1979); Robert Jervis, Richard Ned Lebow, and Janice Gross Stein, eds., *Psychology and Deterrence* (Baltimore: Johns Hopkins University Press, 1985).

49. See, for example, Ole Waever, Barry Buzan, Morten Kelstrup, and Pierre Lemaitre, *Identity, Migration and the New Security Agenda in Europe* (London: Pinter, 1993).

50. Barbara Ehrenreich, "Foreword," in Klaus Theweleit, *Male Fantasies*, vol. 1 (Cambridge: Cambridge University Press, 1987), p. xvi.

51. Campbell, *Writing Security*.

52. Ibid., p. 166.

53. Ehrenreich, *Hearts of Men*, p. 103.

54. Ibid., p. 105.

55. Susan Jeffords, *The Remasculinization of America: Gender and the Vietnam War* (Bloomington: Indiana University Press, 1989).

56. Enloe, *The Morning After*, ch. 3.

57. Ibid., p. 79.

58. See Andrew Parker, Mary Russo, Doris Sommer, and Patricia Yaeger, eds., *Nationalisms and Sexualities* (London: Routledge, 1992).

59. See also Ian Welsh, "Men, Masculinity and the Social Construction of Peace," unpublished paper presented at the Joint Annual Convention of the British International Studies Association and the International Studies Association, London, April 1989.

60. Stearns, *Be a Man*; Elshtain, *Public Man, Private Woman*.

61. The nature and extent of contemporary changes are as yet unclear. I am not endorsing the view that they necessarily constitute a dramatic break with the modern era, heralded by a neomedievalism. Indeed, they may represent an intensification of various aspects of modernity (see Smart, *Modern Conditions*). Nonetheless, these changes do need to be examined in a systemic and global, rather than purely international, context.

62. Linda McDowell, "Life Without Father and Ford: The New Gender Order of Post-Fordism," *Transactions of the Institute of British Geographers* 16 (1991).

63. This is not necessarily the same as a decrease in militarism itself. Women as soldiers may be relegitimizing the military. See Enloe, *The Morning After*, p. 60.

64. Frank Mort, "Boy's Own? Masculinity, Style and Popular Culture," in Chapman and Rutherford, *Male Order*; David T. Evans, *Sexual Citizenship: The Material Construction of Sexualities* (London: Routledge, 1993); Connell, "The Big Picture."

65. Examples can be found in almost any copy of the *Economist* printed in the past few years. See also R. W. Connell, *Masculinities* (Cambridge: Polity Press, 1995), plate opposite p. 146.

66. Connell, *Masculinities*, pp. 206–211.

67. Ibid., p. 211.

68. *Independent (London)*, Sunday, December 2, 1995.

69. Campbell, *Writing Security*.

70. "Japan: The New Nationalists," *Economist*, January 14, 1995, p. 19. Whereas previously Japan incorporated Western standards in order to qualify for entry into the European-dominated "international society of states" (see Hidemi

Suganimi, "Japan's Entry into International Society," in Hedley Bull and Adam Watson, eds., *The Expansion of International Society* [Oxford: Clarendon Press, 1984]), now the stakes are a more dominant position within a more thoroughly globalized capitalist production system.

71. Tickner, *Gender in IR*.

72. Elshtain, *Public Man, Private Woman*.

73. Tickner, *Gender in IR*, p. 39.

74. Ibid., p. 46.

75. Diana Coole, *Women in Political Theory* (London: Harvester Wheatsheaf, 1993).

76. Robert Keohane, "International Relations Theory: Contributions of a Feminist Standpoint," *Millennium* 18 (Summer 1989).

77. Cynthia Weber, "Good Girls, Little Girls and Bad Girls: Male Paranoia in Robert Keohane's Critique of Feminist International Relations," *Millennium* 23 (Summer 1994).

78. Robert L. Rothstein, "On the Costs of Realism," *Political Science Quarterly* 87 (Autumn 1972).

79. Kenneth Waltz, *Theory of International Politics* (Reading, MA: Addison-Wesley, 1979).

80. Nigel Thrift, "On the Social and Cultural Determinants of International Financial Centres: The Case of the City of London," in Stuart Corbridge, Nigel Thrift, and Ron Martin, eds., *Money, Power and Space* (Oxford: Basil Blackwell, 1994).

81. Such images dominate the National Westminster Bank Graduate Recruitment Brochure, 1989, and contemporary advertising in the newspaper the *Economist*. This banking imagery is in stark contrast to the feminized and anti-Semitic images of international banking prevalent at the turn of the century, typified by Frank Lloyd Wright's remarks that New York was a "man-trap of monstrous dimensions," a place fit only for banking and prostitution (quoted in Michael S. Kimmel, "The Contemporary Crisis in Masculinity in Historical Perspective," in Harry Brod, ed., *The Making of Masculinities: The New Men's Studies* [Winchester: Allen and Unwin, 1987], p. 142).

82. Yosef Lapid, "The Third Debate: On the Prospects of International Theory in a Post-Positivist Era," *International Studies Quarterly* 33 (Autumn 1989).

83. Whitworth, "Gender in the Inter-Paradigm Debate"; Peterson, "Transgressing Boundaries."

84. Sylvester, *Feminist Theory*, pp. 149–150. For a discussion of French feminist scholarship on the feminine "other" and its implications for women, see Toril Moi, *Sexual/Textual Politics: Feminist Literary Theory* (London: Methuen, 1985).

85. Richard K. Ashley, "Living on Border Lines: Man, Poststructuralism, and War," in James Der Derian and Michael Schapiro, eds., *International/Intertextual Relations: Postmodern Readings of World Politics* (Lexington, MA: Lexington Books, 1989).

86. Ibid., p. 303.

87. The indiscriminate projection of oppositional characteristics onto disparate groups may account for the apparent affinities between marginalized perspectives, such as the similarity between the so-called African worldview and feminist standpoints. See Mohanty, Russo, and Torres, *Third World Women*.

88. See the introduction in Caroline Ramazanoglu, ed., *Up Against Foucault: Explorations of Some Tensions Between Foucault and Feminism* (London: Routledge, 1993).

89. Suzanne Moore, "Getting a Bit of the Other: The Pimps of Postmodernism," in Chapman and Rutherford, *Male Order.*

90. Peterson, "Transgressing Boundaries," p. 196.

91. This is not the case in some other social sciences, where such perspectives are rapidly becoming the new orthodoxy.

92. There is also the thorny question of to what extent male academics can legitimately speak for feminism. Although there is plenty of room for them to speak for feminism as in *supporting* it, speaking for feminism as in *representing* it is trickier. For a discussion on whether men can be feminists see Joseph A. Boone, "Of Me(n) and Feminism: Whose Is the Sex That Writes?" in Joseph A. Boone and Michael Cadden, eds., *Engendering Men: The Question of Male/Feminist Criticism* (London: Routledge, 1990). It is also worth noting that there are problems of representation within feminism even when all the participants are female.

93. Bordo, "Feminism, Postmodernism and Gender-Scepticism," p. 140.

94. See James Der Derian, "The (S)pace of International Relations: Simulation, Surveillance and Speed," *International Studies Quarterly* 34 (Autumn 1990).

95. Connell, *Gender and Power.*

96. Paula J. Caplan, *Lifting a Ton of Feathers: A Woman's Guide to Surviving in the Academic World* (Toronto: University of Toronto Press, 1994).

97. Fred Halliday warns against subsuming everything under gender. F. Halliday, "Hidden from International Relations: Women and the International Relations Arena," *Millennium* 17 (Autumn 1988).

98. For example, black feminists often have a different perspective on the family than do white feminists because of the different positions of their menfolk. See Mohanty, Russo, and Torres, *Third World Women.*

99. In this chapter I have restricted my remarks on masculinities, IR, and global restructuring to the challenges, resistances, and changes to hegemonic masculinities in metropolitan countries. This is due to the limitations of space and is not to suggest or endorse the view that subordinate masculinities, developing regions of the world, or radical political movements within which men are struggling to dismantle "masculinity" are any less deserving of our attention. Indeed, one of the benefits of examining multiple masculinities is that it enables us to discuss more coherently the contradictory positions of subordinate and oppositional groups of men.

3

"Unacceptable Conclusions" and the "Man" Question: Masculinity, Gender, and International Relations

Steve Smith

Just as this book has had a number of titles, so has this chapter, and these too reflect the development of my thinking about the topic since the original invitation to write this piece. Indeed, little of the first draft, presented at the ISA conference in Acapulco, now survives. The major difference has been that having thought, read, and discussed more, I now want to focus much more on masculinity as a social construction. In writing my original paper, I spent quite a lot of time on the relevance of gender (in effect defined as women) for international relations and then looked at the backlash against feminist work. I concluded with some, frankly, patronizing comments about the problems of gender for feminists (mainly to do with the essentialism of standpoint positions). My concern now is to raise three issues. First, I want to discuss the backlash against feminism precisely because I think it has become even more marked since I wrote the first draft. Second, I want to move on to look at masculinity and international relations, specifically focusing on the issues raised in the introduction about the relationship between masculinity(ies) and the ways in which both the practice of international relations and the discipline of international relations (IR) rely on and support specific forms of masculinity. Finally, I want to try and link this chapter with my developing thinking about social and international theory.

I want to say something about the politics of writing this chapter for exactly the reasons raised in the introduction. My original paper engaged in some (typically) liberal handwringing about writing from a position of male and professional (and class and sexual orientation!) privilege. In response to this, one of the editors (Parpart) reassured me that after all I was a man writing about masculinity, not pronouncing on feminism. But, of course, looking back to that first draft, I was writing about feminism, albeit in the name of writing about masculinity. My privileged position had worked to convince me that writing about the backlash against feminist work was confronting masculinity. A whole set of curtains and conceits allowed me to pronounce on feminism by looking at its effect on some male scholars. I managed to avoid looking at how my own privilege permitted me to write so "authoritatively"; I had not even begun to do what I had been asked to do, which was, after all, to see how definitions and practices of masculinity(ies) were involved in the study and practice of international relations. I was blissfully unaware of how these practices and definitions constructed the space within which my own "authoritative" reflections on feminism could take the shape they did. I relied on precisely the foundations (both epistemological and personal) that I should have questioned—hence the very different focus now of my own thinking and of this version of the paper.

To summarize my current thinking on this issue, I want to acknowledge the privileged position I occupy when writing about gender. This privilege does not extend to any epistemological advantage in reflecting on masculinity and international relations—far from it. But it does make it both problematic and all too easy for me to write about gender and international relations—problematic because I can never escape the hermeneutics of privilege and all the deceptions and delusions that this entails. I can write whatever I want and not suffer the consequences. I can pronounce on gender and its role in world politics or in the profession of IR and yet retreat into the circle of privilege I occupy as a senior male academic. Sure, there are the jibes from the "lads," both "new" and "old," but my tenure and salary will not be affected. In that sense it can be all too easy to write about gender. And, of course, by admitting this I make it even easier! Yet one critical difference arises when I start to think about masculinity and international relations: This privilege stops being a protective shield and instead becomes an explicit example of the problem I have to address—hence, again, the change of focus in this version of the paper. So from worrying about how to write on feminism and gender from a position of privilege, I now have to confront the effects of that position in writing about masculinity. For as Rob Walker has noted, to write about women (or gender) "and" international relations is to miss the point: The former is already contained in the latter. International relations already presupposes certain constructions of gender, and thereby of women; so it is with the concepts of men and masculinity in international relations. And thus I have to address Arthur Brittan's worry about his own responsibility for patriarchy and his own reasons for writing about masculinity.[1]

This leads me to a final introductory point: My concern is not with men (or with women, come to that) but with masculinity(ies) and its role in both the practice and the study of international relations. I do not agree with Tania Modleski's worry that moving from a focus on feminism and women to a focus on masculinity will return men to center stage.[2] I do agree that there are problems in focusing on men, precisely because it denotes an assumed equal weight for men and women that threatens to dilute any feminist project. The focus should be on the construction of gendered social relations, for this, it seems to me, problematizes rather than reinforces patriarchy. Such a focus also undermines any inherent naturalism in the study of social relations, itself a massive blow to appeals to an unproblematized "real" world. In short, I will focus on socially constructed notions of gender and their role in international relations.

Unacceptable Conclusions for Whom?

My first concern is to say something about the reception given to feminist work in the discipline of international relations. The title of this section derives from some comments made by Fred Halliday in his introduction to the special issue of *Millennium* dealing with the question of women and international relations.[3] Aside from the fact that it is interesting to ask why a British journal published the first set of papers dealing with matters of gender and international relations when feminist work is far more advanced in the United States than in the United Kingdom, there are two important aspects of Halliday's paper. First, Halliday, who has the lead article in the special issue, is used to legitimate the entire enterprise; thus a very distinguished male scholar had to be paraded to legitimize the scholarly credentials of the subject. Second, Halliday comments on the implications of feminist work in IR, stating, "It is not as if considerations of gender will alter the teaching and research of international relations as a whole."[4] He goes on to say, "It is, in conventional terms, simply preposterous that questions of gender should play [a role in the definition of human rights] between sovereign states."[5] Talking of the possibility of looking at intersections such as women and nationalism and women and human rights, Halliday continues: "Both lead to what are, in conventional terms, 'unacceptable' conclusions."[6]

The "feminist intervention" in IR has provoked a number of reactions. I want to note four in particular. First, some have openly opposed the intervention. Second, some have adopted the strategy of simply ignoring feminist work. Third, there has been incredulity over "what these feminists are on about." Finally some scholars have attempted to incorporate feminist work within a "wider" focus on gender or identity. Paradoxically, what appears the most hostile of these, namely opposition, has been neither the most widespread nor the most worrying reaction. I believe that ignoring or incorporating feminist work is the far more fundamental danger.

I will begin by looking at the reception of feminist work by the traditional IR community and at the conflict between feminist work and the concerns of other postpositivists.[7] I hope to explore ways of avoiding the dangers inherent in incorporating a feminist project within a wider focus on identity. Finally, I want to mention the dangers of a focus on either men or women rather than on gender.

I have been amazed by the hostile reaction to feminist and gender interventions in traditional international relations in both the U.S. and U.K. academic communities. Usually otherwise decent and open-minded scholars (male and female) simply cannot see the point of gender and IR. The main difference between the two academic communities is one of size. The BISA (British International Studies Association) study group on gender and IR was set up in 1992 and is much smaller than the long-established ISA Feminist Theory and Gender Section in the United States. There is no female professor of international relations in the United Kingdom. Yet *Millennium* published the first special issue on the topic. Looking through the main journals in the United States, I saw that feminist theory and gender did not seem to have broken into the mainstream literature. The absence of a feminist contribution in the celebrated *International Studies Quarterly* special issue is a case in point.[8] Only *Alternatives* seems to encourage feminist contributions. Most feminist work appears in specialist journals such as *Signs, Women and Politics, Women's Studies International Forum, Feminist Studies*, and *Feminist Review*. Mainstream sociology journals, and even mainstream political science journals, seem to be far more open than IR journals to feminist scholarship. Thus if you listed all IR journal articles on the topic of gender and IR, my guess is that the majority would be in British journals. This puzzles me.

Of course, gender issues were originally introduced into IR through the areas of development studies and peace research. This first phase of feminist writing in IR was essentially liberal-feminist in character—easily tolerated as long as it stayed in these areas that were thought to be rather odd and irrelevant. But the *Millennium* special issue led to quite a backlash, a backlash that in my experience is more often discussed by the boys in private than in print. After all, it is not good for one's image to appear to oppose gender concerns, although some people have attacked the enterprise openly. Writing in the *Salisbury Review* (a "radical" conservative magazine) in 1990, IR academic Christopher Coker of the London School of Economics and Politics launched a diatribe against the new master of science course in women and international relations developed by Fred Halliday at the LSE.[9] Although Coker acknowledges that "it is easy enough, of course, to make fun of those radical or not so radical feminists who take life too seriously merely because society fails to take them seriously,"[10] he claims that IR cannot be about women any more than it can be about men. Nor does he accept the argument that IR is "gender neutral" or that there is a female alternative to male behavior. Indeed, he claims that if feminists are right when they point to a more peaceful and less aggressive female nature, then "we must regard women as a far greater danger than men have been. For it was just this attitude that prevented us from deterring Hitler."[11] He concludes, "Whether they love or hate humanity, feminists seem unable to look it in the face. They have to study it, 'sanitizing' their research in university doctorates, of which we may now expect many more in yet another otiose academic field of enquiry."[12]

Coker's article is more interesting for the micropolitics of the journal it appears in than for its arguments. Published in a right-wing magazine, it reflected unease among some of his colleagues about the new master of science course on gender and IR in his own department. This makes it even more interesting that *Millennium*, the LSE-run journal, published the "Women and International Relations" special issue and that Coker's colleague Fred Halliday was the moving force behind both the conference that launched the special issue and the master of science course in question. Of course, Coker's arguments remain relatively mild; far harsher things were and are said about feminist work in the subject. As Lord Max Beloff (a very [in]famous conservative Oxford historian) recently put it, the only contribution of gender studies is "keeping people off the labour market for three or more years. . . . There is no justification for spending large sums of public money to enable third-rate students to attend fourth-rate institutions to study fifth-rate subjects."[13]

There seems to me to be two main reasons for this argument apart from any special problem individuals might have with feminist arguments. The first is that feminist work does threaten many male academics in quite a personal way. To the extent that patriarchy exists or that there is male dominance or a different male nature, male academics either feel rather humble and embarrassed or feel attacked personally and therefore react aggressively. To many academics, feminist concerns are very new and complicated, hence their need to be informed about "the feminist position" on things.[14] Many simply cannot be bothered to do the amount of reading necessary to understand the literature.

The second reason is obvious to feminist writers but still needs saying: Feminist work simply does not relate to the professional agenda of IR. The dominance of realism has demarcated what counts as appropriate questions. IR is so tightly determined, from the tyranny of first-year texts to the conformity of the leading journals, that innovation is difficult and threatening. Students and academics alike are not only told what IR is all about but are also provided with detailed reasons for dismissing those approaches that pretend otherwise. IR theory has thereby performed a central ideological function with very real sanctions for those who try to dismantle it. After all, in the United States and increasingly in the United Kingdom, it matters very greatly where you publish, and this inevitably gives enormous power to editors and referees.

I think, however, that the previously mentioned issues are only part of the answer. The real problem goes much deeper. The disciplining of the discipline is carried out through the dominance of positivistic and neopositivistic epistemologies, which have the power to define what counts as an answer to the questions asked by the discipline.[15] This dominance and the realist agenda filter research; thus only liberal feminist concerns have been considered acceptable in IR theory. Many feminist writings in IR have shared a common fate with a host of radical perspectives determined to challenge the dominance of realism.

What does the resistance to feminist work in the discipline tell us about both IR and masculinity? On the one hand, most feminist concerns simply seem irrelevant to most IR scholars. They can accept that women may fare badly as a result of structural adjustment policies or be exploited in nationalist struggles or by multinationals, but they cannot see what most feminist work has to do with "the real world of international relations." I believe this is primarily because of the widespread view that the "real world" is in some crucial way natural or given. The terms and concepts of IR become reified and treated as if they are part of the natural world. Since most feminist work says little about these concepts and terms, it can be dismissed as irrelevant to the "real world" and therefore to IR scholarship. This problem is far more complex than saying that feminist concerns are not seen as part of the IR agenda. Essentially, we have to shift our focus away from ontology toward questions of epistemology, which matters far more than conventional radical wisdom allows.

Yet arguing for an increased sensitivity toward epistemology does not advance our argument very far. After all, a formidable feminist literature[16] deals with feminist epistemology, centering on to what extent epistemology is gendered. Arguing that epistemology matters implies that there is some foundational epistemology, which of course is exactly what many feminist and poststructuralists would dispute. In short, even if the resistance to feminist work says little about masculinity per se, it may say a lot about masculine views of what counts as knowledge.

Therefore, Halliday's warnings about feminism's unacceptable conclusions for the discipline of IR can be understood in two ways. First, taking feminism seriously would be unacceptable for the discipline as traditionally defined. This brings sharply into focus his claim that "it is not as if considerations of gender will alter the teaching and research of international relations as a whole."[17] Indeed, he concludes his article by expressing the hope that gender will "find recognition as an important and distinct topic within the overall research programme of the discipline, and that it will become an established element in its teaching agenda."[18] Such a view is also found in Robert Keohane's call for the adoption of a feminist-standpoint approach to international relations theory.[19] Both writers seem to be arguing that feminist work can be added to the traditional agenda. Halliday hints at this in his comments about the consequences being unacceptable, but I think he means unacceptable for IR as traditionally defined and, therefore, as it has been practiced. Yet there is a tension here; if the questions asked by feminists regarding IR would lead to unacceptable conclusions, thus transforming IR theory, then how can gender concerns simply add to the research program of the subject? In my judgment Halliday can make the two previously quoted statements because he defines feminist concerns in a very specific and somewhat limited way, as Keohane certainly does.

Second, Halliday's "unacceptable conclusions" may mean that if taken literally, feminist concerns, even liberal feminist concerns, may make IR, as currently defined and practiced, untenable. The issues raised by feminism not only do not fit with the discipline, they disrupt the entire edifice of community and society upon which IR and the other social sciences are built. Their foundations are so embedded in gendered identities, subjectivities, and therefore reified structures of common sense that they simply cannot be amended to take account of gender. Of course, questions of "women and . . ." or a focus on how women experience the effects of international relations can be accommodated, but this really is very superficial stuff. What cannot be accommodated is anything that challenges the identity of the sphere of public economic, political, or social behavior: IR as a discipline is effective only within very specific parameters, and these are of course deeply gendered. It is exactly in the Foucaultian sense that the seemingly natural divisions between the human sciences have to be treated genealogically. They are indeed constructs of social structures, and primary among these is gender.

In this light, there may well be a deep incompatibility between feminist work and IR as a discipline. The only options seem to be either to accept and maybe even celebrate this incompatibility (since the parameters are indeed "only" constructs) or to attempt to transcend the impasse. But each of these responses takes those involved further away from the safe world of the discipline, further into the land of irrelevance and normative analysis. To reiterate a point made elsewhere,[20] positivism's greatest sin was to make us think that normative statements should be avoided, that "proper" analysis dealt with the world as it was and is—not as we thought it should or could be—and that we could understand that world relatively unproblematically. In other words, the identity and location of the observer was not an epistemological issue. That giant con diverted the discipline for at least forty years and is partly responsible for the resistance to feminist concerns. Paradoxically, perhaps old-fashioned and much discredited idealism might have been more responsive to feminist work. But it seems Walker is right: Gender "and" international relations is a nonstarter.

What of the relationship between the "feminist intervention" and other postpositivist approaches? The danger here is of course the one alluded to in the introduction to this volume, namely that of incorporation and thereby a loss of the feminist project. Initially I argued that poststructuralist work threatened to undermine the ontological category of woman and turn it, to use Marysia Zalewski's phrase, to one of "woman."[21]

My central worry was that most poststructuralist work ends up with a notion of subjectivity and identity that is a deconstruction of the concept of "woman." Put crudely, I saw a tension between such core agendas and a focus on woman as a site of oppression. The theoretical, even metatheoretical, impulse to deconstruct the transcendental subject was, I thought, in danger of dissolving the subject of woman as a focus for enquiry and as a starting place for analyzing power and domination. The words used are the best indicator of this tendency: Feminist work seems to me to be primarily and unavoidably woman-centered (whatever its precise form), whereas gender focuses on both sexes. Of course, feminist work may lead to a focus on gender, but surely this has to be through a woman-centered lens. Now, my concern was that work on gender was in danger of taking apart identity in such a way that each gender would have a similar social construction and actual instances of power and domination would be ignored or hidden. Unfortunately, Coker made much the same point in his claim that men too are socially constructed and have to suffer role ascription accordingly.

I am now much less worried by this danger of incorporation, but I do want to maintain that for liberal, radical, and socialist feminisms (and for feminist empiricists and standpoint[s] theorists), poststructuralists do not pay sufficient attention to gender generally and to woman specifically. This tension is old hat in the wider feminist and women's studies literature but has not yet been discussed widely within IR. In essence, then, the various elements of the postpositivist revolution may be incompatible because they have at their core fundamentally different and exclusive ontologies and epistemologies. However standpoint feminism gets defined, it must require some category or categories of woman, and yet it is exactly this move that is dissolved or undermined by many poststructuralist methodologies. To the extent that feminist IR involves a call to start analysis from the position of women, it runs up against exactly the same claims about metanarratives that Lyotard, Baudrillard, and Rorty use to undermine dominant discourses.

Moreover, to the extent that gender analysis leads us into studies of masculinity, there is a danger that we end up seeing the master as being as oppressed as the slave or the bourgeoisie as being as much a victim as the lumpenproletariat. In this light, the postpositivist revolution in IR proceeded for many years without facing up to the problem that its elements are incompatible. Initially, the need to make common cause against a dominant orthodoxy bound the separate elements together; but many feminists have begun to worry that poststructuralist IR is just another manifestation of gendered orthodoxy. To quote an old song, "Meet the new boss; same as the old boss." In my judgment the feminist and the poststructuralist literatures are about to diverge on the question of the orthodoxy to be overthrown.

What interests me in the work of feminists such as Cynthia Weber, Christine Sylvester, and Spike Peterson is their interest in the relationship between the politics of a feminist project and their focus on gender. In the years since I first started work on this chapter, I too have become less convinced that the focus has to be on "women," and I therefore am less worried about the dangers of incorporating the feminist project. In that sense I side more with Kathy Ferguson than with Tania Modleski. The most productive focus is on gender, not women or feminism, because only this focus allows the examination of precisely the construction of identities in IR that shape what happens to actual women and men in IR. The problem exists in exactly the kind of assumptions I made in the first draft of this chapter, namely that a focus on gender might ignore the very different lives and opportunities of actual women. I too bought into naive assumptions about identity construction, reinforcing a process that treated them both as more fixed and as less ambiguous than they are. Now I am more interested in calling into question the very identities that I previously wanted to protect so as not to undermine the emancipatory project of feminism. I still remain concerned that there is an attempt within some aspects of the postmodernist project to downgrade questions of gender and, by calling into doubt all social constructions of gendered identities, to divert attention from the power differences between men and women. This diversion can be achieved by focusing more on male than on female scholars. An easy thing to do, this practice reinforces exactly the private/public split that earlier generations of feminist writers fought long and hard to overcome and shows how deeply the politics of writing go. But in the work of, for example, Lacan, Derrida, Lévinas, and Foucault, there is space for analyzing gender in a way that does not reinforce this split.

The third group of writers I want to discuss is one that focuses not on gender as such but on women or men, usually, given the nature of work on gender in IR, the former. I have particularly in mind standpoint feminists. Despite many variants, their central claim involves the assumption that the standpoint(s) of women is related either to biosocial or to situational factors. Women have standpoints because they are biologically women or, in other versions, because they are socially constructed women. Biology versus social construction is the classic tension between sex and gender. If there is any biological causation involved, the implication is that there is something irreducibly biologically determined about not only the female (feminine?) standpoint. There can be lengthy debate over the extent of this reductionism and over the domain it explains, but clearly there is some foundationalist claim being made here. If this claim is true, then the corollary must be that the masculine standpoint is also rooted in biology.

All of this quibbling about biology seems rather bland and is easily dismissed as old hat, but note its consequences for feminist IR. Any biological basis for social behavior makes transcending that behavior impossible. I do not mean simply whether men behave differently than women but rather the subversive statement that to the extent that standpoint theorists believe men and women think differently because they are differently sexed rather than because they have differently inscribed social entities, one implication of taking gender seriously is that deep issues of epistemology are fundamentally gendered. This leads to the dilemma that, to use Thomas Nagel's phrase, it is impossible to have "the view from nowhere" because nowhere cannot exist. Accordingly, there is no way of resolving metatheoretical disputes, particularly those about ethics and what counts as knowledge. Equality thus becomes not merely contestable but essentially incontestable.

Not surprisingly, most feminist scholars seem unwilling to accept these "unacceptable" conclusions. If accurate, the view that equality is incontestable would lead to the impossibility of transcending gender-imposed differences in concepts and understandings with the result that feminist work in IR could never relate to malestream work. Maybe feminist IR is not trying to relate to the mainstream in this way, but in that case, it will not be surprising if malestream work is taken more seriously. And in an obviously patriarchal world, guess which knowledge claims would be seen as portraying the "real world."

The obvious route out of this dilemma is to move away from biological reductionism toward the notion of socially structured standpoints. Thus the focus of thinking about gender in IR should not be on women or men but on the patterns of socially constructed gender relations; or to put it in the form of a question, What forms of masculinity and femininity are entailed by the processes and structures of international relations? In this sense it is neither the sexed body nor the individual that matters; our focus for analysis should not be the body or the individual but the patterns of gendered social relations. Such a focus would allow us to think about what it might mean to be a man in the U.S. Army today or a female factory worker in the Philippines. It would direct our attention to the international processes that help construct what it means to be male or female, as well as pointing to the dependence of the practices of international relations on other gendered structures and processes. This approach would undermine the claims of those who see IR as a separate discipline with distinctive structural charac-

teristics and subject area and thereby contribute to making IR less isola-
tionist as a discipline and more humble in its intellectual pretensions.

The "Man" Question and
International Relations

Speaking of being humble, when I look at the nature of masculinity in international relations I have to reflect, as does Arthur Brittan, on why I am
doing this and on how much responsibility I should feel for patriarchy. This
is not easy, especially since I know all too well the dangers of self-delusion.
It would be easy to pretend that admitting the problem was all I needed to
do. But I want to make a more fundamental point, which is that discussing
masculinity is really very easy on some levels because I can speak frankly
while continuing to enjoy the benefits of being a senior male academic. Do
I get the best of both worlds by being "right on" or "politically correct"—
a term used only by those who oppose such "correctness"—and then going
back to my privileged and comfortable position in the profession? To be
candid, there is no simple way to answer this worry precisely because I can
never be sure of my freedom from self-delusion. All I can say is that I am
aware of privilege and how it works. I see around me many extremely able
female graduate students and colleagues, every bit as "able" (a gendered
term if ever there was one!) as their male counterparts, and I know that
their career chances will, as a group, be far less promising than those of
comparable men. And in the wider political world I see every day of my life
how power works to the advantage of males. I try to correct imbalances and
to undermine patriarchy whenever I can, but I would, wouldn't I? All I can
say is that just as writing about masculinity is painful, so is it humbling, and
I guess that is not a bad start as bad starts go. If only more male professors
of IR felt humble about their privilege, the discipline might be a lot more
gender aware and progressive.

I want to look at the "man" question in terms of both the practice of IR
and the discipline of IR. Interestingly, each poses the question of whether
the focus should be on men or masculinity. As to the practice of international relations, my concern is with the kinds of men produced by the current practices of international relations. I want to make four main points
about masculinity and international relations.

First, in talking about masculinity we are doing something far more radical than confining our analysis to women or gender. We are taking on far
more one would think; that is, we are calling into question the entire state
apparatus. Thus, as noted in the introduction, the "man" question, not the
"woman" question, is the one to be asked. The problem is not simply
women's exclusion from the international arena but rather the forms of
masculinity (and femininity) that associate certain categories of men with

existing state structures and international processes. The focus, then, is on the nature of masculinity(ies) in gendered structures.

My second point is that to analyze masculinity(ies) and power risks an incredible backlash, since any move to point to the socially constructed nature of masculinity axiomatically undermines the "naturalness" of the existing power divisions between men and women. Assumptions about what it means to be a man (let alone a "real" one) run very deeply in men; their ideological status is powerfully protected by a series of auxiliary appeals to a "natural" set of differences or to some equally commonsensical views about biology and male and female physical and emotional characteristics. Probing masculinity, and specifically probing it in a way that makes it appear that the existing social order could be other than it is, is a full, frontal attack on centuries of domination and privilege. Compared to the stakes involved here, feminism is a much less radical attack on male domination.

Third, I want to note the extent to which masculinities in international relations are both socially and historically constructed. Just as Tilly can claim that the state made war and war made the state, so is it the case that the processes of state formation and warmaking created certain forms of masculinities. This assumption, of course, runs counter to popular notions of any fixed biological essentialism for masculinity, but the crucial move is to develop understandings of masculinity(ies) that both problematize the concept and refuse to treat it as in some way fixed or biologically determined. Such a move allows us both to link work on masculinities to other social constructivist theories of international relations and to remove any epistemological or ontological foundations from theories that rely on accounts of "man's true nature." Recent work on masculinity in gender studies, such as that by Bob Connell and Victor Seidler,[22] supports this move by treating masculinity as a plural. The focus then moves from men to questions about the kinds of masculinities (and femininities) that specific patterns of gender relations involve; these patterns can then be investigated to see how they are themselves instantiations of other social relations.

Finally, I want to turn to one example, men and war, to probe the kinds of masculinities produced or implicit in international relations. Here I can draw on the excellent work by many feminists, most notably Jan Pettman, Jean Elshtain, Cynthia Enloe, and Ann Tickner.[23] This example is of course doubly useful, since it is both central to debates about the differences between the genders and central to IR's main concerns. The first question is whether men are naturally aggressive. Much of the literature seems to imply this is so, but then why do military organizations have to instill in new recruits such a clear pattern of aggression? In my view, the kind of masculinities required by military organizations has nothing to do with any natural masculinity but rather has meaning only in opposition to the feminine (whether practiced by biological females or males). Thus masculinity in the military is itself constructed as a gendered relationship between a "real" man and other forms of both masculinity (i.e., queer) and femininity (i.e., girl). A tremendous amount of ideological work has to go into getting soldiers to behave as required, and we can only begin to appreciate these complexities if we see masculinities as produced within very complex gendered relations (see Chapters 5 and 7).

Different forms of masculinity seem to be required in different aspects of international relations, for example, in war fighting as opposed to war planning or in nationalist movements as opposed to peacekeeping. At one stage the man is meant to be rational and in control and at another to allow his "natural" aggression to come out. In some instances he is meant to act as protector of the "other," the female-and-child; in other war situations it is accepted that the spoils of war include the rape of the conquered. Under any criteria, masculinity is a far more complex process than any biological or essentialist theory can ever allow. Moreover, these varying conceptions of masculinity derive their meaning not from some absolute standard but from their linkage to other gendered male/female and male/male relations.

In my view hegemonic masculinity dominates the practice of international relations. This hegemonic view is marked by its homophobia, an acceptance of men dominating women, and a strident heterosexuality. Now this is where we have to pose the question raised by Brittan: To what extent are all men responsible for this ideology? Not all men would accept this definition of masculinity, but it clearly constructs a system through which all men derive some benefits. Thus although I may abhor such a version of masculinity, I nonetheless continue to enjoy the benefits it bestows on me.

For these reasons, the versions of masculinities that play out in international relations seem to be a more fruitful course of inquiry than looking at whether men have a different view than women of security, the nation, or war. They almost certainly do have different views, but my interest is not so much in establishing these differences or in locating them within some essential maleness or femaleness as it is to inquire how these views derive from social constructions of masculinity. Thus, for example, the excellent and illuminating work of Carol Cohn[24] on the language of intellectuals in the field of defense is important not because she tries to say anything about some essential masculinity but because she takes an almost anthropological approach to the worlds of defense planners; she treats them as almost another culture. Occupations such as defense planning require a very specific kind of masculinity, one far removed from the forms of masculinity required in other male roles. The focus, then, is rightly on masculinity and not on men. As Caroline Ramazanoglu puts it, "Changing men is not simply about men developing new identities, but about the structural transformation of gendered power relations."[25] Specific kinds of men are created by international relations because its practices become instantiated in certain forms of masculinity, themselves existing within wider gendered relations.

When we turn to the discipline of IR, the situation becomes not so much what forms of manliness and manhood are constructed as what the responsibilities are of men in this and similar gendered structures. I want to make three main points:

First, the discipline is clearly very gendered in both its working practices and its power structure. This ranges from patterns of sexual harassment in the workplace to promotion prospects to child-care arrangements to salaries. At first sight, the gendered nature of the discipline may be seen as having nothing to do with masculinity, since appeal is always made to objective standards of employment or promotion. Thus few male academics support discrimination against women. But they might well define the academic enterprise in such a neutral way that it effectively excludes most women. I am thinking not so much about issues such as child care, which are often at least in the public arena, but more that the standards for promotion take little account of most women academics' different career patterns; thus, on the one hand, there may be liberalism over child-rearing responsibilities, but the same liberal terrain will ensure that promotion and tenure are based on the same "objective" standards for both sexes, thereby discriminating in a wider sense against women with children. This discrimination raises significant questions about the responsibilities of men in such gendered structures.

My second concern is that all too often the subject matter of IR is seen as genuinely gender-neutral; thus work on gender, whether done by men or (usually) by women, is seen as irrelevant or ideological. This perception has been a matter of considerable concern for feminists working in IR departments, as well as for profeminist men. If the analysis of gender by women makes waves, think what the reaction will be to male scholars who seek to question the givens of masculine identity in IR. For all analysts of gender, be they men or women, the most serious problem is that the discipline will not easily accept their questions as legitimate. The belief in a "real" world that presents itself to us is so deeply entrenched in the positivism that dominates the discipline that questions about the construction of the identities that are the furniture of that world are simply deemed irrelevant.

Third, I believe masculinity is deeply entrenched in the ways in which we think about IR, because the subject is virtually always male. I do not mean the obvious reference to "him" or "he" but the rather more radical thought that the methodologies and epistemologies of IR are always based on so-called male attributes. This raises some important issues, since our assumptions about masculinity do a lot of the work in explaining notions such as "rational" decisionmaking; evaluating evidence "logically"; and explaining concepts such as "certainty," "cause," and "constraint." The model subject is usually implicitly Cartesian, and thus whatever the topics of our inquiries into IR, analysis is nearly always undertaken on terms that reflect dominant masculine notions of knowledge and knowledge-making. And of course, attempts to put forward alternative views are usually met with hostility. The debates about feminist epistemology illustrate this only too well. But my point is also that the discipline is so locked into masculinist epistemology that these ways of knowing literally stop us from asking and answering questions about the very identities that lie behind these assumptions. To paraphrase Wittgenstein, whereof we cannot speak, thereof we must remain silent.

All of these points raise the issue of men's responsibilities in these gendered structures. This issue is genuinely difficult, however much the intention is to be progressive. One obvious route forward is for men to try to confront their own actions and beliefs with the same degree of doubt over their identity(ies) that they see feminist colleagues applying. But of course this gets back to certainty and foundational knowledge and, in so doing, calls far more into question than one's gendered identity; it potentially calls the entire structure of scholarship into question. My own hard-fought conclusion is simply to try to be as self-conscious about the assumptions I am making about gender or any other form of identity and to see how far I can take that process. I have to admit that I soon run up against some fairly powerful internal constraints in my thinking, not because I do not want to reflect on my own masculinity and the role it plays in both my scholarship and my professional life but rather because I do not want a tolerance of difference to go as far as a position of "anything goes." Or to put it very personally, I do believe in certain "standards" of scholarship despite recognizing that they are fundamentally gendered. My own work is now in the area of epistemology, and I find it difficult to call everything about knowledge claims into question. So although I can well see how knowledge is gendered, I have a (naive?) belief in the possibility of communicative competence, or at least of the existence of standards of academic discourse that can tolerate difference and yet have epistemological rules (if not foundations in the strict empiricist or rationalist sense).

I also feel that men in gendered structures need to do what they can (usually far more than they admit) to resist dominant forms of masculinity, be they in relationship to feminism or to gay/lesbian sexual identity. I do not accept the kind of reaction that pays lip service to equality (usually defined as equality of opportunity) but actually defines the parameters for action very narrowly. Crucially for the purposes of this book, these parameters rarely include self-consciousness about one's own masculinity or the gendered standards of scholarship.

Conclusion

In this chapter I have attempted to look at two main instances of masculinity in international relations, the reaction to feminist work in IR and the kinds of men and masculinities produced within the practice and discipline of IR. As to the first, my central conclusion is that feminist work, and here I do mean "feminist" rather than "gender" or "women-centered," has been as accepted into the discipline of IR as might have been expected. It has been trivialized and attacked, marginalized and dissolved. Feminist scholarship is simply too radical for the mainstream, which cannot take it on board without a fundamental shift in emphasis, and too conservative (or limited in scope) for the poststructuralists, for whom it appears as merely yet another metanarrative. As a result, both tend to downplay feminist work; it has "unacceptable" conclusions for each of their projects. Whereas this outcome is not surprising for the mainstream, it is more so in the case of the poststructuralists given their own ostensible focus on all forms of domination and hierarchy. Unhappily, both approaches share an antipathy to the feminist project.

IR as a discipline is the historically constructed space within which thinking about international relations is possible. That space operates by holding some things such as gender constant and by defining concerns about gender as irrelevant or as outside the scope of the subject. Yet the reaction to feminist work within IR gives cause for thinking that whatever the IR approach, feminist concerns will always have unaccepted conclusions for the field.

Regarding the second main instance of masculinity, I have concluded that the practice of international relations requires very specific constructions of masculinities and that the discipline of IR poses clear challenges to men working in these gendered structures. The constructions of masculinity embedded in the practices of international relations are often contradictory and constructed in reference to other gendered identities. They are neither natural nor biologically determined, and they represent instantiations of power relations between the genders. Furthermore, there is a hegemonic masculinity at work that has as much to say about male-male relations as male-female relations, imbued as this masculinity is within a dominant heterosexual and homophobic culture. In this sense, men as well as women are victims of the dominant definitions of masculinity; often, in a world of war, they are literally victims.

Within the discipline of IR the problem is both masculinity as reflected in ways of knowing and thinking and men in the way they confront (or do not confront) their own privilege. The analysis of masculinity as socially constructed fundamentally destabilizes the discipline as we know it. If feminism has led to unacceptable conclusions, then an analysis of the socially constructed nature of masculinity seems likely to threaten the discipline even more profoundly, especially those who still believe in a positivist approach to the natural and social worlds. This approach really would be undermined if the very identities and units of its models and worlds were not the fixed or theoretically primitive categories that have been assumed. As for the obligations of men in the gendered structure of IR, my conclusions seem to me to be both weak and as much as I can say! At the end of the day, the most constructive way forward is for men to reflect on their own privilege and situation as much as possible and to inquire into the construction of their own masculinity; but I do not want to pretend that this is an easy option. As Caroline Ramazanoglu has noted, personal reflection and struggle is not enough—the work has to extend to the wider social structures within which the dominant conceptions of masculinity operate.[26]

My analysis of the unacceptable conclusions and the "man" question leads me to five overall concluding comments about masculinity(ies), gender, feminisms, and international relations. First, the focus in future should be on gender rather than on women or men. Gender allows one to study the patterns and interrelationships between masculinities and femininities. I do not imply that the gender roles are equally oppressive; heterosexual men in general are not as oppressed as a gender as are women or as groups such as blacks and gays. Second, gender roles are socially constructed and defined by their relationship with one another. As long as they are not defined too tightly, there is room for agency, however limited its space. There is certainly room for taking responsibility for one's part in continuing to make masculinity what it is. Third, seeing gender as socially constructed opens up the possibility of linkages with other social constructivist theories and the wider identity literature. Here the important move is to focus not on the individual but on the nature of the social relations that define and create individuals. Fourth, gender constructions must be historicized so that IR can account for the varying ways that gender relations are entailed by wider social, cultural, economic, and political factors. Finally, IR practitioners and theorists should still search for the patterns of gendered power relations in international relations, but the question should not be Where are the women (or even the men)? but Where are the gender relations? Only when we ask these questions will the discipline of IR be able to demonstrate just how much international relations depends on patterns established by socially constructed definitions of what it is to be a man or a woman in the contemporary world. Such a focus would be able to deal both with the hierarchy of men and women and with the competing accounts of masculinity(ies) that so structure international relations. This hierarchy and these competing accounts are not simply additional frills; they are logically entailed by the practices at the core of our discipline. Yet these logical entailments have never been exposed for the ideologies they are. It is about time that IR scholars and practitioners treated identities such as these less as the starting points for analysis and more as a central core of international relations. The good news is that gender relations and identities are socially constructed and are therefore amenable to change; the bad news is that "we" made them that way and "we," whether in our practice of international relations or our study of it, go on remaking them.

Notes

1. Arthur Brittan, *Masculinity and Power* (Oxford: Basil Blackwell, 1989), p. 200.

2. Tania Modleski, *Feminism Without Women: Culture and Criticism in a "Postfeminist" Age* (London: Routledge, 1991), p. 5.

3. Fred Halliday, "Hidden from International Relations: Women and the International Arena," *Millennium* 17, 3 (1988), pp. 419–428.

4. Ibid., p. 426.

5. Ibid., p. 425.

6. Ibid., p. 423.

7. See Yosef Lapid, "The Third Debate: On the Prospects of International Theory in a Post-Positivist Era," *International Studies Quarterly* 33, 3 (1989), pp. 235–254; and Steve Smith, "The Self-Images of a Discipline: A Genealogy of International Relations Theory," in Ken Booth and Steve Smith, eds., *International Relations Theory Today* (Cambridge: Polity Press, 1995), pp. 1–37.

8. See Rob Walker and Richard Ashley, eds., "Speaking the Language of Exile: Dissidence in International Studies," special issue of *International Studies Quarterly* 34, 3 (1990).

9. Christopher Coker, "Women and International Relations," *Salisbury Review* (June 1990), pp. 23–27.

10. Ibid., p. 23.

11. Ibid., p. 26.

12. Ibid., p. 27.

13. Lord Max Beloff, "Elite and Proud of It," *Times Higher Education Supplement* (August 9, 1996), p. 13.

14. For a clear analysis of this problem, see Marysia Zalewski, "Well, What Is the Feminist Perspective on Bosnia?" *International Affairs* 71, 2 (1995), pp. 339–356.

15. Steve Smith, "Positivism and Beyond," in Steve Smith, Ken Booth, and Marysia Zalewski, eds., *International Theory: Positivism and Beyond* (Cambridge: Cambridge University Press, 1996), pp. 11–44; and Smith, "The Self-Images of a Discipline."

16. See Sandra Harding, especially *The Science Question in Feminism* (Milton Keynes, England: Open University Press, 1986); Mary Hawkesworth, "Knowers, Knowing, Known: Feminist Theory and Claims of Truth," *Signs* 14, 3 (1989), pp. 533–557; Linda Alcoff and Elizabeth Potter, eds., *Feminist Epistemology* (New York: Routledge, 1993).

17. Halliday, "Hidden from International Relations," p. 426.

18. Ibid., p. 427.

19. Robert Keohane, "International Relations Theory: Contributions of a Feminist Standpoint," *Millennium* 18, 2 (1989), pp. 245–253. See also in reply to this, Cynthia Weber, "Good Girls, Little Girls and Bad Girls: Male Paranoia in Robert Keohane's Critique of Feminist International Relations," *Millennium* 22, 2 (1994), pp. 337–349.

20. Steve Smith, "The Forty Years Detour: The Resurgence of Normative Theory in International Relations," *Millennium* 21, 3 (1992), pp. 489–506.

21. Marysia Zalewski, "The Women/'Women' Question in International Relations," *Millennium* 23, 2 (1994), pp. 407–423.

22. Victor Seidler, *Rediscovering Masculinity: Reason, Language and Sexuality* (London: Routledge, 1989); R. W. Connell, *Masculinities* (London: Routledge, 1995).

23. Jan Pettman, *Worlding Women: A Feminist International Politics* (St. Leonards, NSW: Allen & Unwin, 1996); Cynthia Enloe, *Bananas, Beaches and Bases: Making Feminist Sense of International Politics* (London: Pandora, 1993), and *The Morning After: Sexual Politics at the End of the Cold War* (Berkeley: University of California Press, 1993); Jean Elshtain, *Women and War* (New York: Basic Books, 1987); J. Ann Tickner, *Gender in International Relations* (New York: Columbia University Press, 1992).

24. See Carol Cohn, "Sex and Death in the Rational World of Defense Intellectuals," *Signs* 12, 4 (1987), pp. 687–718, and "War, Wimps and Women: Talking Gender and Thinking War," in M. Cooke and A. Woollacott, eds., *Gendering War Talk* (Princeton: Princeton University Press, 1993).

25. Caroline Ramazanoglu, "What Can You Do with a Man? Feminism and the Critical Appraisal of Masculinity," *Women's Studies International Forum* 15, 3 (1992), p. 346.

26. Ibid., p. 347.

4

Masculinity and the Fear of Emasculation in International Relations Theory

**Lucian M. Ashworth
and Larry A. Swatuk**

Perhaps the most widely discussed news story in the Western world in 1994 was a "malicious" wounding of a husband by his wife. It led to a media circus, produced a new verb—"to bobbitt"—and caused men from all different walks of life and educational backgrounds to turn pale and cross their legs. Malicious woundings, not to mention murder, go unreported daily in the United States. This one caught the attention of the Western world only because it involved a penis and hence dredged up male fears of emasculation.

This chapter deals with this fear of emasculation as it manifests in the development of mainstream international relations (IR) theory. We examine the classical debate between conservatism (which eventually fed into realism) and liberalism (idealism or liberal internationalism) from a gendered perspective.[1] Since the inception of international relations as a field of study, liberalism/idealism has (unsuccessfully) sought to displace conservatism/realism as the dominant mode of inquiry and method of analysis (Swatuk 1991). However, the gendered nature of this dialectic has been neglected.

One critique of this interparadigm debate is that by limiting mainstream debates to arguments and claims to truth as made by realists and liberals, more critical and particularly feminist approaches are marginalized (see Holsti 1985 as compared to George 1994 and Runyon and Peterson 1991). We seek to build on this criticism by focusing on the masculinist bias in mainstream theory. We argue that by couching these debates within the veiled context of what it means to be properly masculine, realist and liberal IR approaches are not only gendered and androcentric but are indeed mutu-

ally constitutive. Realism and liberalism define themselves not only in relation to each other's theoretical claims but in mutual disdain of dominant
Western conceptions of femininity. For example, from a realist perspective,
to be an idealist is to be irrational and prone to moralizing, which has no
place in the hard-hearted world of power-maximizing states (see Levi
1969). To base one's theory on the "ought" rather than the "is" is therefore
to engage in "weak" or "failed" theory-building (Carr 1939; Morgenthau
1985). For realists, liberals are not "man enough" for the dangerous and
deceitful world of international affairs.

A common liberal counterattack has been to respond with an increasingly scientific and androgynous theory based upon impersonal concepts
such as regimes, interdependence, or "the end of history" (Keohane 1984;
Burton 1972; Fukuyama 1992). For liberals the truly masculine man is one
who discards pseudoscientific notions of the immutability of power or of
defects in human nature and accepts the superiority of progress, rational
analysis, and technological advance.

Each theory emerges from an androcentric, even racist, conception of
social relations.[2] These theories have sought to render themselves scientific
with each aspiring to an objective analysis of international relations by
drawing selectively from recorded and prehistoric events (see Keegan
1993; Macdonald 1987). Most important, by confining the debate to
proper forms of masculinity, both conservatism and liberalism are better
able to resist critical challenges to the dominant paradigm, thereby con-
tributing, as Rowena Chapman suggests, to the production of "a hybrid
masculinity which is better able and more suited to retain control" (quoted
in Chapter 6).

To understand this contemporary split between masculinities in orthodox
IR, we describe the ideological background of orthodox IR theory, looking
back to the conflict between conservative and liberal ideas in Western
thought. Then we examine how this earlier liberal-conservative split influenced the development of masculinities associated with liberal and realist
IR and how each, in seeking theoretical hegemony, pursues a strategy that
partially involves the emasculation of the other. Before proceeding with that
discussion, however, we must first say a few words about gender in international relations.

Gender and International Relations

Traditionally, gender has been seen as a physical, unchanging attribute.
Physical properties unique to a particular sex (and especially supposed
physical properties of the brain) were meant to produce different gender
properties.[3] We argue, rather, that gender is constructed by associating particular behavioral traits with one or the other of the sexes.

Gender as a social construct is not a predetermined set of conditions and behaviors but rather varies significantly in time and space and within and among cultures. Gender is not dichotomous but is rather a continuum of undisclosed shape and size (see, for example, Threadgold and Cranny-Francis 1990). Masculinity and femininity are not simply biological categories. One must prove one's femininity or masculinity, and the criteria for proof changes in time and space (see, for example, Brod 1992). Rather than being an inescapable biological necessity, gender represents a cultural standard that not all are able to (or even want to) reach. "Failed" men and women, those who do not live up to their prescribed gender roles, are a constant reminder of both the power and arbitrariness of gender roles. This view of gender as cultural has been gaining acceptance over the past decade, and increasingly, current analysis of the relationship between masculinity and femininity is based on this approach (Sylvester 1994, 4; Ramazanoglu 1992, 340–342). Physical emasculation, as illustrated by the Bobbitt case, graphically demonstrates masculine fears of a loss of masculinity (through a loss of physical maleness), but fears of emasculation can extend to the worry about losing those traits that society regards as masculine (see Chapter 6).

By regarding gender as learned, we side with the early, against the later, Freud. Gender roles are learned by children through observing the adults around them, not through any process linked to the particular physical attributes of the sexes, as Freud would later claim (Freud 1905, 1925–1931). This position allows us to refuse the concept of two monolithic and homogeneous genders and to see multiple forms of both masculinity and femininity. Even so there are generally consistent and hegemonic conceptions in the West of what masculinity and femininity are. Mary Anne Warren, in *Nature of Woman*, defined Western conceptions of gender with two lists of psychological traits. The feminine included gentleness, empathy, compassion, nurturance, sensitivity, and unselfishness; masculine traits centered on ambition, independence, aggressiveness, and rationality (quoted in Vetterling-Braggin 1982, 5–6).

For international relations theory, this categorization is interesting because it separates the normative and moral from the objective and active. Morality is taken seriously, as de Tocqueville claimed in the nineteenth century, in the feminine realm (quoted in Elshtain 1981, 131); to be masculine is to privilege looking and objectivity over feeling and empathy (Code 1991, 139–150, 170–172). To take morality in international theory seriously is to portray a feminine characteristic. By contrast, to look beyond the normative (to be independent and rational) toward an "objective" understanding is to be masculine.

The historical representation of masculinity and femininity in Western social thought as binary opposites profoundly affects the analysis and praxis of politics at all levels: from the household (i.e., man as breadwinner) to the civil state (i.e., the domestic, knowable realm) to the anarchical interstate system (i.e., the unknowable "other"). In all cases, politics is dependent on a gendered definition of power where control and domination" are rewarded and compromise and trade-offs are only for those weak of will and body (Runyon and Peterson 1993). Similarly, economics has come to be equated with modern notions of rational man over temperamental [i.e., feminine] nature (Merchant 1980, 1989). The character of the global political economy in the late twentieth century, therefore, reflects the exploits of the masculine, which is controlling, rational, self-reliant, risk-taking (Marchetti 1989). Similarly, ideas, institutions, and material conditions have commingled to objectify and commodify women and entrench them as states to be protected, as natural resources to be exploited, as "other" markets to be captured, and as producers of and primary caregivers to the next generation of labor.

Central though this binary conception of gender is to much of Western thought, it presents an illusory dichotomous opposition between genders that obscures important distinctions within masculinity and femininity. Interestingly enough, once the idea of fractures within Western conceptions of masculinity and femininity is accepted, the division between what is masculine and what is feminine tends to be less clear. Fractures within masculinity have played a crucial part in defining the relationships between the two orthodox paradigms in IR: namely realism and liberal internationalism. The division of orthodox IR into two different masculine camps has led to a competition between two aspiring hegemonic masculinities over which is more masculine (real and objective) and which should be regarded as inferior and feminine (subjective and normative).

The Secret Prehistory of International Relations

Realism and liberalism claim an objectivity—a divine view from a *nunc stans*—that the subjectivity of their origins denies. Realism claims an understanding of the innate laws of human nature that govern all human action; liberal IR assumes that it understands the nature of human progress in accordance with the doctrines of reason. In this sense, both paradigms also represent an irreconcilable split between two masculinities: the former highlighting an aggressive human nature, the latter the powers of rational man.

Orthodox IR was and remains a product of the conflict between conservatism and the forces supporting what became the Enlightenment reaction to conservatism. It is both an andro- and Eurocentric enterprise that in its post-Westphalian form has used selective global and historical examples to universalize the experiences of European statesmen.

The construction of distinct domestic and international spheres was as much a result of the partial victory of the Enlightenment as it was a product of post-Westphalian institutional changes. By conservatism we mean the ideology that supported the hierarchical and fundamentally aristocratic order that succeeded the political order of the high Middle Ages. Post-medieval conservatism maintained the notion of a secular hierarchy supported by tradition and order.[4] The interaction of this conservatism and the liberal Enlightenment produced the realist/liberal split that divided both the subject of international relations and the manifestation of masculinity within that subject.

The crucial contrast for the conservative advocate was between the orderliness of life within a legitimate social hierarchy and the state of nature that exists between states or in a state of anarchy within a disordered state. According to the conservatives, hierarchy was necessary to protect subjects from domestic disorder and from invasion and attack from outside. The dominant warrior-aristocrat saw himself both as a moral protector of his subjects and as the scourge of outsiders who threatened his social hierarchy. He was presented as a father figure presiding over and protecting his family. Indeed, Robert Filmer's justification for monarchical rule was based on his interpretation of monarchy as a political offshoot of fatherly rule going back to the sovereignty of Adam (Filmer 1652, 110–112; and 1680, 12–24). The conservatives believed the warrior should be courteous and honorable at home but aggressive and uncompromising in the state of nature that exists outside of a properly ordered society. That this warrior ethic was something to be aimed at meant that there was plenty of room for "failed" men, whether they were the tyrannical "bad father" or those who were just weak. The church represented an avenue for expressing a different kind of fatherly conduct, for which the secular warrior could not serve as a paradigm.

A sort of domestic-international split existed within conservative practice and self-image, albeit defined more on the behavior of the elite than institutionally. Social hierarchy and traditions meant the warrior-aristocrat within a society had a strict and circumscribed role. This equally referred to relations between European aristocrats, who shared similar traditions and hierarchies and therefore respected each other as honorable men. Thus war between European sovereigns, even when infected with religious strife, was governed by laws and codes of honor that reflected the conservative elite's self-image as chivalrous heir of a timeless tradition. Beyond this system of shared values the aristocrat ceased to be a man of honor and instead became a protector and propagator of his values (Raleigh 1661, 58).

In addition to these international and social levels, conservatism recognized a third level of political activity that was both prior to and an influence on the constitutional form of the state. Across Europe, the family unit, living in a home and headed by the father, had emerged as a new kind of social unit prior to and just after the end of the Middle Ages. By the seventeenth century the open and public dwellings of the Middle Ages were giving way to an idea of a home occupied, primarily, by one family. Within the family the notion of parental, and particularly fatherly, responsibility toward children replaced older communal forms of living (see Rybczynski 1986, chs. 1–3). The conservative age of the sixteenth and seventeenth centuries marked a transition between the modern conception of a private (nonpolitical) home life and the medieval conception of the house and family as fully integrated parts of public existence. Although the family remained public in the conservative age, its existence as a recognizable and basic unit of society made it a paradigm for the proper ordering of society. Hierarchies of masculinities and men were related to kinship hierarchies and the social order.

The twin pillars of conservative society—tradition and order—drew on this model of the family. The great success of conservatism in the more stable parts of Europe was due to the compatibility and mutual support of tradition and order in constitutionally secure (hence "domestic") intrastate situations. In interstate relations, there were neither traditions nor order, and consequently conservatism assigned this arena to the hypermasculinity of the uncontrolled warrior. This hypermasculinity outside of domestic society assumed the supremacy of the human desire to dominate through the use of unrestrained force and the primacy of war as a means of achieving ends. War was, however, not meant as an end in itself but as the means by which the traditional and legitimate order of the dynastic state would be preserved. The goal of war was peace, albeit a particular kind of peace—defined by a hierarchical order and aristocratic elite interests—but peace nonetheless (R.W., nd, 2; and Bland 1647, 12).

Conservatism did not lack for philosophical supporters. Social theorists as diverse as Francis Quarles, Thomas Hobbes, Gottfried Leibniz, and Robert Filmer provided intellectual reasons for the conservative orthodoxy. They all stressed the importance of order to human well-being and contrasted it with the disorder of egalitarian living outside of a social hierarchy (Leibniz [1683] 1988 , 186; and Quarles 1642, 1). Order, in the form of a hierarchical authority headed by a single sovereign, was thus a guarantor of peace and prosperity for all. What limited the claim of any order, especially "tyrannical" orders established by usurpers, was the importance of tradition, and in particular those traditions tied to monarchical behavior and the corresponding rights of subjects (see Tuck 1993, ch. 2).

Although tradition and order were often compatible, the potential for dispute between them always existed. Machiavelli, who was in some respects a precursor of conservative political theory, treated tradition and order as compatible in the normal and proper relations discussed in *The*

Discourses but saw them as fundamentally different concepts in the break-down and reforming of order outlined in *The Prince*. In good times conservatives valued both order and tradition, but when under attack from anti-conservative forces in troubled times, conservatives favored order as an abstract and nontraditional entity. This is seen most clearly in Hobbes's defense of order, which could just as easily have been a defense of Cromwell's protectorate—a defense of the Royalist course.

Hobbes reconstructed conservatism, replacing tradition with instrumental reason as the legitimator of conservative authority. He argued that each *man* seeks power in order to receive goods in the future but that each individual's power is incompatible with the power of other individuals. The only power that matters is the surplus power that any one individual has over his contemporaries. What mattered in human affairs, Hobbes believed, was relational power between people, and following from this he concluded that the struggle for power was universal (Hobbes [1651] 1968, ch. 10, p. 41, and ch. 11, p. 47). In the state of nature or in a civil war, this struggle impoverishes human existence. There is, therefore, a need for all to give up individual freedom in exchange for the peace and order in which people's prosperity can flourish. Since voluntary agreements are open to defection and abuse, only a sovereign, in whom power is concentrated, can establish peace and order between warring individuals. Covenants, according to Hobbes, need the sword to enforce them (ch. 17, p. 85).

Hobbes's interpretation of the masculine ruler is related to but subtly different from the masculinity of the high-conservative aristocrat. In high conservatism, the masculine aristocrat is free to use his sword in defense of the realm and of order but hangs it up to be the good father at home. Hobbes's masculine sovereign holds on to his sword at home and imposes order upon his subjects—for their own good—by displaying the sword (phallus?) as a threat. The father figure becomes the disciplinarian rather than the caring moral instructor. Hobbes offers two visions of society; civilization is possible only in the latter. Life can be either the destructive struggle between masculine warriors in a state of nature or the ordered rule of an absolutist warrior or warrior caste in charge of an absolutist state.

Yet despite what appears a rather modern realist view of power relations, Hobbes remained as much wedded to the idea that the family provides the paradigm for the ordering of society as any of his conservative contemporaries (Hinton 1968, 55–57). Ideas of relational power, the struggle for existence, and the existence of chaos outside of social order rested in the idea of the family as a necessary paradigm for any theory of society that claimed to be natural. Men's dominion over women—and over other "failed" men—was for Hobbes based upon the male ability to use power to extend and protect the family (Hobbes [1651] 1968, ch. 20). Hobbes's political theory has to be seen, therefore, as a refining of the idea of the hypermasculine warrior.

To the eighteenth-century European mind, conservatism was fast losing its legitimacy. Conservative absolutism no longer rested on claims of tradition but instead appeared to rely on the arbitrary use of power. Writers of the time searched once more for a transcendental basis for proper government, and where the medieval mind saw God and the Renaissance mind saw tradition, the Enlightenment mind latched onto rational and progressive thought. Tradition was rejected as a basis of government and replaced by the idea that through the exercise of common human reason we could construct a rational constitution and proper collective ways to live. Whereas tradition spoke for the order of a state under a sovereign, reason constructed rules of justice that were right for all people at all times (see, for example, Kant [1795] 1978, 18). The liberal Enlightenment's rejection of the warrior as part of an atavistic class was matched not only by concerns of rational justice but also increasingly by a privileging of the institutions (and men) that created material prosperity.[5]

Whereas conservatism based domestic society on tradition and saw relations outside of the domestic as being directed by the need to maximize power, liberals looked to reason. The conservative ideal type was the warrior, who ruled by right of tradition at home and fought to maximize power abroad. The warrior's concern was always security whether that be the security within the static constitution of society or the security afforded to him by power in the world outside tradition. The liberal ideal type was the manager, who used reason to properly oversee justice, the organs of state, and the economy. Both conservatism and liberalism were masculine paradigms, but whereas conservatism was based on the hypermasculinity of the father-warrior, liberalism was founded on the rational masculinity of the objective decisionmaker. Like conservatism, liberalism looked to its own precursors (or supposed precursors), particularly—for a later age—Kant and Grotius, to bolster their theoretical positions (Swatuk 1991).

From the eighteenth century to the early twentieth, conservatism gave way domestically to the forces of liberal change. Tradition was no longer regarded as necessarily the best judge of what should be the domestic form of society. Instead, liberal conceptions of a progressive reason justified the newly emerging liberal societies. Yet conservative notions survived in the sphere of international politics. It is telling that whereas bourgeois elites in the nineteenth century took over the running of domestic affairs in the major Western states, particularly in France and Britain, a close-knit aristocratic club still ran foreign affairs (Lauren 1976, 23–32). As a consequence, Western societies at the close of the nineteenth century were marked by the exercise of a managerial, rational masculinity in issues related to their internal politics but by a pugnacious hypermasculinity in their foreign relations.

The gradual victory of liberalism in the domestic sphere of the major Western states by the end of the nineteenth century can be contrasted with the survival of conservatism in the running of foreign affairs. The attempts of John Bright and others to spread liberalism to the international sphere had not been successful. Yet the conservatism that survived in foreign policy was the reformed model of Hobbes, steeped in instrumental rationality and shorn of the moral imperatives of high conservatism. Conservative morality had been a product of a recognition of common traditions and could exist either domestically or between European elites that shared a similar way of life. Liberalism had squeezed out conservatism from the domestic and subordinated tradition to reason. Conservative morality, therefore, had no place in modern life, but conservative ideas of a foreign policy based on competition among sovereign states over relational power still existed.

By the turn of the century, liberals in both Britain and France, spurred on by increases in economic activity across state boundaries, were beginning to agitate against the conservative norms inherent in foreign policy. In France two émigré Russian writers, I. S. Bloch and Jacques Novicow, questioned war and the conservative foreign policy structures that supported it. In Britain, J. A. Hobson attacked British imperialism, including the upper classes and their foreign policy establishment, and Norman Angell's classic work *The Great Illusion* refuted conservative foreign policy assumptions (Bloch 1899; Novicow 1912; Hobson 1902; Angell 1909–1910).

Although these were very different attacks on the conservative foreign policy establishment, the implication that the rationally informed and the trained (whether professional or educated public) were superior to the brave-by-birth amateur runs through this turn-of-the-century liberal genre. The liberal idea of an educated public centered on the image of the man in the street and on the professionally trained diplomat. It was, therefore, fundamentally masculine. Women were still in the home, albeit a liberal home that had lost the political role that had at least kept women visible to the conservative political theorist.

The subject of international relations was partially a product of this rising tide of liberal resentment against an atavistic foreign policy establishment in the Britain and France of the decade before World War I. A similar process can be seen in the United States in which the target was the realpolitik of an American foreign policy best personified by Theodore Roosevelt.[6] Yet the real spur toward the creation of the discipline of international relations as a liberal opposition to conservative foreign policy was World War I. To liberals in both Britain and North America, the cause of the war had been the conservative foreign policy that stressed the utilization of instrumental reason within an international anarchy in which power was the ultimate goal (the milieu of the male warrior)(see, for example, Dickinson 1926). By stressing the creation of organizations based on liberal reason, which would lead to an international rule of law, and the elimination of the conservative foreign policy elite, liberals hoped to bring the benefits of the domestic liberal order to the relations between states (Angell 1921, chs. 3–5; Woolf 1916). The formation of the League of Nations—thanks to the political pressuring of Woodrow Wilson and his cabinet in the United States and to British liberals such as L. T. Hobhouse, J. A. Hobson, Lord Bryce, and Lowes Dickinson—was the first tangible step in what seemed an unstoppable progress toward the elimination of conservative-dominated foreign affairs (Morris 1972; Hobson 1915; Hobhouse [1917] 1931). The establishment of the discipline of international relations has to be seen as part of that liberal onslaught against the last vestiges of conservatism.

That the liberal dream of a science of international relations, which would bring foreign affairs under the direction of Enlightenment reason, should end in the liberal nightmare of a subject dominated by a conservative-inspired, hypermasculinist, reformulated paradigm must be regarded as one of those all-too-common ironies of history. Crucial to this domination by realism is the accusation by realists that liberals were "feminine" or, worse, "failed men." Thus in effect, realism's domination of IR is based on an "emasculation" of liberalism (see Chapter 8).

Masculinity in IR:
"Emasculation" as Discrediting

The realist/liberal split, which creates the orthodoxy in IR, is more often than not treated as a debate based on logical argument. The problem with this claim is that it does not conform to what we know of the interaction between realism and liberalism in the first half of this century. Realism, rather than liberalism, was associated with appeasement, whereas the realist critiques of liberal international theory, particularly those crucial works written by E. H. Carr and Hans Morgenthau, do not properly address the liberal arguments of the pre–World War II period (Ashworth 1994, ch. 7).

By looking at the realist/liberal antimony in gender terms, we can begin to explain why realism, despite its unconvincing academic argument against the utopianism or idealism of liberalism, was able to supersede liberal internationalism, after 1945, as the dominant paradigm in IR. The realist/liberal dispute, rather than being a logical argument between objective paradigms, is a dispute between two different conceptions of the masculine world. In this dispute both sides presented the other as not properly masculine with the realists going so far as to associate liberal internationalism with feminine traits. In terms of the study of post–World War II international politics, realism has succeeded in presenting liberalism as an idealistic, feminine, and therefore "failed masculine" interpretation. This presentation of liberalism by realism has been so successful that even a feminist IR scholar such as Christine Sylvester regards idealism (i.e., liberal internationalism in its early-twentieth-century form) as a male plagiarism of femininity

(Sylvester 1994, 7, 83–84). We argue instead that both realism and liberalism are forms of hegemonic masculinity.

In order to make a distinction between these competing hegemonic masculinities, we refer to the form taken with realism as *hypermasculinity* and to that found with liberal IR as *rational masculinity*. Realism's hypermasculinity is adopted from conservative thought via the conservative approach to foreign policy of the nineteenth century. As Rebecca Grant mentioned, it is this man-as-warrior idea (along with the conception of a split between what is moral behavior inside a state and what is moral outside) that underpins the realist conception of a separate "anarchic" realm of competing states—and that ultimately excludes women from this realm (Grant 1991, 18).

Realism in IR consciously adopted Hobbes's conception of human nature (e.g., Morgenthau 1946) without accepting the original conservative qualifier that this view presupposed a patriarchal government based on the family. Four points emerge to distinguish this masculine approach from liberal IR. First, reason is seen as fundamentally instrumental and has no transcendental quality. Reason, for the realist, does not lead us to a particular goal of human society. This is important because it reduces reason to a mere tool for achieving preset ends, and these ends are found in a basically pugnacious human nature. Whereas individuals are capable of altruism and self-sacrifice, Morgenthau and Niebuhr claimed, human groups manifest only the pugnacious element (Morgenthau 1985, 39; 1952, 985–986; Niebuhr 1932, xi–xii, 25–27). Even those, such as Waltz, within the realist paradigm who have doubted Morgenthau's pessimism do finally see a common and power-hungry human nature at work in the relations between groups (Waltz 1979, ch. 5).

As recognized by Ann Tickner in her examination of Morgenthau's work, realism claims that human nature makes international relations an issue of competing aggressive ambitions—a combination of two of the characteristics mentioned earlier that form part of the various hegemonic interpretation of Western masculinity (Tickner 1991). These ambitions are achieved by employing a common rationality that is nonetheless a slave of human pugnacious desires. Although objective, common rationality divorced from the social contexts that it is applied to is also a masculine trait, this rationality is significantly different from the one employed by liberal internationalists. For liberals consider this realist approach to be faulty science and, implicitly, failed (i.e., nonhegemonic) masculinity.

Second, and following from realism's conception of an aggressive human nature, realism assumes that people's ambitions lead them to attempt to maximize their power relative to others. In fact, realists often argue, the struggle for power underlies all human political interaction (Morgenthau 1985, 31–32; 1946, 195; Carr [1939] 1964, 67–75; Waltz 1979, 126–128). For some, such as Waltz, this leads to a mechanistic model of international affairs, but to earlier realists, Niebuhr and Morgenthau, for example, this develops into a sense of tragedy. The human condition is one of slavery to the masters, but every man aspires to be a master. Those who believe that intelligence can manage to end war therefore ignore the tragic character of human nature, which leads us on—as with Macbeth, Oedipus, Creon, and Rigolletto—toward actions our intelligence would rather avoid (Morgenthau 1946, 169; Niebuhr 1935; Carlton 1990, 195–196). This sense of the (often, but not always) tragic warrior-hero is a particular feature of hypermasculinity. The largely independent hero is dragged into tragedy by social forces or character flaws, and against his rational intelligence (see Hanke 1992; cf. Gerzon 1984). This is not to say there cannot be female tragic heroes, but Western conceptions of gender have usually embedded these women's tragedies within a social or family context (e.g., Antigone, Hecuba, Portia, La Traviata, or Ophelia). Rational masculinity, by contrast, does not have a sense of tragedy.

Finally, realism gives morality a dependent role. This is not to say that realists do not care about morality, for people like Reinhold Niebuhr obviously do, but the struggle for power is placed before moral considerations. Indeed, Morgenthau even claims that morality is a product of the settling of power struggles within a society (Morgenthau 1946, 115–118).[7] Thus realism tends to see moral claims as a superimposed and external force, one that often has trouble being heard above the clamor of the struggle for power (see Levi 1969). In effect, realists have taken Augustine's conception of the relation between heaven and earth and reversed it. Whereas Augustine said that morality came from heaven and was incompatible with the secular world and that the dictates of heaven were more important, realists claim that the dictates of the nonmoral "city of man" take priority.

Ironically, this is where realism, which sees itself as the heir of the thought of such conservatives as Machiavelli and Thomas Hobbes, shows a marked dissimilarity with conservatism but a powerful link with nineteenth- and twentieth-century Western conceptions of masculinity. Conservative thought at its height showed the masculine warrior as a moral being, whereas in realism people do not generally behave morally. This, perhaps, can be explained by a shift in what was regarded as a masculine trait. In Machiavelli, John Knox, Fox Morcillo, and the other writers of the conservative period, morality was an aspect of the father-ruler and thus was a masculine trait. By the nineteenth century it was widely seen as the woman's task to instill morality into the very young. The conservative view of the father as a moral teacher was replaced with the idea that morality was learned from the mother. The masculine public sphere was, by contrast, hedged around with the nonmoral "realities" of political life. This can be explained by the removal of the home as a model for political organization and its being placed in a private sphere of its own. A crucial point for the mid-twentieth-century realist thinkers was the need to refute "uninformed" moralizing and show the world as it "really" was (Waltz 1979).

Liberal internationalism as it emerged in the twentieth century—as a critique of the handling of foreign affairs—pushed a more powerful form of rationality than that found in realism. In line with liberal thought as it has emerged in economics and large parts of political economy, liberal internationalism assumed that through an increased rational examination of our condition, we would wish to cooperate more and conflict less. This was as true of those writers written off by realists as idealists during the 1940s as it is of the reemergent liberal internationalism best typified by Francis Fukuyama (cf. Woolf 1940; Angell 1909–1910; Fukuyama 1992).

This faith in the power of rationality was dismissed by Morgenthau and Carr as fundamentally misguided. Here the key thinkers in the realist tradition may have glossed over their opponent's argument without giving it a fair reading. Most liberal internationalists agreed with the realists that humans were innately pugnacious, but they supplemented this view with the argument that through learning we may be able to deflect human behavior toward greater cooperation and material improvement. More important than human nature, therefore, is the manner in which we look at the world (Angell 1909–1910, 157–158, 160, 164–165, 221; 1933, 456–457, 472; Woolf 1916, 124–125, 180; Beitz 1979; Banks 1984, 3–20). From the masculine trait of looking at the world "objectively" comes the notion of managing international problems "objectively." To more rightist liberals such as Fukuyama, this might mean the promotion of free-market values. To more social liberals such as Angell or Woolf, this would mean using structures of international governance to manage social conflict.

A spin-off from the liberal internationalist view of reason is a faith in progress—a faith that is, interestingly enough, more naively optimistic in modern liberals such as Fukuyama than it is in early-twentieth-century liberal internationalism. Reason is a constant, the argument largely goes, but over time the rules governing social behavior will change (e.g., Burton 1972, 28–47). As our behavior changes with the development of technology, so (liberals argue) our understanding of the interconnectedness of society increases. The result is progress. As we progress we tame nature (Angell 1909–1910, 144–145; 1914, 14–15; Fukuyama 1992, xiv–xv; Wells 1922). Nature, therefore, becomes an object to be controlled.

Finally, realist commentators on liberal "idealism" often stress the vacuous moralism in liberal internationalism, yet there is no moralism in liberal internationalism at all. Rather, morality is regarded as merely an offshoot of what it is rational to do. To behave morally is to behave in such a way as to objectively benefit society as a whole (Angell 1909–1910, 66, 322; Beitz 1979; Fukuyama 1992). In both realism and liberal internationalism, morality becomes a subjective and feminine trait that is opposed to objective and value-free (masculine) thought. For realists, within the context of interstate power politics, feminine morality is subordinate to hypermasculinity. Although it may have a place in the "domestic" sphere, it has no business beyond the home front. Among liberal internationalists, gender is purportedly not an issue. But as has been suggested, liberal internationalism is dependent on a technical and rational understanding of interstate relations—in other words, on a subjective, knowing, rational, Cartesian man.

Realist claims that liberals are moralists serve the role of emasculating liberalism. That these claims have been successful despite their obvious fallacy points to the power of using emasculation as a tool of academic (and policy) argument. It would be wrong, however, to regard charges of emasculation as solely a realist tool. Liberal internationalists, in a way, have tried to do the same to realists and, before realism, to conservatives. They have done this by claiming that realism is atavistic. In this form of emasculation the assumption is that to be a potent male means to be up with the times. To be behind the times is to be not fully rational and, by implication, to be subjectively linked to a dead past. An old-fashioned masculinity, in these terms, becomes subjective and partially feminine (see, for example, Norman Angell 1909–1910; Burton 1972).[8]

The arguments between realists and liberal internationalists, a conflict between competing hegemonic masculinities, show attempts by both, but particularly the realists, to emasculate the other. The question still remains, Why has realist hypermasculinity remained dominant in spite of post–World War II global economic growth and technological development (factors that seem to support liberal internationalist hypotheses about progress)? Perhaps this has something to do with the changed international conditions in the late 1940s. Cynthia Enloe's dissection of the gendered mechanics of the Cold War suggests that a particular form of masculinity assisted the militarization of the societies involved in the East-West conflict (1993, ch. 3). The form of hypermasculinity found in realism, with its emphasis on the natural aggressiveness and ambition of men, fitted the militarized peace associated with the Western response to a perceived Soviet threat. Under these conditions, when hostility between East and West appeared so real, it was hard to claim that realist hypermasculinity was obsolete. And as John Keegan points out in his history of warfare, economic growth and technological development are as often the handmaidens of power politics as they are the agents of rational men (Keegan 1993). In the post–Cold War era, however, rational masculinity appears to be on the rise, at least in the West, and ready to challenge once again the dominance of hypermasculinity (see Chapters 6 and 8).

Conclusion:
The Costs of an All-Masculine Debate

Whereas we think it important to avoid what Halliday calls "precipitate totalization,"[9] we also think it worthwhile to recognize the very real connections between the domination of masculine paradigms in intellectual debate, on the one hand, and personal insecurity in the late twentieth century, the development of industrial capitalism, and ecological destruction, on the other. The recognition of these connections is nothing new; both Peterson and Tickner unpackage IR in this way (Peterson 1992, 32; Tickner 1992). However, the relation between these connections and the dispute between realist and liberal forms of masculinity must also be recognized (see Chapter 1).

The shift from hierarchical to spatial world orders that occurred after the Middle Ages created an international realm in which the hypermasculinity of the warrior developed and finally flourished as realist hypermasculinity within the discipline of international relations. The intellectual response to conservatism from the Enlightenment produced a conception of reason that laid the foundations of the "rational man" of the following centuries of capitalist development. Finally, the liberal conception of progress as the natural outgrowth of increasing rationality produced the critical liberal conception of the gradual mastery of man over nature.

The consequences are readily itemizable: (1) realist hypermasculinity is responsible for the emergence and eventual militarization of the state system with its imagery of protector/protected, inside/outside, and order/anarchy—a situation in which security for the few is bought at the cost of insecurity of the many (Luckham 1983); (2) liberal masculinity's notions of competition, individuality, and rational economic man has meant prosperity for the few and exploitation of the many (Wallerstein 1974; Amin 1974); (3) liberal conceptions of progress have fostered a split between man and nature where nature is to be dominated and is consequently responsible for the widespread degradation of the global environment (Crosby 1986); (4) both liberal and realist conceptions of masculinity have been responsible for the fostering of the belief in the discovery of predictable regularities through which "science" can reveal eternal truths about "man" and "nature." This has allowed (hu)manity to ignore the myriad warning signs of imminent catastrophe (Peterson 1992; Tickner 1992).

Yet IR is a product of the interaction between these two powerful forms of masculinity. In order to reform IR at its gendered base, it is necessary to bring in what its foundation left out. IR has been constructed on the idea of a split between the international and the national, which has left little place for the home. Admittedly, when the home was part of theorizing about the international, in the conservative era, it served a particular masculine outlook. There is a space for a more emancipatory project to reintroduce the home into discussions of the international, and indeed this is what feminists, greens, and other critical scholars of international relations have been doing (see Chapter 5).

Finally, amid all the claims of proper academic debate coming from mainstream realist and liberal IR, it is important not to forget the place that emasculation plays in maintaining and displacing paradigms. If taking feminine traits seriously can help men in IR realize the extent to which associations with the feminine are used to discredit competing masculinist paradigms, then on that score alone, it is worth doing.

Notes

1. For the sake of convenience and at risk of giving offense to many, we regard realism as, to a large extent, a product of a postmedieval, pre-Enlightenment body of thought that we have labeled conservatism. Similarly, and perhaps even more problematic for some, we are using idealism, liberalism, and liberal internationalism interchangeably—where "idealism" was the term of abuse used by realists for liberal internationalists. In the third section of the chapter, we explore these linkages in more detail.

2. On androcentrism see Tickner (1991) and Runyon (1992). On the racist, or at least culturally biased, nature of Western inquiry, see Said (1993) and Spivak (1987).

3. These approaches and perspectives are most often found in studies of pop science that have such catchy titles as *Brain Sex* and *Women Are from Venus, Men Are from Mars* (see Moir and Jessel 1993).

4. For contemporary statements supporting this position see especially Botero [1589] 1956, 14, 51, 84; and Quarles 1642. For a good modern commentary see Tuck 1993.

5. This process was particularly marked in Britain, where writers as diverse as Adam Smith, Jeremy Bentham, and Herbert Spencer turned to material prosperity as a mark of both happiness and progress (Smith [1776] 1937, 81; Spencer [1857] 1972, 38–52, 168–174). See also the report in *Times* for May 1, 1851, on the Great Exhibition.

6. For a discussion of this tradition of realpolitik in turn-of-the-century America, see John P. Mallan (1956, 216–299).

7. This is a centerpiece of Waltz's criticism of the interdependentists. For Waltz, post–World War II cooperation and prosperity was a function not of reason or progress but of the bipolar distribution of power. Moreover, according to Waltz, this is one of the reasons we are to fear the end of the Cold War, for the numerous points of cooperation fostered under bipolarity are now potential points of conflict (see Waltz 1979, ch. 7).

8. There are similarities here with Niva's "tough and tender" new world order masculinity (Chapter 6 of this volume). The liberal internationalist, like the tough and tender (American) male, is not afraid of technology, change, or cooperation. He is a tough but fair negotiator when in pursuit of trade arrangements; he is capable of "empathetic cooperation," of "learning," and of navigating his way via the use of technology around a "dynamically dense," postindustrial world order (see Haas 1983; Keohane 1984; Ruggie 1975). In contrast, realists (particularly those like John Mearsheimer) who fear the end of the Cold War, who fear change and stand ready to lash out blindly in defense of a known but passé world order are retrograde in the extreme. To liberals, this type of masculinity (which new world order American males, as Niva suggests, have successfully linked to "traditional"—par-

ticularly non-Western, non-caucasian—cultures) cannot meet the complex needs of (post)modern, (post)industrial social systems.

9. Precipitate totalization is "the tendency, once connections between different levels of social and political practice have been established, to see all as the expression of a single mechanism or process" (Halliday 1991, 167).

Bibliography

Amin, Samir (1974) *Accumulation on a World Scale*. Cambridge: Cambridge University Press.

Angell, Norman (1909–1910) *The Great Illusion: A Study of the Relation of Military Power in Nations to their Economic and Social Advantage*. Toronto: McClelland and Goodchild, 1911.

_____ (1914) *The Foundations of International Polity*. Toronto: William Briggs.

_____ (1921) *The Fruits of Victory*. New York: Garland, 1972.

_____ (1933) "Educational and Psychological Factors." In Leonard Woolf, ed., *The Intelligent Man's Way to Prevent War*. London: Gollancz.

Ashworth, Lucian M. (1994) "The Liberal Solution to the Problem of War in International Relations: Progress, Human Freedom and Rationality in the Peace Theories of Norman Angell and David Mitrany." Unpublished Ph.D. thesis, Dalhousie University.

Banks, Michael (1984) "The Evolution of International Relations Theory." In Michael Banks, ed., *Conflict in World Society: A New Perspective in International Relations*. New York: St Martin's Press.

Beitz, Charles R. (1979) *Political Theory and International Relations*. Princeton: Princeton University Press.

Bland, Francis (1647) *The Souldiers March to Salvation*. York: np.

Bloch, I. S. (1899) *Is War Now Impossible?* London: Grant Richards.

Botero, Giovanni (1589) *The Reason of State*. London: Routledge, 1956.

Brod, Harry, ed. (1992) *The Making of Masculinities: The New Men's Studies*. New York: Routledge.

Burton, J. (1972) *World Society*. Cambridge: Cambridge University Press.

Carlton, Eric (1990) *War and Ideology* London: Routledge.

Carr, E. H. (1939) *The Twenty Years' Crisis 1919–1939*. New York: Harper Row, 1964.

Code, Lorraine (1991) *What Can She Know? Feminist Theory and the Construction of Knowledge*. Ithaca: Cornell University Press.

Crosby, Alfred W. (1986) *Ecological Imperialism: The Biological Expansion of Europe, 900–1900*. New York: Cambridge University Press.

Dickinson, Goldsworthy Lowes (1926) *The International Anarchy 1904–1914*. New York: Century.

Elshtain, Jean Bethke (1981) *Public Man, Private Woman: Women in Social and Political Thought*. Princeton: Princeton University Press.

Enloe, Cynthia (1993) *The Morning After: Sexual Politics at the End of the Cold War*. Berkeley: University of California Press.

Filmer, Robert (1652) "Observations upon Aristotle's Politiques." In David Wooton, ed., *Divine Right and Democracy: An Anthology of Political Writing in Stuart England.* Harmondsworth: Penguin, 1986.

_____ (1680) *Patriarchia: Or the Natural Power of Kings.* London: Walter Davis.

Freud, Sigmund (1905) "Three Essays on the Theory of Sexuality." In *The Complete Psychological Works of Sigmund Freud, Volume VII.* London: Hogarth, 1953.

_____ (1925–1931) "Femininity." In *New Introductory Lectures on Psycho-Analysis.* London: Hogarth, 1974.

Fukuyama, Francis (1992) *The End of History and the Last Man.* New York: Free Press.

George, Jim (1994) *Discourses of Global Politics: A Critical (Re)Introduction to International Relations.* Boulder, CO: Lynne Rienner.

Gerzon, Mark (1984) *A Choice of Heroes: The Changing Face of American Manhood.* Boston: Houghton Mifflin.

Grant, Rebecca (1991) "The Source of Gender Bias in International Relations Theory." In Rebecca Grant and Kathleen Newland, eds., *Gender and International Relations.* Bloomington: Indiana University Press.

Haas, Ernst B. (1983) "Words Can Hurt You: Who Said What to Whom About Regimes." In Stephen Krasner, ed., *International Regimes.* Ithaca: Cornell University Press.

Hanke, Robert (1992) "Redesigning Men: Hegemonic Masculinity in Transition." In Steve Craig, ed., *Men, Masculinity and the Media.* London: Sage.

Hinton, R.W.K. (1968) "Husbands, Fathers and Conquerors: 2: Patriarchalism in Hobbes and Locke." *Political Studies* 16, 1: 55–67.

Hobbes, Thomas ([1651] 1968) *Leviathan.* Harmondsworth: Penguin.

Hobhouse, L. T. ([1917] 1931) "The Future League of Peace." In J. A. Hobson and Morris Ginsberg, *L. T. Hobhouse. His Life and Work.* London: George Allen and Unwin.

Hobson, J. A. (1902) *Imperialism: A Study.* London: Nisbet.

_____ (1915) *Towards International Government.* New York: Macmillan.

Holsti, Kal (1985) *The Dividing Discipline.* Boston: Allen and Unwin.

Kant, Immanuel (1795) *Perpetual Peace.* Indianapolis: Bobbs-Merrill, 1978.

Keegan, John (1993) *A History of Warfare.* Toronto: Vintage Books.

Keohane, Robert O. (1984) *After Hegemony: Collaboration and Discord in the World Political Economy.* Princeton: Princeton University Press.

Lauren, Paul Gordan (1976) *Diplomats and Bureaucrats: The First Institutional Responses to Twentieth Century Diplomacy in France and Germany.* Stanford: Hoover Institution Press.

Leibniz, Gottfried Wilhelm ([1683] 1988) "Excerpts from Two Letters to Landgraf Ernst of Hesse-Rheinfels Concerning Absolute Power and Resistance." In Leibniz, *Political Writings.* Cambridge: Cambridge University Press.

Levi, Werner (1969) "The Relative Irrelevance of Moral Norms in International Politics." In James Rosenau, ed., *International Politics and Foreign Policy.* New York: Free Press.

Luckham, Robin (1983) "Security and Disarmament in Africa." *Alternatives* 9: 203–228.

Macdonald, Sharon (1987) "Drawing the Lines: Gender, Peace and War: An Introduction." In Sharon Macdonald, Pat Holden, and Shirley Ardener, eds., *Images of Women in Peace & War: Cross-Cultural & Historical Perspectives.* London: Macmillan.

Mallan, John P. (1956) "Roosevelt, Brooks Adams and Lea: The Warrior Critique of the Business Civilization." *American Quarterly* 8: 216–299.

Marchetti, G. (1989) "Action-Adventure as Ideology." In I. Angus and S. Jhally, eds., *Cultural Politics in Contemporary America.* New York: Routledge.

Merchant, Carolyn (1980) *The Death of Nature: Women, Ecology, and the Scientific Revolution.* San Francisco: Harper & Row.

_____ (1989) *Ecological Revolutions: Nature, Gender and Science in New England.* Chapel Hill: University of North Carolina Press.

Moir, Anne, and David Jessel (1993) *Brain Sex: The Real Difference Between Men and Women.* London: Mandarin.

Morgenthau, Hans (1946) *Scientific Man Versus Power Politics.* Chicago: University of Chicago Press.

_____ (1952) "Another Great Debate: The National Interest of the United States." *American Political Science Review* 46, 4: 961–988.

_____ (1985) *Politics Among Nations*, 6th ed. New York: Knopf.

Morris, A. J. (1972) *Radicalism Against War, 1906–1914: The Advocacy of Peace and Retrenchment.* Totawa NJ: Rowman and Littlefield.

Niebuhr, Reinhold (1932) *Moral Man and Immoral Society.* New York: Charles Scribner.

_____ (1935) "The Pathos of Liberalism." *The Nation* 11 (September): 117–119.

Novicow, J. (1912) *War and Its Alleged Benefits.* London: Heineman.

Peterson, V. Spike (1992) "Security and Sovereign States: What Is at Stake in Taking Feminism Seriously?" In Peterson, ed., *Gendered States: Feminist (Re)visions of International Relations Theory.* Boulder, CO: Lynne Rienner.

Peterson, V. Spike, and Anne Sisson Runyon (1993) *Global Gender Issues.* Boulder, CO: Westview Press.

Quarles, Francis (1642) *Observations Concerning Princes and States, Upon Peace and War.* London: John Sweeting.

Raleigh, Walter (1661) *Aphorisms of State.* London: Thomas Johnson.

Ramazanoglu, Caroline (1992) "What Can You Do with a Man? Feminism and the Critical Appraisal of Masculinity." *Women's Studies International Forum* 15, 3: 339–350.

Ruggie, John Gerald (1975) "International Responses to Technology: Concepts and Trends." *International Organization* 29, 3: 557–584.

Runyon, Anne Sisson (1992) "The 'State' of Nature: A Garden Unfit for Women and Other Living Things." In Peterson, *Gendered States.*

Runyon, Anne Sisson, and V. Spike Peterson (1991) "The Radical Future of Realism: Feminist Subversions of IR Theory." *Alternatives* 16: 67–106.

R.W. (nd) *The Anatomy of Warre.* London: John Dalham and Richard Lownde.

Rybczynski, Witold (1986) *Home: A Short History of an Idea.* New York: Viking.

Said, Edward (1993) *Cultural Imperialism.* New York: Alfred A. Knopf.

Smith, Adam (1776) *An Inquiry into the Nature and Causes of the Wealth of Nations.* New York: Modern Library, 1937.

Spencer, Herbert (1857) "Progress: Its Law and Cause." In Herbert Spencer, *On Social Evolution*. Chicago: Chicago University Press, 1972.

Spivak, Gayatri Chakravorty (1987) *In Other Worlds*. New York: Methuen.

Swatuk, Larry A. (1991) *Between Choice in a Hard Place: Contending Theories of International Relations*. Halifax: Centre for Foreign Policy Studies.

Sylvester, Christine (1994) *Feminist Theory and International Relations in a Postmodern Era*. Cambridge: Cambridge University Press.

Threadgold, Terry, and Anne Cranny-Francis, eds. (1990) *Feminine, Masculine and Representation*. London: Allen and Unwin.

Tickner, J. Ann (1991) "Hans Morgenthau's Principles of Political Realism: A Feminist Reformulation." *Millennium* 17, 3: 429–440.

_____ (1992) *Gender in International Relations: Feminist Perspectives on Achieving Global Security*. New York: Columbia University Press.

Tuck, Richard (1993) *Philosophy and Government 1572–1651*. Cambridge: Cambridge University Press.

Vetterling-Braggin (1982) *Femininity, Masculinity and Androgyny: A Modern Philosophical Discussion*. Totowa, NJ: Littlefield Adams.

Wallerstein, Immanuel (1974) *The Modern World System*. New York: Academic Press.

Waltz, Kenneth N. (1979) *Theory of International Politics*. Reading, MA: Addison-Wesley.

Wells, H. G. (1922) *Men Like Gods*. North Hollywood: Leisure.

Woolf, Leonard (1916) *International Government*. London: George Allen and Unwin.

_____ (1940) *The War for Peace*. London: Routledge.

5

Six Masculine Roles in International Relations and Their Interconnection: A Personal Investigation

Craig N. Murphy

This chapter began with a puzzle about why many of the male scholars in international relations who are sympathetic to feminist studies of gender and international affairs, men who even lend such studies institutional support and who certainly have learned a great deal from them, nonetheless do not put the study of gender at the center of their own research programs (although see Murphy 1996). They often remain consumers rather than producers of scholarship on gender in international affairs. The question is a personal one; I am part of that group. As a consequence, part of my research for this chapter involved thinking about my own motivations and rummaging through my own experience of gender and international affairs. That reflection, in turn, has given me some tentative ideas about gender and power in world politics that I report here. I probably could have begun to answer my original question simply by building on Nancy Hartsock's (1990) analogy to Albert Memmi's (1967) analysis of "the colonizers who refuse" and then find that their lives become "a long series of adjustments" until they fully recognize their own complicity in the unequal social order and leave the colony. However, gender relations and colonial relations differ enough that a simple analogy to Memmi's endpoint seems inappropriate. Instead of disengagement, male scholars sympathetic to feminist analysis can expect a path of "adjustments" that eventually brings them to place gender in a more central position in their own work.

This tentative attempt to bring gender into my own analysis begins with an outline of a variety of fundamentally different "masculine" roles played in international affairs, including some that are examples of the sort of "devalued masculinities" that Ann Tickner (1992, 63–64, 139–140) argues may be transvalued by a feminist understanding of international relations. I then consider how these roles may relate to each other in the gendered structuring of power internationally and how the interests of men who play different roles may make them more likely or less likely to sympathize with the challenge offered by feminist understandings. Finally, I return to the question of sympathetic male scholars' reluctance to put gender at the center of their work, returning to Hartsock's analogy and offering some justification for what little we "sympathetic colonizers" have done so far.

Six Masculine Roles in World Politics

Although the attributes of the roles outlined here can be distinguished by more conventional social science methods, my own knowledge of them is linked to my upbringing as the son of a career serviceman in the U.S. Air Force during the Cold War. Most men and women who grew up outside the military do not have the same peculiar knowledge of this set of roles; nor do they carry the same emotional baggage about these roles that burdens those of us who, as Mary Edwards Wertsch (1991) puts it, grew up "inside the fortress." However, I suspect that this emotional baggage does not threaten objectivity; it does, however, offer an unusually intimate view of one aspect of gender in world politics.

As has been pointed out by so many of those who have investigated issues of gender and international affairs, the socially constructed link of the military with men and the socially constructed exclusion of women from the military's defining work (combat) is at the core of gendering international affairs. Thus Tickner (1992, 27) begins her discussion of "traditional" international relations with a famous passage from Simone de Beauvoir: "It is not in giving life but in risking life that man is raised above the animal: that is why superiority has been accorded in humanity not to the sex that brings forth but to the one that kills." Of course, there is no inherent reason for males to be that privileged sex; men have to be made from children who do not know how to risk their lives and who do not know how to kill. Whereas most male children and some female children are subjected to socialization processes designed to transform them into particular types of men, the male children of the military, its "junior warriors," tend to experience a starker and more direct form of the "necessary" socialization than that imposed on the average boy. We male military children also may be more likely to become conscious of that socialization in part because of the unattainability of the stark ideal of masculinity to which we were being shaped as boys and in part, as Wertsch (1991, 142) argues, because the nature of military life tends to make our uniformed fathers distant and seemingly uncaring, leading us to question whether they are worthy of emulation. Thus military sons are likely to have the benefit (or curse) of a deeply engaged, critical "dynamically objective" view of some of the starker connections between masculinity and international affairs.

Certainly, the masculine role that military sons learn about *first* is of central importance, namely being the *good soldier*. I learned it from family discussions about Dwight Eisenhower, whose picture hung in my room until I was a teenager. For many years I displayed it like an icon over the pillow on which I slept. It wasn't a picture of Eisenhower the president but of Eisenhower in his five-star uniform, Eisenhower the supreme allied commander in the war against fascism. The recent hoopla around the fiftieth anniversary of D day brought back memories about the picture and its importance to me. Veterans recalled Eisenhower not only as courageous, decisive, and successful but also as a "soldier's general," as a man who never chewed out the dough boys (the enlisted men) who had messed up. He saved his ire for their commanding officers, the ones who, according to the rulebook, really bore the responsibility.

My father and many of his uniformed friends believed this sense of responsibility was perhaps the more important of two characteristics that distinguished men like Eisenhower from men who filled a second role, that of *civilian strategist*; these men often also work as scholars of international relations. The dinner-table conversations of American military families in the early 1960s were hardly sites of empathetic understanding of the men who gave us "protected hamlets" and "winnable nuclear war." These civilian strategists were faulted for their pridefully maintained distance from field soldiers and from the civilian victims of their grand strategies, a distance that erased accountability. My father and his friends could be just as conscious of, and just as humorous about, the hypermasculine language of Cold War strategy as Carol Cohn (1990) is in her "'Clean Bombs' and Clean Language." But unlike Cohn, the soldiers believed the taproot of this discourse lay not in military culture but in the world of the civilian strategist. In their minds, the various Dr. Strangeloves who occupied MIT and Harvard chairs, filled the pages of *Orbis* and *Foreign Affairs*, and sat in or on the edge of the National Security Council needed all that hypermasculine display to compensate for their lack of opportunity to display the more fundamental "masculine" attributes of courage and responsibility. Of course, in the worldview I learned as a child, uniformed servicemen far from the field—at the Pentagon or White House—were believed to suffer the same problem and might be expected to compensate in the same way.

Limited opportunities to display courage, but not limited opportunities to display responsibility, also characterized the third key role I learned about as a military brat, the role that I myself had to play as a *military son*. Few international relations specialists recognize this role as essential, although most who have read Cynthia Enloe's (1990) *Bananas, Beaches and Bases* recognize that the wives and partners of military men play indispensable roles in the constitution of world order. Mary Edwards Wertsch (1991), who acknowledges her debt to Enloe, has done a significant service in organizing existing research on the much wider range of essential social support provided to American military men by *all* the members of their families. One of Wertsch's key observations may seem bizarre to those brought up "outside the fortress," but it is second nature to anyone who grew up within it: The Cold War American military demanded that the wife and children of an officer or enlisted man see the combat readiness of that man as their own overriding purpose. Military families did not exist to nurture and support their children; military children existed to nurture and support military men. As Pat Conroy, the military-brat novelist who has provided some of the most realistic portraits of American military families, recalls in introducing Wertsch's study,

> My mother explained that my loneliness was an act of patriotism. She knew how much the constant moving bothered me, but she convinced me that my country was somehow safer because my formidable, blue-eyed father practiced his art at air stations around the South. We moved every year preparing for that existential moment (this is no drill, son) when my violent father would take to the air against enemies more fierce than his wife or children. That was the darker part of my service to my country. . . . Military brats . . . spent their entire youth in service to this country (Wertsch 1991).

Wertsch's original research on the children of military men allows us to say something about the gender differentiation in that childhood service. For Cold War–era military sons the job was to be, as Wertsch puts it, "the mirror of the warrior" in the nonwarrior world, the world in which the possibility of death in combat was not omnipresent. These military sons typically were the subject of a peculiar kind of constant attention, an unrelenting surveillance designed to ensure that they continuously displayed the good soldier's courage, competence, and sense of responsibility. As one of my high school friends used to joke, it was as if everyone we knew carried a copy of the Boy Scout code and constantly checked it to see if all our actions conformed.

There is a whole host of microreasons that even boys who grew up, as I did, in one of the less-authoritarian and less-violent military families would experience what seemed like relentless pressure to conform to an utterly conventional and unrealistic standard of masculine behavior. The pressures came, for example, from quite conscious efforts of military families to maintain good relations with locals in foreign countries where the United States had bases or even at home in communities where the military would be only a temporary resident. But there may be more macro-, "functional," and perhaps unconscious reasons for the distinctive roles played by Cold War military sons, whose constant visibility as junior warriors Wertsch contrasts with the invisibility felt by most military daughters. It is as if the constant pressure on the military son to display the whole range of the good soldier's masculine virtues would reassure noncombatant society that good soldiers would continue to be produced even though everyone had good reason to fear that few men could live up to so unrealistic a model of behavior. At the same time, the differentiation of the military son's public display of warrior virtues from the military daughter's hidden display of rather similar virtues (courage in confronting loss, competence, and responsibility) reinforced the myth of the inherently masculine nature of the good soldier's role.

Even if the boyhood actions of Cold War military sons may have helped maintain the myth of the essentially male nature of warrior virtues, we did not do much to reproduce the Cold War's good soldiers. Relatively few of us joined the military. In part, I believe, this is because the experience of growing up in a military family explodes one of the other key myths sustaining military power. This myth is, as Judith Hicks Stiehm (1989), among others, argues, an essentially gender-based one: Soldiers—male soldiers—must exist to protect those who "cannot protect themselves," the women and children. Children of military men did not need the new generation of feminist studies of international relations to recognize that militaries do not exist to serve and protect women and children. Our own childhood service contradicted that principle. Even the American military itself told us the opposite, namely that we and our mothers existed to assist military men, who in turn, we were told, actually served some higher principle associated with our country—freedom, democracy, and so on. Some of those Cold War military sons, and probably equal numbers of Cold War military daughters, who could believe that myth actually did make careers in the military. (And often they then worked to overturn the gender-based restriction on combat duty that the other myth of the military's purpose served to reinforce.) For most of the rest of us—those who came to question whether the United States could consistently pursue its higher goals—a military career (or for that matter, even a diplomatic career that would require relatively uncritical support of U.S. policy) was foreclosed.[1]

Many of us who realized this foreclosure as teenagers experienced it as an acute loss. For many of us an international government-service career had long seemed a way to turn our rootlessness within our own country—as well as our superficial knowledge of the other countries in which our fathers had been stationed—into a strength. For me, as for many other Cold War military brats, the decisive point came during the war in Vietnam. Sometime between spring 1968 and summer 1969, when I was fifteen, I shifted from being a vocal supporter of the war to being a less vocal, but more adamant, opponent. In retrospect I do not think that the key was the persuasiveness of Eugene McCarthy, George McGovern, Martin Luther

King, or Bobby Kennedy—or even my reaction to Kennedy's and King's assassinations. I was more affected by attempting to understand something closer to home: the fate of a young man, a family friend, who had been shot down over Laos and declared missing in action. The more I listened to what my father and his senior-officer friends had to say about the case and the more I learned by rummaging through air force publications and news accounts of the widening war, the more certain I was that our friend had been dead from the moment his plane was shot down. He was "missing in action" simply because he died carrying out a mission over Laos at a time when the United States was not supposed to be fighting a war there.

Soon after, when our friend was finally declared dead (not on the basis of any new information on his case but after Nixon officially began bombing Laos), his parents gave me many of his clothes and books. This is when I came face-to-face with the fourth of what might be considered essential masculine roles in world politics, that of another type of good soldier, what might be called the *good comrade*. In the last months of his life our family friend was studying Albert Schweitzer, reading about Buddhism, and taking notes on the history of Vietnam. He seemed as disillusioned about U.S. war goals as I was. What seemed to keep him going was that old sense of responsibility tied to a particular military competence—a sense of responsibility toward his comrades, those other young American men whose lives depended on his skills. He shared a key part of what Hartsock (1982) identifies as the culture of the "barracks community," which has always been one part of the Western social institution of war. The poets of the "Great War"—Robert Graves (1917), Siegfried Sassoon (1918), and others—helped many men and women of the twentieth century recognize this much older masculine role. The war poets spoke for worldly wise young men who recognized the venal futility of World War I but who continued to fight simply to protect one another.

Half a century later the poets' image of disillusioned men in battle was bound to make more sense, and to appear more honorable, to an American military son than a fifth masculine role that I learned at about the same time. Let me call it, with perhaps undue derision, the role of the *fashionable pacifist*. During the year that I became increasingly saddened with U.S. policy in Vietnam, my father was in charge of the air force's Reserve Officer Training Corps (ROTC) unit at Dartmouth College. An effort to remove ROTC was at the center of campus politics and was sometimes rhetorically linked to a simultaneous, basically unrelated effort to admit women to the college's undergraduate programs. One of the most vocal advocates of both policies was an articulate and self-righteous young man who was ever ready to speak (and equally teary eyed) about the plight of Vietnamese peasants living in the path of U.S. bombers and the plight of able American co-eds condemned by male chauvinism to attend Mount Holyoke, Smith, or Bryn

Mawr rather than Dartmouth. A few of those women were always an ador-
ing part of the audience when he spoke. Some years later I recognized the
same role in Gilbert and Sullivan's *Patience,* which satirizes Oscar Wilde
and the other "aesthetic young men" of the nineteenth century. Gilbert and
Sullivan's aesthetic poet, Bunthorne, like so many of the fashionable pacifists of the Vietnam War era, seemed to appeal first and foremost to young
women. Bunthorne projected "sensitivity" and "concern," acting out one
of the "devalued masculinities" to achieve the same ends pursued by more
conventional rakes.

Sometime later I discovered another masculine, peacemaking role with a
very different valance. It is the one that Tickner (1992) uses to point to the
way feminist theorizing about international relations can serve to trans-
value "devalued masculinities." She calls the role that of the mediator, following the usage by Mark Gerzon (1984), who developed a model of this
role by interviewing one of the key players in the Harvard Negotiation
Project. I want to differentiate this role by calling it that of a *Sisyphean
peacemaker,* a phrase suggested by Tickner's identification of this role with
the work of social psychologist Herbert Kelman. Kelman has played a
relentless and largely unsung role in Arab-Israeli peace negotiations for over
twenty years. He has always acted with the determination and good humor
that Camus (1955) says we should attribute to Sisyphus and is much like
Camus's own mythical hero, the doctor who confronts and tries to relieve
suffering in *The Plague* (1948). Ethan Bronner (1993) describes Kelman in
Jerusalem soon after the historic announcement of the Palestinian-Israeli
agreement on Gaza and Jericho as elated but hardly willing to rest and
already strategizing about how to avoid the inevitable setbacks and about
how, if possible, to move to the next stage of reconciliation.[2]

Tickner sees the mediator as a relatively nongendered model of human
behavior, but in Camus's formulation, or even in the way the role is performed by someone like Kelman, it shares the putatively masculine characteristics of the good soldier: courage, competence, and a deep sense of
responsibility. However, the Sisyphean peacemaker has very different ways
to express his courage and competence. Kelman, for example, almost always
wears a worn tin peace symbol on his lapel. A few years ago at a reception
for associates of Harvard's Center for International Affairs, of which
Kelman is part, I commented to him that it took some courage to wear that
symbol in this particular company, a courage similar to that of a young man
whose path around the room was just then being marked by horrified stares
due to the pink triangle on his jacket. Kelman laughed and said that it was
not a matter of courage at all. He had started wearing his peace symbol
many years before when he kept finding himself drawn into conversations
with other Harvard Center associates who were earnestly discussing strategies for victory in Vietnam; the pin provided a way to abridge the long con-

versations that would follow his colleagues' horrified discovery that Kelman did not share their hawkish views. Of course, the fact that he did nothing to hide those views in that particular company remains an act of courage. Kelman's dovishness provided a reason for other men, the civilian strategists that typify the Harvard Center, to question his competence and responsibility, his understanding of the "tough" choices that face "real [states]men."

Masculine Roles and
the Gendered Structuring of World Power

Gerzon, and even Tickner, seem to imagine that great changes in world affairs are possible if more of the men involved in world affairs model themselves on "mediators" like Kelman. I am less sure. It seems to me that there are two logics connected to the set of masculine roles in world affairs that would have to be transcended before we would see the kind of positive transformation that so many analysts of gender in international affairs seem to desire. On the one hand there is a functional logic of global power in which gender is only one dimension of inequality, and on the other there is a hierarchical logic of masculinity that connects the six roles.

The functional logic of power links *civilian strategists,* who invent plans for "world order," with good soldiers, who help carry out those plans and tend to identify with them, and with good comrades, who help to carry out those plans but do not identify with them. As recent feminist scholarship has demonstrated, the activities carried out by these men are supported by women in a whole host of roles that are rarely recognized as part of world affairs. Men and boys, military sons and Sisyphean peacemakers, also play roles similar to some played by women; these men help maintain the war-ravaged society and help clean up the mess left by "high politics."

Mary Kingsley, a turn-of-the-century British explorer of Africa, summarized those supportive roles in a letter written from the Boer War hospital where she served to a friend:

> It is a personally risky game that I am playing here and it is doubtful—one nurse and one orderly who have only been on two days are down themselves—but . . . I was and am and never shall be anything but a mucker—all this work here—the stink the washing the enemas the bed pans the blood is my world, not London Society politics and that gallery into which I so strangely wandered—into which I don't care a hairpin if I wander again. Take care—you who can do so much more than I in what St. Loe [John St. Loe Strachey] calls the *haut politique* and remember that it is the haut politique that makes me have to catch large powerful family men by the tails of their shirts at midnight stand over them when they are stinking—tie up their jaws when they are dead—5 or 6 jaws a night I have had to tie up—*Dam[n]* the haut politique. (Quoted in Blunt 1994, 135)

Strachey's world of high politics was not synonymous with world affairs. Rather, it was the interelite politics of the upper classes of the world's most powerful nation. Within that high politics, the most frequently heard voices *against* war were those of the Bunthornes, the fashionable pacifists who, in Kingsley's view, ultimately served the war machine even more than she did. They did so by shielding themselves from the horrors of the battlefield and by oversimplifying war's moral ambiguities in order to give their audiences the "clear solutions" they craved.

Yet Strachey's somewhat fashionable simplifications do have something to tell us about the network of fundamental masculine roles and the structuring of world affairs through the functional logic of power. Strachey (1906) shared a view later popularized by the now-better-remembered, younger John Strachey (1956, 1959), a man who saw as many horrors in what he thought was a "good" war, World War II (Strachey 1941), as Kingsley saw in her "bad" war. In their slightly different ways and at different times, both Stracheys emphasized that the global social orders civilian strategists designed, good soldiers willingly protected, fashionable pacifists obscured, good comrades died for and military families prepared for, and Sisyphean peacemakers cleaned up after were all embedded in geographic structures of political and economic inequality where the high politics of imperial elites governed the less powerful in their own societies and in colonies abroad. Today, we international relations scholars have much more sophisticated and nuanced ways to describe this logic of global inequality, but the basic image remains valid. I believe that the logic of international inequality is served by the aforementioned network of six masculine roles. Further, I believe that a second, hierarchical logic of masculinities is what connects the roles and that it inhibits critical reflection on both logics by many of the men who fill those roles.

The logic of masculinities is hierarchical in the sense that the masculine virtues of one of the roles—that of the good soldier—are privileged by the entire network of distinctions that define the different types of masculinity in the United States. This is not to say that men in the other roles would prefer to be acting as good soldiers but that the courage, competence, responsibility, and fairness that define the good soldier's role are reflected in different forms in the other roles as well. The roles inhibit critical reflection only because none allow those who fill them to be as fully courageous, competent, and responsible as they would like to believe themselves to be.

The good soldier must don a mask of unswerving support for the inegalitarian social order whose defense gives meaning to his life even though, more often than not, he has taken on the role only because it offers the best opportunities for advancement available to him as a member of a disadvantaged race or class (Wertsch 1991, 17). In a world that defines "masculinity" in great part as being competent, as being in charge, one of the virtues required of a good soldier is unswerving loyalty. The soldier risks being "unmanned" if he recognizes his real subservience. Thus the inegalitarian social order that the good soldier serves is masked by the positive content of patriotism and its association with manly competence.

Similarly, the hypermasculine-sounding civilian strategist fears his own lack of opportunity to display the courage that seems to ensure the manhood of the good soldier. The good comrade has developed and affirms an alternative, "devalued" masculinity that allows him critical reflection but leaves him to serve as cannon fodder. In a similar vein, Ashis Nandy (1983, 43–45) argues that even when that other kind of devalued masculinity affirmed by society's Bunthornes becomes an honest "statement of protest," as he believes it did in Oscar Wilde's case, the vast distance from most masculine norms ensures not that men who play that role are marginalized into political ineffectiveness but that they become reluctant to reflect on their ineffectiveness. It may take more than simply a larger act of courage for the good comrades and former Bunthornes to place themselves as only one very small part of a political movement of the marginalized that, united, would have the possibility of becoming effective.

The men who fill two roles that share many aspects with roles often filled by women—the military sons and the mediators—may be in a better position to make politically effective critical reflections on both the larger functional logic of power and the hierarchical logic of masculinity in world affairs. As Nandy says of men in a structurally similar position within colonial societies,[3] they can see prospects for their own identity beyond the reenactment of a rigid hypermasculinity; they already know that the "nonmasculine" can be involved in the roles that they value so highly. This makes them more likely to see the gender logic(s) of an inegalitarian social order in the course of identifying its other logics of power. This is, perhaps, one explanation for the distribution of sympathy among men in the field for feminist analysis of international relations. Although I doubt that military sons make up a large enough group to account for much of this sympathy, I suspect that men in the field who identify more with the mediator's role than with that of the civilian strategist are more likely to be sympathetic to reflection on gender in international affairs simply because the threat to their masculine identity and competence is not as great.

Reluctance to Put Gender at the Center of Men's Work

Even though men in international relations who identify with the mediator's role may feel less threatened, the threat is still there. It is reflected in three factors that, I believe, could account for the reluctance of the men who sympathize with gendered approaches to international affairs to put that dimension at the center of their own work. These factors are (1) attachment to a macroperspective that leads men to see gender equality more as a means to achieve global equality than as a goal in itself; (2) a fear of what might be called Bunthornism, or seeming to be opportunistically choosing to study a fashionable field that challenges conventional ideas of masculinity (a fear that is similar to that felt by Albert Memmi's [1967] "colonist who refuses"); and (3) a deep fear of looking too closely at the microstructuring of masculinity(ies).

The first factor is linked to the connection I have hypothesized between the "mediator" masculine identity and the men who are the most sympathetic to the new scholarship on gender in international affairs. The same group of men is likely to be willing to reflect on the larger structures of power in world affairs, the broad structures of inequality of which gender inequality is only one element. In fact, looked at through the very-wide-angle lens that can encompass all of humanity, gender inequality might appear less crucial than class as one of the great lines of division between the powerful and the weak. Certainly, as the UNDP's *Human Development Reports*[4] have argued, income is a better indicator of potential influence or power than it is of quality of life. From this perspective, gender inequality seems less important than inequalities linked to geography or class. If we could wave a magic wand and eliminate gender inequality (by raising women to the level of men) but leave class and geographic inequality in place, a woman in the bottom fifth of population in Africa might be able to increase her income two- or threefold. Yet eliminating either class inequalities (giving her the same income as women in the top quintile in her country) or global geographic inequalities (giving her the same income as women in the bottom quintile of the industrialized countries) would increase her income some twelve- to thirtyfold. If we look at gender from the global level—from which "the details crucial to lower-level analysis . . . become blurred and indistinguishable, or even irrelevant" (Von Laue 1987, xiii)—it might even seem strange to put gender at the center of the study of global structures of power.

Even so, male scholars who view international affairs could still conclude that the removal of gender inequalities would be an essential means toward the "larger" end of removing global inequalities of geography and class. Establishing gender equality in education in Africa might indeed do more than any other single policy to increase African incomes and, thus, Africa's power. Similarly, the elimination of gender discrimination in assigning combat duty in industrial countries might help break down the patriotic myths that can mask the coercive role played by armed forces in the maintenance of global inequality. Thus men who see gender equality merely as a means to a larger end of removing global inequality might still support the entry of women into the male world of the civilian strategist and welcome feminist studies of international affairs to the extent that they support this goal. The same men might also want to encourage the studies of women and development or gender in the military but still feel no compelling reason to undertake those studies themselves.

One can add to the logic of that position a bit of the psychology of various masculinities: A need constantly to demonstrate a sense of *competence* may make us shy away from anything that would require us to focus on anything other than the macro- or global vision that we have worked so hard to develop. Indeed, a sense of competence seems a pivotal part of most masculinist assumptions and may be a yet understudied aspect of masculine concepts of power.

Men who are sympathetic to the study of gender in international affairs still are reluctant to put the issue of women's inequality at the forefront of their research simply because it feels artificial and awkward to do so. Contemporary scholars who identify with mediators or Sisyphean peacemakers, rather than with civilian strategists seem to want close links between their own identity and the particular issues they study. For Kelman the determinant is his Jewish identity (see Kelman 1977). For Adam Curle (1975), the first holder of the University of Bradford's Chair of Peace Studies, it was long experience as educational planner mostly in newly independent Commonwealth nations in Africa and Asia. Most male scholars do not have the same sense of authenticity when approaching issues of gender inequality in international affairs. The women who first highlighted these issues certainly have a greater right of ownership, and male scholars may fear becoming opportunistic Bunthornes if they pursue gender issues too far.

This position differs from the one Memmi treats as the most ethical one for the colonist who refuses. Male scholars who think of themselves as getting out of the way of the women who have more right to these issues are doing something quite different from colonists who leave the colony in which their presence is key to the colonized's oppression. Nevertheless, like Memmi's sympathetic colonists, sympathetic male scholars are bound to confront different stages of cognitive dissonance when they attempt to develop an understanding of something they once did not recognize at all.

However, although it may be relatively easy for a sympathetic male scholar to claim that a certain lack of authenticity, a sense of Bunthornism, prevents him from studying the way women's inequality contributes to the structuring of international affairs, the case is not so easily made when the same scholar is asked to consider the role of masculine identities in international affairs. He can point to the questionable contribution of the men's movement to larger understandings of gender and power and to the many feminist scholars who question the contributions made by men studying masculinity with the goal of improving gender equality (Ramazanoglu 1992). But both arguments actually reinforce the need to do a better job, and male scholars who recognize the need to study masculinity in international relations do have an authentic reason for taking on that task.

However, to do so we have to let our masculine identity(ies) become the basis for research in the same way that other kinds of identity issues push forward the research and writing of so many of the mediators. Many would argue that the commitment of the contemporary field of international relations to an antiseptic and disinterested form of "objectivity" inoculates us against the itch of such questions. I am not so sure. Not only do we have the model of different kinds of objectivity—the kinds that come from commitment—in the work of men like Kelman, we also have the clear, coherent introduction of the idea of "dynamic objectivity" in a great deal of the recent feminist scholarship. Dynamic objectivity is a methodological position that, perhaps somewhat surprisingly, has received significant support by "mainstream" international relations scholars, even if that support has come as part of an attempt to tame or direct feminist scholarship (Sylvester 1994, 134–138).

In the end, I suspect that there is also the issue of finding the courage to look at some of the "authentic" things at that microlevel where all of us know something about the construction of masculinity, and this is the level at which we have to look to see the details crucial for understanding the ways gender structures global affairs. To put it another way, many of us would have to face very real fears if we did, and those fears are exacerbated when they are placed in the context of the masculinist drive for competence and control.

I do not want to overplay this issue. Men who privilege the pain associated with becoming "masculine" in this society are justly satirized, as in the Austin Lounge Lizards song,[5] as the guys who "with drums in their hands and hearts on their sleeve" are "sharing their pain and learning to grieve." Nonetheless, a childhood in the American military gives me some sense of the violence—psychological as well as physical—that can go into shaping a child into the more extreme gender roles that can be found in the United States and, I suspect, in most of the rest of the world. I was spared much of that violence, yet it is still very familiar to me when I read about it, whether in the clinical abstractions of a social psychologist or in the urgent realism of Pat Conroy's fiction. American military families are more prone to violence and more prone to try to create extremes of masculine identity than the average American family, but the mechanisms for creating gender difference that can be found in military families differ only in degree from those that appear in the rest of American society (LaGrone 1978).

Ashis Nandy's (1983, 65–71) wonderfully sympathetic analysis of Rudyard Kipling's upbringing gives some sense of the ubiquity of the process, at least among the privileged classes in societies that dominate many others: "close-yet-distant relationship with his Victorian parents . . .

school [that] emphasized the military and masculine virtues. Ragging was common, the cultural compulsion to enter sports enormous. . . . [Kipling suffered] bullying and ostracism . . . as an alien-looking 'effeminate.'" For an adult male, for whom a masculine sense of courage and competence is bound to play some part in personal identity, the resurrection of the fears that may be attendant on the ways he "became a man" is certain to be uncomfortable. This discomfort is hardly an excuse for not investigating the role of gender in international affairs, but it may be part of an explanation for some men's seeming reluctance to explore the link between the personal and the global that the study of gender in international affairs encourages and perhaps even requires.

Notes

I am grateful to the editors for encouraging me to explore gender and international relations from a personal as well as an institutional perspective. I also want to thank Bart J. Cannon and Andy Quan for sharing their work in progress and my sister, Claire B. Murphy, who helped me clarify many of the hypotheses presented here.

1. As Wertsch argues, here is a key aspect of military-brat psychology that led many of us to "foreclose" a career in government service when we became aware of the recurrent hypocrisy of U.S. foreign policy. Probably the more mature and more rational response would be to simply remain conscious of the contradictions and to find grounds for compromise within various government roles. Unfortunately, military brats tend to share a rather rigid idealism, "*one that never betrays the cause. Not even in the short-run. Not even for a moment. Not even when bending over a little or backing off for awhile, might serve the cause better over the long term. . . . It takes time to perceive the subtleties and gray areas, and still longer to learn to function with the flexibility and compromise that characterize civilian life*" (Wertsch 1991, 375–376). Rigid idealism was still very much a part of most Cold War–era military brats when they made their initial career decisions.

2. Kelman (1979 and 1992) provides a good introduction to his motivations and his approach to mediation.

3. Native men in colonial societies are more likely to seek ways to define themselves that go beyond the colonizer's unidimensional hypermasculinity.

4. The rough comparison that follows is based on figures in the UNDP's 1992 *Human Development Report*, especially Tables 1.3 and 3.1–3.7.

5. "Paint Me on Velvet," Flying Fish Records, Durham, North Carolina, 1993.

References

Blunt, Alison (1994) *Travel, Gender, and Imperialism: Mary Kingsley and West Africa*. New York: Guilford Press.

Bronner, Ethan (1993) "Harvard Teacher Provided Early Mideast Forum." *Boston Globe*, September 30.

Camus, Albert (1948) *The Plague.* New York: Modern Library.
_____ (1955) *The Myth of Sisyphus and Other Essays.* New York: Knopf.
Cohn, Carol (1990) " 'Clean Bombs' and Clean Language." In Jean Bethke Elshtain and Shelia Tobias, eds., *Women, Militarism, and War: Essays in Politics, History, and Social Theory.* Savage, MD: Rowman & Littlefield.
Curle, Adam (1975) "The Scope and Dilemmas of Peace Studies." Inaugural Lecture for the University of Bradford Chair of Peace Studies.
Enloe, Cynthia (1990) *Bananas, Beaches and Bases: Making Feminist Sense of International Relations.* Berkeley: University of California Press.
Gerzon, Mark (1984) *A Choice of Heroes: The Changing Face of American Manhood.* Boston: Houghton Mifflin.
Graves, Robert (1917) *Fairies and Fusiliers.* London: Heinemann.
Hartsock, Nancy (1982) "The Barracks Community in Western Political Thought: Prolegomena to a Feminist Critique of War and Politics." *Women's Studies International Forum* 5, 3/4.
_____ (1990) "Foucault on Power: A Theory for Women." In Linda Nicholson, ed., *Feminism/Postmodernism.* London: Routledge.
Kelman, Herbert C. (1977) "Foreword." In Simon H. Herman, *Jewish Identity: A Social Psychological Perspective.* Beverly Hills: Sage.
_____ (1979) "An Interaction Approach to Conflict Resolution and Its Application to Israeli-Palestinian Relations." *International Interactions* 6, 2: 99–122.
_____ (1992) "Informal Mediation by a Scholar/Practitioner." In Jacob Bercovitch and Jeffrey Z. Rubin, eds., *Mediation in International Relations: Multiple Approaches to Conflict Management.* New York: St. Martin's Press.
LaGrone, Don M. (1978) "The Military Family Syndrome." *American Journal of Psychiatry* 135, 9.
Memmi, Albert (1967) *The Colonizer and the Colonized.* Boston: Beacon Press.
Murphy, Craig (1996) "Seeing Women, Recognizing Gender, Recasting International Relations." *International Organization* 50, 3 (Summer): 513–538.
Nandy, Ashis (1983) *The Intimate Enemy: Loss and Recovery of Self Under Colonialism.* Delhi: Oxford University Press.
Ramazanoglu, Caroline (1992) "What Can You Do with a Man? Feminism and the Critical Appraisal of Masculinity." *Women's Studies International Forum* 15, 3: 339–350.
Sassoon, Siegfried (1918) *Counter-Attack, and Other Poems.* New York: E. P. Dutton.
Stiehm, Judith Hicks (1989) *Arms and the Enlisted Woman.* Philadelphia: Temple University Press.
Strachey, John (1941) *Digging for Mrs. Miller: Some Experiences of an Air Raid Warden.* New York: Random House.
_____ (1956, 1959) *Contemporary Capitalism* and *the End of Empire.* New York: Random House.
Strachey, John St. Loe (1906) "Introduction." In Strachey, *The Manufacture of Paupers: A Protest and a Policy.* London: John Murray.
Sylvester, Christine (1994) *Feminist Theory and International Relations in a Postmodern Era.* Cambridge: Cambridge University Press.

Tickner, J. Ann (1992) *Gender in International Relations*. New York: Columbia University Press.

UNDP (1992) *Human Development Report*. New York: Oxford University Press.

Von Laue, Theodore H. (1987) *The World Revolution of Westernization: The Twentieth Century in Global Perspective*. New York: Oxford University Press.

Wertsch, Mary Edwards (1991) *Military Brats: Legacies of Childhood Inside the Fortress*. New York: Fawcett Columbine.

6

Tough and Tender: New World Order Masculinity and the Gulf War

Steve Niva

The "Man" Question in the Gulf

On the morning after the Gulf War[1] cease-fire on March 1, 1991, while the remnants of still-burning Iraqi vehicles and corpses littered the deadly highway out of Kuwait, U.S. president Bush, in what he called a "spontaneous burst of pride," announced: "By God, we've kicked the Vietnam syndrome once and for all."[2] Bush hardly needed to utter the words; from the beginning of the American military mobilization Vietnam became such a common historical referent in official and popular discourse about the Gulf War that it often seemed as if the Vietnam War was being refought in the desert sands near the Gulf.[3] By referring to the defeat of Iraq and the defeat of the "Vietnam syndrome" in the same breath, Bush revealed that the popular historical legacy of the Vietnam War had also been targeted for a supposedly surgical strike. For decades Bush and many other American national security elites had wanted to put an end to the reluctance on the part of many Americans to support U.S. military interventions in the Third World and refurbish their pride in American military prowess. In Bush's clinical argot, this reluctance was an obstacle and a deficiency on the part of the American population, a syndrome to be kicked as one would drugs or alcohol. Through the successful military campaign to drive Iraq from Kuwait, Bush believed he had also driven this malaise from the American body politic.

The desire to overcome the temporary inhibitions against overt U.S. military interventions (the Vietnam syndrome) had been nurtured during the 1980s largely as a result of the Reagan administration's overt militarization of foreign policy, its strident rhetoric about America "standing tall" in world affairs, and its carefully staged prime-time bombings and mini-invasions of small Third World nations such as Libya and Grenada. Not uncoincidentally, this new foreign policy orientation corresponded with an outpouring of films and television programs in which militarized heroes such as the high-tech and megabodied Rambo and Delta Forces redeemed the "wounds" of Vietnam by winning out over hapless Third World peoples, often Arab-Muslim "terrorists" and "fanatics." Thus it was not surprising that, as Edward Said caustically observed, once American troops began mobilizing in the Gulf after the Iraqi invasion, it was as if "an almost metaphysical intention to rout Iraq had sprung into being, not because Iraq's offense, though great, was cataclysmic, but because a small non-white country had disturbed or rankled a suddenly energized super-nation imbued with a fervor that could only be satisfied with compliance or subservience from 'sheikhs,' dictators and camel-jockeys."[4] When Bush triumphantly took the podium to announce the end of the Vietnam syndrome, it seemed as if this entirely unlikely celluloid hero was indeed answering Rambo's infamous question: "Do we get to win this time?"

A crucial component of the complex cultural codes and construction of national identity that tied Vietnam to the Gulf War and helped propel American public support for a newly militarized foreign policy had to do with gender relations in the United States. In particular, the push to overcome the Vietnam syndrome was as intimately related to restoring American manhood as it was to restoring the national belief in military intervention. Whereas asserting his virility was certainly evident in President Bush's calculated effort to slay his wimp image through his martial duel with Saddam Hussein, the broader national effort to restore American manhood is related to what Susan Jeffords has brilliantly outlined as the "remasculinization" of American culture and foreign policy in the wake of the social upheavals brought about by the Vietnam War.[5] These social upheavals, which included the rise of the civil rights and women's movements, challenged the dominant political and social paradigms that many believed were responsible for the disastrous war in Vietnam; among these paradigms were the prevailing ideals of American manhood and the traditional nuclear family structure, in which men were the breadwinners and heads of household while women were full-time wives and mothers. Many men, particularly white and middle class, emerged from that period feeling besieged and threatened. Consequently, for many of these men, redeeming the Vietnam War became intimately bound up with redeeming their own identity and traditional roles as men (see Chapter 8).

It took a full-scale war to set in motion the redemption of Vietnam and a more fulfilling revival of American manhood, but the new paradigm of masculinity was not simply the restoration of the pre-Vietnam ideal of patriarchal American manhood. What emerged during the Gulf War was a new paradigm of masculinity that combined toughness and aggressiveness with some tenderness and compassion. This new blend of manhood not only was the product of the gender realignments since Vietnam and the 1960s but was also profoundly shaped by the political, social, and cultural context in which the Gulf War took place. The old bipolar configuration of global power and norms had given way to a new unipolar world, in particular to renewed claims to universalism and benevolence, and grave proclamations of responsibility on the part of the United States.[6] With the Gulf War, the United States asserted itself as the social paradigm for international society—the upholder of international law and normality *and* the model for gender relations—in order to prop up its sagging hegemonic claims. As a result, a new paradigm of legitimate manhood, or rather a "new world order" masculinity, emerged from the Gulf War.

Drawing on feminist literatures on international politics and the emerging body of work that critically examines the social construction of masculinity, in this chapter I explore in more detail the emergence of this "new world order" masculinity by asking what Kathy Ferguson has called the "man" question in the context of the Gulf War (see the introduction).[7] Asking the "man" question has to do with "making it possible to view male power and female subordination, and/or maleness and femaleness per se, as a phenomenon in need of explanation and redress."[8] Recognizing that masculinity is neither given as a fact of nature nor monolithic but rather socially constructed in specific political contexts and changing over time enables us to treat masculinity as an important component of complex struggles to define and control individual and collective identities as well as domestic and international political orders. Taking masculinity as a central focus is not to deny that one can also explore the Gulf War through the more familiar political, economic, military, or ethical paradigms that have been employed to interpret and highlight its important dimensions. Rather, this focus raises new questions and makes connections that may enable us to uncover, in Foucault's words, "the fine meshes of the web of power"[9] that subordinate women and produce those masculinities organized around self-control and domination that pervade contemporary world politics. I will discuss the role of gender in international politics and the importance of addressing the politics of masculinity before examining the new world order masculinity that emerged from the Gulf War.

Feminism, Masculinity, and International Politics

As we know, the Gulf War was largely a man's war. With few exceptions, men were the newscasters, commentators, reporters, and even critics we heard and saw in the media. Male leaders met and spoke in male-dominated international forums or smaller meetings. Men planned battles and organized political strategies. In addition, mobilization for the war was replete with male bonding and macho posturing, and as the saying goes, the men were ultimately separated from the boys. These rather banal facts are rarely recognized in popular and academic discourse about war and international politics, which, quite literally, present us with disembodied, ungendered understandings of international politics and war.

That it is exceedingly difficult in international politics to recognize men as men, as gendered subjects with specifically gendered identities, bodies, desires, and insecurities, is symptomatic of a broader impoverishment of political discourse about international politics and warfare. This discourse is distinguished by a narrow preoccupation with the strategic calculations of supposedly unified "state actors" and decisionmaking elites and is reinforced in international relations theory by a self-limiting desire to imitate the natural sciences in form if not content; during the course of this imitation, decisionmakers often discount the importance of social identities, culture, and gender in the production of international political events and power relations (see Chapter 2).[10] However, a growing number of feminist writers and works have begun to em-body our understanding of world politics by revealing the highly gendered and masculinist character of the study and practice of world politics.[11] This diverse body of work demonstrates the multiple ways that women affect and are affected by international politics and has pointed to the pervasive structuring of world politics by gender hierarchies that more often than not have privileged men and men's needs at the expense of women. These scholars also argue that such diverse international political issues as colonialism, military mobilization, foreign policy decisionmaking, and national security interests have been and continue to be shaped by a complex set of gender ideologies and social relations.

This work is increasingly concerned with making *gender* visible in international politics. Taking gender seriously requires more than simply recognizing how international politics affects women or how men occupy, by and large, the positions of power in international political orders, although this is a necessary first step. Feminist work insists that every public power arrangement depends upon relations between men and women that are grounded in socially constructed understandings of femininity and masculinity. These relations and gender identities form an important basis upon which and for which international political projects are launched, standards of legitimation are articulated, and social orders are mobilized. As a result, feminist scholarship has shifted from "adding 'sex as a variable' to understanding gender as an analytic category."[12] As a category of analysis, gender does not refer to biological differences between men and women but to a set of socially constructed and defined characteristics, meanings, and practices associated with being a man (masculinity) and being a woman (femininity). Notions of femininity and masculinity vary across time and place and have been historically related to male domination.[13]

By taking gender seriously as a category of analysis and recognizing that genders are not natural or given but created, feminists are increasingly "coming to realize that the traditional concepts of masculinity and femininity have been surprisingly hard to perpetuate: it has required the daily exercise of power—domestic power, national power, and . . . international power."[14] This recognition has had important implications for expanding the understanding of power relations that constitute international political life and warfare but also for feminist theorizing about power. Concerning the latter, in 1983 Nancy Hartsock observed that "feminists have been more willing to focus attention on women's oppression than on the question of how men's dominance is constructed and maintained," and consequently "the subject of power has not received sustained feminist attention."[15] Many feminists have and will continue to focus on the pressing issues of women's oppression, particularly the connections between international political violence and domestic violence, the gendered effects of global economic structures and the growing global networks of prostitution and feminized domestic servitude.[16] But recent feminist theory suggests the need to pay more attention to power, relations among men, and the social construction of masculinity that underpins patriarchal political orders.

Recognizing that men are, in fact, gendered has not been easy because, as Cynthia Enloe notes, "that masculinity is socially constructed, often with the help of self-consciously honed public policy, has been hard for many people to accept."[17] Not only is the term "man" used as an unmarked universal category to stand for humanity in general but much energy has been invested in persuading us that men "naturally" do what they do, a sentiment summed up most typically in the excuse that "boys will be boys" (see Chapter 5). In addition, the social sciences have been about men and men's experience without explicitly saying so. As Jeff Hearn and David Morgan point out, "An invisibility [is] constructed through and within a wider framework of male dominance."[18] This framework has sought to keep men's activities apart from critical scrutiny and to dismiss the feminist contention that the overall relationship between men and women in the contemporary era is one involving power and domination.[19]

The invisibility of men as gendered subjects has been increasingly challenged in recent feminist theorizing and scholarship as well as through an emerging body of work by men that is often referred to as "the new men's studies." This work reveals the manifold ways in which men are indeed gendered.[20] However, it often downplays its theoretical and political inheritance from feminism, focusing too singularly on masculinity, ignoring the place of different constructions of masculinity within the broader gendered context of male privilege and domination.[21] Cynthia Enloe has wisely warned that a concern for making masculinity visible should not shift attention from its effects on women's lives, resulting in a reinvigoration of old-style patriarchy in a new, more "enlightened" guise.[22]

Making men visible as men in international politics can start first from the recognition that masculinity (like femininity) is a relational construct, incomprehensible apart from the totality of gender relations in which men's power over women is an organizing principle of masculinity. In addition, it is important to recognize that not all men share equally in male privilege or that being male is automatically associated with power. Universal notions of male dominance and patriarchy have been justly criticized for their inability to recognize the impact of race, class, sexualities, and the global division of labor and power on the social construction of various masculinities. Following Carrigan and colleagues, the notion of a "hegemonic masculinity" is a useful way to recognize power relations among men as well.[23] Hegemonic masculinities define dominant ways of "being a man" in opposition to practices ascribed as feminine as well as in opposition to various subordinated and devalued masculinities, such as those associated with gay men, men of color, or men of different classes. Scholars of international politics must identify the hegemonic masculinities that are constitutive of and empowered by particular international political orders. In the rest of this chapter I explore the emergence of a new hegemonic masculinity in the context of the Gulf War.

Masculinity and the Vietnam Syndrome

Recognizing the gendered dimensions of international politics and war is not so much about identifying a precise cause of state policies or violence but rather about identifying the way international politics and war draw upon, define, and shape ongoing social relations and identities through their legitimization of state power and violence. The editors of a major work on gender and war suggest as a point of departure that "war must be understood as a gendering activity, one that ritually marks the gender of all members of society."[24] In international political crises and war, socially constructed distinctions between genders and different social groups are often accentuated through appeals to unity in defense of national security. In this context, Jean Elshtain has argued that war formalizes a notion of collective identity by bringing into being men and women as particular identities through promoting certain understandings of manhood and womanhood necessary to defend the nation.[25] Susan Jeffords has amended Elshtain's formulation by suggesting that "it is not so much that war 'creates' identities as it provides a forum for the articulation of identities already implicit within the systems of dominance and power within patriarchy."[26]

If we follow this insight, then, in order to understand the contours of the new paradigm of manhood that emerged from the Gulf War, it is necessary to outline the gendered relations that were mobilized and shaped in the United States during this war. As mentioned at the outset, the gendered division of power and social relations mobilized during the Gulf War in 1990–1991 was a product of what Susan Jeffords identifies as the "remasculinization" of American society following the U.S. defeat in Vietnam. The dual desire to redeem the "loss" in the Vietnam War and to roll back the challenges to dominant paradigms of American manhood gave rise to a "regeneration of the concepts, constructions and definitions of masculinity in American culture and a restabilization of the gender system within and for which it is formulated."[27] This reformulation of masculinity and gender relations aimed to revive a masculinity that could reinforce and legitimate a more aggressively militarized foreign policy.

The American defeat in Vietnam generated a twofold crisis that made explicit the links between foreign policy and particular conceptions of masculinity. On the one hand, it revealed the limits of America's political and military ability to successfully intervene militarily in Third World countries. The defeat in Vietnam created a crisis in American foreign policy by raising fundamental questions about the dominant political and military paradigms of how war could be conceptualized, organized, and fought and fostered; once again, there was a suspicion of overseas military intervention on the part of the American populace.

On the other hand, this questioning was intimately related to the social and political crisis that followed the American defeat in Vietnam, which had shattered the nation's long record of martial victories and the sense of purpose that accompanied these victories. From the first of these wars, against Native Americans, most American warfare has been framed in terms of what historian Richard Slotkin has called the national mythology of "regeneration through violence," where military conquest has been seen as a sign of American moral superiority and victory as a regenerative force.[28] The defeat in Vietnam led to a crisis of national purpose and a temporary collapse of institutions that had upheld the prevailing social order; out of this defeat emerged movements of cultural and social, as well as political, experimentation and liberation. The crisis of Vietnam challenged dominant paradigms of American manhood on a number of grounds. First, the temporary disdain for military service halted the accepted male socialization process in which masculine virtue was reproduced by fighting and sacrificing for one's country. In addition, men could no longer justify patriarchal authority on the basis of their role as military guardians of the nation. Second, the prevailing paradigm of American manhood was further destabilized by the women's movement, which challenged sexism and male privilege in many domains of social life (symbolized by the equal-rights-amendment movement) and raised critical questions about many of the values associated with manhood. In particular, the women's movement challenged the Cold War institution of the male-dominated nuclear family, which was based on distinctive gender roles and economic relationships in which men were breadwinners and heads of the family and women were full-time mothers and wives.[29]

The pressure to reinvent American manhood and redefine men's role and responsibilities in family and society unavoidably threatened a masculine selfhood that up to this time had been defined in sharp contrast to perceived feminine characteristics, roles, and responsibilities and had valorized competition, aggression, and dominance. No longer could men aspire to the likes of TV dad Ward Cleaver, the unemotional family patriarch who set and enforced the rules, competed in the public sphere with other men for jobs and influence, and occasionally metamorphized into John Wayne in order to protect the nation. And women could no longer be counted on to watch the hearth, take responsibility for the emotional life of their children and husbands, and faithfully wait on the home front while men went off to defend their country, homes, and honor.

However, this crisis did not lead to a national renegotiation of gender relations or an open discussion of the changing identities, roles, and responsibilities of American men, on the one hand, or to a critical rethinking of American domestic and foreign policies, on the other. Instead, attempts to heal the wounds of Vietnam were appropriated during the next decade by a reassertion of American military power in foreign policy and a realignment of gender differences in favor of a vigorous masculinity that defined itself once again in sharp opposition to what was perceived to be feminine. This remasculinization of American culture and politics was an important component of the Reagan-era militarization of foreign policy and its highly gendered appeals for a reassertion of American power and patriotism throughout the 1980s. Symptomatic of this remasculinization was the emergence of warrior myths in movies such as the Rambo trilogy and attempts to refight the Vietnam War in a wide variety of cultural productions that functioned "as a way for men to heal the wounds of military defeat in Vietnam and to simultaneously alleviate the perceived threats from feminism and the many other social and economic changes of the past twenty years" (see Chapter 5).[30]

Gender relations in this period were increasingly portrayed as oppositional and militarized as a battle of the sexes or as the gender wars. The battle lines were drawn to such a degree that even liberal-progressive men like Robert Bly, a leading antiwar poet of the Vietnam era and current guru of the mythopoetic wing of the "men's movement," blamed the erosion of men's confidence in recent years on "the attacks launched against men by the separatist part of the women's movement and the Vietnam War."[31]

Although Bly's men's-movement project seeks to promote the sensitive and caring heterosexual male, which has been celebrated by some as the "new man," it is built on affirming masculinity as something categorically distinguished and in many ways superior to femininity.[32] Thus women and their gains over the past few decades inevitably became a target of the male resentment increasingly adrift in American culture during the 1980s—often referred to as the "backlash." This resentment has even been incorporated by the new man's fear of the emasculating potential of the "new woman."

In less than two decades, the legacy of Vietnam had been reformulated in American popular culture and American foreign policy to become the Vietnam syndrome. No longer did the Vietnam War conjure up images of napalmed Vietnamese children or returning American body bags or criticism of militarized values and imperial pretensions. No longer did the slogan "no more Vietnams" mean opposition to direct military involvement in regional Third World conflicts. Instead, the problem of Vietnam had become framed in terms of those wimps and sissies—hippies and bureaucrats alike—who tied the hands behind the backs of the real men trying to win the war and serve their country. Accordingly, the lesson of Vietnam became reduced to the belief that "limited war" and suspicions about military intervention were dangerous. In this new formulation, the victims of the war were not the roughly 2 million Vietnamese who died or even those half a million American GIs who were killed for the sake of geopolitical "credibility" and the domino theory. The *real* victims were those American Vietnam War veterans who had been denied a hero's welcome, particularly by the women they had supposedly been protecting. Indeed, the carefully staged parades in June 1991 following the Gulf War victory were designed precisely to compensate these men for the parades they never received.[33]

New World Order Masculinity

To the list of Iraqi president Saddam Hussein's monumental miscalculations on August 2, 1990, can be added his woeful underestimation of the resolve of an America imbued with a manly fervor to put to rest the Vietnam syndrome. It is doubtful that ten or even five years earlier the United States would have mobilized for war to the same degree as it did in summer 1990. Of course, it helped that as a result of the 1979 Islamic revolution in Iran, which removed one of the historic pillars of the U.S.-dominated order in the Gulf, the United States had been hard at work developing the Rapid Deployment Force and an accompanying global network of bases and infrastructure to enable massive military intervention in the Gulf.[34] More important, in the post–Cold War conjuncture with the Soviet Union collapsing, no one could challenge the assertion of U.S. military muscle, block U.S. control of the United Nations, or provide any alternative to U.S. global designs.

As many others have argued, the Iraqi invasion of Kuwait provided a most appropriate occasion for the United States to project its hegemony in the post–Cold War period. However, if we recognize, as David Campbell has powerfully argued, that the construction of security threats in international politics is intimately shaped by and helps shape the construction of national identities, which are composed in part through dominant paradigms of being a man and a woman, then we can see that the Iraqi invasion posed a challenge not only to U.S. hegemony in the Gulf or to the post–Cold War order under way but also to a refurbished American manhood that was ready, as President Bush neatly summarized, to "kick ass."[35]

From the first U.S. troops landing in Saudi Arabia in the wake of the Iraqi invasion and occupation of Kuwait, the Gulf War provided a showcase for the remasculinized American man, who was able and willing to meet dangerous threats in far away places and defend not only his country but also international law and order. The time was right for the international redemption of the American soldier and the Bush administration. Military spokespeople and media analysts alike joined the chorus of accolades for the new respectability of American soldiery. However, the masculinity on display in the Gulf was not simply a carbon copy of the one-dimensional and hypermacho Rambo or his Delta Force colleagues. The new hegemonic masculinity had not only been shaped by the post-Vietnam realignment of gender relations in the United States but had also been recast to fit the exigencies of the new world order proclaimed by President Bush. The new man was no longer the traditional nuclear family patriarch.

Perhaps the most important element of this new masculinity was its slight feminization through the construction of a tough and aggressive, yet tenderhearted, masculinity. As Robert Stam points out, "The administration, and the media, were careful not to make colonialist fantasy and jingoistic militarism the sole locus of identification for the American spectator, however; they also provided more cuddly, more stereotypically 'feminine' and 'progressive' points of identification."[36] For example, President Bush, the commander in chief in the midst of war preparations, still managed to hunt and fish at his Maine coastal estate and attended church services with his family. General Colin Powell, a polished and articulate African American military man, openly wept at his Harlem high school reunion. General Norman Schwarzkopf spoke of his love for the opera and his family and even donned traditional Saudi robes on occasion in a display of multicultural sensitivity. More generally, military spokespersons expressed their constant worry about the safety of "our troops" in the Gulf. This openly articulated sense of manly vulnerability and human compassion, rather than bravado or stern invincibility, was reinforced by the proliferating yellow ribbons draped over houses and street signs and displayed prominently at pro-war gatherings.[37]

As George Mariscal points out, that American soldiers and men could be both tough and tender was reinforced by the general refusal to cast the enemy as feminine.[38] Iraqi leader Saddam Hussein was consistently portrayed as the anachronistic hypermacho opponent who in the end could not match the liberal and compassionate U.S. man. The administration and media outlets' constant references not to Iraq or the Iraqi people but to Saddam personalized the war and demonized the leader. No longer the "moderate" and "pragmatic" leader of just one year before, Saddam was suddenly transformed into an Oriental Hitler and held out as a paradigm of Arab and Iraqi men. Saddam Hussein and the type of masculinity he represented were seen as simply not man enough to compete with the new American man, who was tough and highly militarized but also sensitive and compassionate.

In addition to emphasizing the contrast with Saddam Hussein and his regressive model of manhood, the new hegemonic vision of U.S. masculinity also accentuated the technological and civilizational superiority of the U.S. military and society. The military's new "technowar" paradigm for capital-intensive, high-technology warfare highlighted the differences between economies and political systems and, thus the superiority of Western men over other men. The old John Wayne image of the warrior was replaced by blending the technologically sophisticated heroes of Tom Clancy's "technothriller" novels with the megamasculine Rambo.[39] Infantrymen took a backseat in war coverage to computer programmers, missile technologists, battle-tank commanders, high-tech pilots, and those appropriately equipped and educated for new world order warfare. As Gibson points out, this emphasis enabled the reassertion of the primacy of the heroic male warrior in a way that was accessible to middle- and upper-class men whose heroes are the educated professionals who fight with their minds and with the most advanced technology science can develop.[40] They, too, could consider themselves part of the broader war effort and rest assured that they were "man enough" to fight and defeat the enemy.

The contrast between the tough but tender and technologically sophisticated Western man and the hypermacho Arab villain from an inferior civilization owes its considerable pedigree to the discourse of Western superiority that Edward Said called Orientalism.[41] Scholars, diplomats, military strategists, and experts of various sorts have colluded over time to produce this discourse, which can be drawn upon to generate a stock of justifications and racist sentiment about the Middle East. The Gulf War provided a showcase example of the way cultural prejudices can be mobilized in the service of a moral crusade with obvious racist overtones.[42] Like his colonial predecessors, the American man had what it took to take the lead in establishing the rules and norms not only for the Middle East, a task its anachronistic and despotic men were obviously unable to accomplish, but also for international law and order.

The construction of a new hegemonic masculinity designed to meet the challenges of the new world order was not accomplished on the terrain of masculinity alone. An important component of the new softer and civilizationally superior masculinity was the way in which conceptions of femininity and womanhood were included in a new model of gender relations. Whereas both the pre- and the post–Vietnam War man sharply differentiated himself from women and their activities, the Gulf War's new man sought to include women in his world, even if restricting them to strictly noncombatant roles. Cynthia Enloe has pointed out that the military's reliance on 200,000 women in uniform and thousands of other women in the Gulf War operation helped make the "myth of the wartime family even more potent."[43] Not only did the presence of women send out a message about the broadmindedness of American men as opposed to their regressive opponents, it also helped secure women's support for the war effort and a further militarization of their lives.

The increasing visibility of American women in the military also enhanced the portrayal of the U.S. intervention as something different than old-style imperial interventions by reassuring the international community of the civilized nature of the intervention. This was perhaps most tellingly symbolized in the constant repetition of one of the most typical scenes of the Gulf crisis: the Orientalist framing of the U.S. woman soldier alongside the veiled Arab-Muslim woman, a portrayal that affirmed the superiority of "our" women over "their" women.[44] It mattered little that this framing depended on a generalization of the veiled woman as an ideal-type Arab-Muslim woman and thus overlooked the vast heterogeneity of women's lives and practices throughout the region.[45] This framing also conveniently overlooked the fact that the veiled women in question were most often the subjects of countries and social orders that the United States was ostensibly defending. Another issue that received widespread press coverage—the Saudi women's protests against driving prohibitions—was also appropriated within this Orientalist framework. This event was widely interpreted as representing the liberating influence of the United States despite the fact that many of the Saudi women who participated actually opposed U.S. intervention and had intended the protest as a message against the U.S. policy of supporting corrupt and regressive dictatorships in the region, such as their own.[46]

Throughout the Gulf War the United States declared itself the arbiter of international law and order of final resort and claimed to act on behalf of the world community and universal values. At a time when sagging material and economic bases of hegemonic power had led to questions about the ability of the United States to remain dominant in a changing global order, the Gulf War became a stage for the reconstitution of U.S. identity, purpose, and meaning.[47] As a result of this war, the United States temporarily remains the dominant power for creating the values, symbols, and norms for the "international community" and has managed to promote itself as the provider of a social paradigm that defines what is normal and what cannot be included in the "family of nations." The Gulf War also reinforced the dominant U.S. role in the security market, where it sought to legitimate itself as the provider of enlightened military power. The Gulf War established authoritative proof that military force could be used effectively in a just cause. Not surprisingly, immediately following the Gulf War, a new paradigm of humanitarian intervention went into operation first in Iraqi Kurdistan and then in Somalia.[48] The new tough and tender masculinity that emerged with the Gulf War was ready for the new operational requirements of the post–Cold War world (dis)order.

Beyond the Gendered Gulf

Born and raised in the tumultuous aftermath of Vietnam and reaching maturity in the Gulf, the tough and tender new world order masculinity appears triumphant for the moment. This new paradigm of masculinity, or hegemonic masculinity, has emerged not only through the remasculinization of America but also through a remasculinization of international order. Although by no means corresponding to the actual practice of most men, this new masculinity has been established as a norm through which social orders can be maligned, populations mobilized, and incredible destruction legitimated. It is less than ironic that this new tenderhearted and supremely "civilized" masculinity presided over one of the most lopsided slaughters in modern warfare with between 100,000 and 200,000 Iraqi soldiers and civilians killed and fewer than 400 coalition soldiers killed, many of them due to "friendly fire."[49] Whether the Gulf War established a lasting framework for militarized masculinity remains to be seen. New wars and conflicts will no doubt offer new opportunities for masculinity(ies) to be reconceived and appropriated for new strategic contexts and challenges.

In the aftermath of this war, a crucial role left for the critic, as James Der Derian has suggested, is to focus on the "after-image" of the war, which he defines as "the still unfinished product of the war between matter and perception that would determine the dominant memory of this conflict."[50] If a goal of the state's project and war machine was to help provide a new foundation for American hegemony in a changing world order and if gender was central to the construction of this hegemony, then taking stock of this configuration must be a concern for those interested in raising critical questions about the content and meaning of the proclaimed new world order. A number of important studies of media censorship and its collusion with the Pentagon, as well as critical discussions of U.S. hegemonic interests in the Middle East, cast doubt on the U.S. claim of selflessly upholding international law and order through waging war on Iraq. There is still the all-important task of considering "the means by which current societies reproduce themselves culturally and ideologically."[51] The construction of a new masculinity that was both tough and tender, assertive yet civilized, played a central role in this reproduction.

A number of different interpretations of this new masculinity can be offered. For some, this new tough and tender masculinity signaled a hopeful sign that men could change and that in many ways this new man signified an advance for women. For example, after the Gulf War the liberal feminist Ellen Goodman crowned General Norman Schwarzkopf as a new model of male leadership. He was not strong but silent like John Wayne, not sensitive but wimpy like Alan Alda, and not a brawny no-brain like Rambo. Rather, General Schwarzkopf exemplified "a man who is on speaking terms with his emotions, willing to express his fears, but not paralyzed by them. . . . A good man, as they say, is hard to find. Make some room for men who are still strong but no longer silent."[52]

This chapter offers a more critical and perhaps more realistic interpretation of this new masculinity. Although it is important to recognize that masculinity is not biologically given or monolithic, it is also critical to understand that a change in gender meanings is not necessarily better for men or women. The concept of the new man—as well as its offspring, the new world order—may simply be a patriarchal mutation, a redefinition of masculinity in men's favor through an expansion of the concept of legitimate masculinity and thus an extension of masculinity's power over women and deviant men who do not measure up to this new paradigm.

In sum, this new combination of manful aggressiveness *and* sensitivity may have less to do with redefining masculinity than with realigning the general association of maleness with power. The challenges to American manhood resulting from the Vietnam War and the ensuing social upheavals may have fragmented American masculinity, but the remasculinization of American politics and the recent new world order reconfiguration of American manhood may have instead produced "a hybrid masculinity which is better able and more suited to retain control."[53] This new masculinity can counter critics who claim it seeks to denigrate women or sharply define itself against the feminine. It can hold itself out as superior to and more easily justify its actions, however ill-intentioned, against those men and masculinities in different social and cultural contexts that are still associated with traditional patriarchal social orders. And it can do all of this without having to radically question the persistent fact that men, particularly elite Western men, still dominate the major institutions, decision-making bodies of international authority and power that, however enlightened their agendas and concerns, still shape the agenda of world politics.

Making masculinity visible in international relations is not about insisting that all men should simply be nice guys to women and other men or that they conform to some stereotypical image of a more genuine and progressive manhood. It is about making ourselves visible and accountable as men and making our sexualities and gender identities a basis for discussion and analysis instead of assuming that men and masculinity naturally occupy the identities and practices that constitute international politics. For power is not simply about domination and brute control but also about the identities, meanings, and practices of subjects that define political orders and shape political conflicts. Power not only shapes human activity but also reinforces and legitimates more obvious material power relations. Power also works not through a fixed structure or predictable array of dispositions but rather through a mobile array of strategies and tactics that adjust to changing circumstances.

Foucault writes that "power is tolerable only on condition that it mask a substantial part of itself. Its success is proportional to its ability to hide its own mechanisms. . . . For it, secrecy is not in the nature of an abuse; it is indispensable to its operation."[54] As men we operate within changing definitions and practices of masculinity that hide the mechanisms of our power and naturalize the privileges that we have learned to take for granted. Although some of us write and speak sympathetically about feminism and women, unless we raise questions about those definitions and practices that constitute us as men, we are unlikely to disturb many of the actual power relations that are constitutive of both the "old" and the "new" world order.[55]

Notes

1. Throughout this chapter I use the term Gulf War to cover the period from the Iraqi invasion of Kuwait on August 2, 1990, to the cease-fire agreements signed in early March 1991. Since any prefix before "Gulf" has been contested in recent history through attempts to label it the Arab or Persian Gulf, I will attempt to subscribe to neutrality by keeping "Gulf" prefix-less. However, many in the Middle East and elsewhere refer to the events following August 2, 1990, as the Second Gulf War because they followed, and in many ways grew out of, the devastating war between Iran and Iraq during the 1980s. See the preface to Dilip Hiro, *Desert Shield to Desert Storm: The Second Gulf War* (New York: Routledge, 1992).

2. Maureen Dowd, "War Introduced Nation to a Tougher Bush," *New York Times*, March 2, 1991.

3. Two particularly good discussions of the conflation of the Vietnam War with the Gulf War are John Carlos Rowe, "The 'Vietnam Effect' in the Persian Gulf War," *Cultural Critique* (Fall 1991); and Marilyn Young, "This Is Not a Pipe/This Is Not Vietnam," *Middle East Report* no. 171 (July-August 1991), pp. 4, 21.

4. Edward Said, *Culture and Imperialism* (New York: Alfred A. Knopf, 1993), p. 295.

5. Susan Jeffords, *The Remasculinization of America: Gender and the Vietnam War* (Bloomington: Indiana University Press, 1989). I thank Ann Sisson Runyan for first suggesting this book as a starting point for this chapter.

6. These claims are encapsulated quite clearly in Joseph Nye's recent book *Bound to Lead: The Changing Nature of American Power* (1990; rev. ed. New York: Basic Books, 1991). Edward Said has said of this rhetoric that its "most damning characteristic is that it has been used before, not just once (by Spain and Portugal) but with deafeningly repetitive frequency in the modern period, by the British, the French, the Belgians, the Japanese, the Russians, and now the Americans." See Said, *Culture and Imperialism*, p. xvii.

7. Kathy Ferguson, *The Man Question: Visions of Subjectivity in Feminist Theory* (Berkeley: University of California Press, 1993).

8. Ibid., p. 6.

9. Michel Foucault, *Power/Knowledge: Selected Interviews and Other Writings,* ed. Colin Gordon (New York: Pantheon Books, 1980), p. 116.

10. This is surely a caricature, but support for this caricature can be found in a variety of important critical diagnoses of the theoretical and epistemological limitations and disguised ideologies of mainstream international relations theory. See Yale Ferguson and Richard W. Mansbach, *The Elusive Quest: Theory and International Politics* (Columbia: University of South Carolina Press, 1988); J. Ann Tickner, *Gender in International Relations: Feminist Perspectives on Achieving Global Security* (New York: Columbia University Press, 1992); Jim George, *Discourses of Global Politics: A Critical (Re)Introduction to International Relations* (Boulder, CO: Lynne Rienner, 1994); R.B.J. Walker, *Inside/Outside: International Relations as Political Theory* (Cambridge: Cambridge University Press, 1993); and Christine Sylvester, *Feminist Theory and International Relations in a Postmodern Era* (Cambridge: Cambridge University Press, 1994).

11. Some of the most important feminist works and collections on international politics are Cynthia Enloe, *Bananas, Beaches and Bases: Making Feminist Sense of International Politics* (Berkeley: University of California Press, 1989), and *The Morning After: Sexual Politics at the End of the Cold War* (Berkeley: University of California Press, 1993); Rebecca Grant and Kathleen Newland, eds., *Gender and International Relations* (Bloomington: Indiana University Press, 1991); Tickner, *Gender in International Relations*; V. Spike Peterson, ed., *Gendered States: Feminist (Re)Visions of International Relations Theory* (Boulder, CO: Lynne Reinner, 1992); Anne Sisson Runyan and V. Spike Peterson, *Global Gender Issues* (Boulder, CO: Westview Press, 1993); Sylvester, *Feminist Theory and International Relations in a Postmodern Era;* and Simona Sharoni, *Gender and the Israeli-Palestinian Conflict: The Politics of Women's Resistance* (New York: Syracuse University Press, 1994).

12. V. Spike Peterson, "Introduction," in Peterson, *Gendered States*, pp. 17–18.

13. See Joan Wallach Scott, "Gender: A Useful Category of Historical Analysis," in Elizabeth Weed, ed., *Coming to Terms: Feminism, Theory, Politics* (New York: Routledge, 1989). Although I use the terms men and women without quotation marks or other complex circumlocutions, I do so with reservations not only concerning the socially constructed and thus contextually specific nature of these categories but also recognizing that these are not necessarily mutually exclusive categories. For further discussion of this point see Terry Threadgold and Anne Cranny-Francis, eds., *Feminine, Masculine and Representation* (London: Allen & Unwin, 1990).

14. Enloe, *Bananas, Beaches and Bases*, p. 3.

15. Nancy C.M. Hartsock, *Money, Sex and Power: Towards a Feminist Historical Materialism* (Boston: Northeastern University Press, 1983), p. 1.

16. See Maria Mies, *Patriarchy and Accumulation on a World Scale: Women in the International Division of Labour* (London: Zed Books, 1986); and Maria Mies, Veronika Bennholdt-Thomsen, and Claudia von Werlhof, eds., *Women: The Last Colony* (London: Zed Books, 1988).

17. Enloe, *The Morning After*, p. 20.

18. Jeff Hearn and David Morgan, "Men, Masculinities and Social Theory," in Hearn and Morgan, eds., *Men, Masculinities and Social Theory* (Cambridge, MA: Unwin Hyman, 1990), p. 7.

19. Barbara Ehrenreich documents this evasion in *The Hearts of Men: American Dreams and the Flight from Commitment* (New York: Anchor/Doubleday, 1983).

20. In addition to works already cited, some of the works that address men and masculinity include Harry Brod, ed., *The Making of Masculinities: The New Men's Studies* (New York: Routledge, 1992); Michael Kimmel, ed., *Changing Men: New Directions in Research on Men and Masculinity* (Newbury Park, CA: Sage, 1987); Rowena Chapman and Jonathan Rutherford, eds., *Male Order: Unwrapping Masculinity* (London: Lawrence and Wishart, 1988); Klaus Theweleit, *Male Fantasies*, vols. 1 and 2 (Minneapolis: University of Minnesota press, 1989); Michael Roper and John Tosh, eds., *Manful Assertions: Masculinities in Britain Since 1800* (New York: Routledge, 1991); R. W. Connell, *Masculinities* (Berkeley: University of California Press, 1995); and Andrea Cornwall and Nancy Lindisfarne, eds., *Dislocating Masculinity: Comparative Ethnographies* (New York: Routledge, 1994). Also see the review of some of this work by Caroline Ramazanoglu, "What Can You Do with a Man? Feminism and the Critical Appraisal of Masculinity," *Women's Studies International Forum* 15, 3 (1992).

21. See the critical discussion of "men's studies" by Jalna Hanmer, "Men, Power and the Exploitation of Women," and Joyce E. Canaan and Christine Griffin, "The New Men's Studies: Part of the Problem or Part of the Solution?" in Hearn and Morgan, *Men, Masculinities and Social Theory*; and also L. Segal, "Slow Change or No Change: Feminism, Socialism and the Problem of Men," *Feminist Review* 31 (1989).

22. Enloe, *The Morning After*, p. 20.

23. See Tim Carrigan, Bob Connell, and John Lee, "Toward a New Sociology of Masculinity," in Brod, *The Making of Masculinities*; see also R. W. Connell, *Gender and Power* (Stanford, CA: Stanford University Press, 1988).

24. Margaret R. Higgonet et al., eds., *Behind the Lines: Gender and the Two World Wars* (New Haven: Yale University Press, 1987), p. 4.

25. Jean Bethke Elsthain, *Women and War* (New York: Basic Books, 1987), p. 166.

26. Jeffords, *The Remasculinization of America*, p. 182.

27. Ibid., p. 51. Another useful work on the link between revivified masculinity and overcoming the Vietnam syndrome in American culture and politics is J. William Gibson, "American Paramilitary Culture and the Reconstitution of the Vietnam War," in Jeff Walsh and James Aulich, eds., *Vietnam Image: War and Representation* (New York: St. Martin's Press, 1989).

28. See Richard Slotkin, *Regeneration Through Violence: The Mythology of the American Frontier 1600–1860* (Middletown: Wesleyan University Press, 1973).

29. Elaine Tyler May argues that this uniquely American social institution, the nuclear family, was a product of the Cold War. See her *Homeward Bound: American Families in the Cold War Era* (New York: Basic Books, 1988).

30. J. William Gibson, "Paramilitary Fantasy Culture and the Cosmogonic Mythology of Primeval Chaos and Order," *Vietnam Generation* 1, 3–4 (Summer-Fall 1989), p. 16.

31. Robert Bly, "The Vietnam War and Erosion of Male Confidence," in Reese Williams, ed., *Unwinding the Vietnam War: From War into Peace* (Seattle: Real Comet Press, 1987), p. 162, cited in Lorrie Smith, "Back Against the Wall: Anti-Feminist Backlash in Vietnam War Literature," *Vietnam Generation* 1 (Summer-Fall 1989).

32. Bly's recent work, most notably his popular *Iron John: A Book About Men* (Reading, MA: Addison-Wesley, 1990), offers a recipe for "recovering" the ability to express those "softer" emotions that he claims have been "lost" by men over the course of human history. The typically unemotional and physically aggressive "macho man" is judged not nearly man enough, and Bly calls for launching a quest to recover some original "manliness" through new initiation rites and male bonding that allow reentry into the "new man's" world. For critical commentary see Kay Leigh Hagan, ed., *Women Respond to the Men's Movement: A Feminist Collection* (New York: Harper Collins, 1992).

33. For a good discussion of this reformulation of the Vietnam War, see Lynda E. Boose, "Techno-Muscularity and the 'Boy Eternal': From the Quagmire to the Gulf," in Miriam Cooke and Angela Woollacott, eds., *Gendering War Talk* (Princeton: Princeton University Press, 1993); and John Carlos Rowe, "The 'Vietnam Effect' in the Persian Gulf War," *Cultural Critique* (Fall 1991).

34. Although planning for the Rapid Deployment Force began in the wake of the Islamic revolution and the Soviet invasion of Afghanistan, after Iraq's attack on Iran in September 1980 the United States was able to extract more extensive Saudi participation in U.S. plans, including the sale of five AWACS electronic surveillance planes and a system of bases across the Gulf and in Saudi Arabia that were "overbuilt" to accommodate rapid U.S. military intervention. There was also a Gulf-wide air defense system built to U.S. and NATO specifications that was ready for U.S. forces to use in a crisis and that cost $50 billion. By 1988, the U.S. Army Corps of Engineers had designed and constructed a $14 billion network of military facilities across Saudi Arabia that included port facilities and support bases. In 1983, the Pentagon transformed the Rapid Deployment Force into Central Command, or CENTCOM, which largely organized and directed Operation Desert Storm. See Joe Stork and Martha Wenger, "From Rapid Deployment to Massive Deployment: The US in the Persian Gulf," *Middle East Report* (January-February 1991); and Joe Stork, "Reagan Re-flags the Gulf," *Middle East Report* (September-October 1987).

35. See David Campbell, *Writing Security: United States Foreign Policy and the Politics of Identity* (Minneapolis: University of Minnesota Press, 1992).

36. Robert Stam, "Mobilizing Fictions: The Gulf War, the Media, and the Recruitment of the Spectator," *Public Culture* 4, 2 (Spring 1992), p. 121.

37. For further discussion of the role of yellow ribbons in the Gulf War and an eloquent elaboration of many of the themes addressed in this section, see George Mariscal, "In the Wake of the Gulf War: Untying the Yellow Ribbon," *Cultural Critique* (Fall 1991).

38. Ibid., p. 103.

39. J. William Gibson makes this point in "Redeeming Vietnam: Techno-Thriller Novels in the 1980's," *Cultural Critique* (Fall 1991).

40. Ibid., p. 200.

41. Orientalism refers to the way European and U.S. perceptions of "the orient" have constructed an image of Arabs and the "Arab mentality" as irrational, despotic, violently unpredictable, and in sharp contrast to the supposedly superior forms of self-assured "universal" reasonableness of "the West," an image entirely in line with the West's beliefs in its own civilizational superiority and fully compatible with its imperial policy interests. See Edward Said, *Orientalism* (New York: Random House, 1979), and *Covering Islam: How the Media and the Experts Determine How We See the Rest of the World* (New York: Pantheon, 1981).

42. Kevin Robins discusses this point in more detail in "The Mirror of Unreason," *Marxism Today* (March 1991).

43. Enloe, *The Morning After*, p. 175.

44. Ibid., p. 170.

45. For feminist critiques of the stereotypical and Orientalist depictions of Arab and Muslim women see Leila Ahmed, "Western Ethnocentrism and Perceptions of the Harem," *Feminist Studies* 8, 3 (1982); Rema Hammami and Martina Reiker, "Feminist Orientalism and Orientalist Marxism," *New Left Review* 20 (1988); and Simona Sharoni, "Middle East Politics Through Feminist Lenses: Toward Theorizing International Relations from Women's Struggles," *Alternatives* 18 (1993). See also the broader discussion of Western depictions of non-Western women in Aihwa Ong, "Colonialism and Modernity: Feminist Re-presentations of Women in Non-Western Societies," *Inscriptions* 3, 4 (1988); and Chandra Talpade Mohanty, "Under Western Eyes: Feminist Scholarship and Colonial Discourses," in Chandra Talpade Mohanty, Ann Russo, Lourdes Torres, eds., *Third World Women and the Politics of Feminism* (Bloomington: Indiana University Press, 1991).

46. See the discussion in Eleanor Abdella Doumato, "Women and the Stability of Saudi Arabia," *Middle East Report* no. 171 (July-August 1991), pp. 4, 21; and Judith Ceasar, "Saudi Dissent: Rumblings Under the Throne," *Nation*, December 17, 1990.

47. An extremely important work that addresses this issue and many others, including the dubious moral certainties proffered by the Bush administration, is David Campbell, *Politics Without Principle: Sovereignty, Ethics, and the Narratives of the Gulf War* (Boulder, CO: Lynne Rienner, 1993).

48. For a critical discussion of this new intervention paradigm see the special issue "Humanitarian Intervention and North-South Politics in the 90's" of *Middle East Report* no. 187–188 (March-April/May-June 1994), pp. 2–3.

49. For an extensive discussion of the numbers of Iraqi dead and wounded and the attempts by the U.S. administration with collusion by the mainstream media to underplay these numbers, see David Prochaska, "'Disappearing' Iraqis," *Public Culture* 4, 2 (1992).

50. James Der Derian, "Cyberwar, Videogames, and the Gulf War Syndrome," in *Antidiplomacy: Spies, Terror, Speed, and War* (Cambridge, MA: Blackwell, 1992), p. 178.

51. Jochen Schulte-Sasse and Linda Shulte-Sasse, "War, Otherness, and Illusionary Identifications with the State," *Cultural Critique* (Fall 1991), p. 68.

Important studies of the media's role in the Gulf War and censorship include Douglas Kellner, *The Persian Gulf TV War* (Boulder, CO: Westview Press, 1992); and John R. MacArthur, *Second Front: Censorship and Propaganda in the Gulf War* (New York: Hill and Wang, 1992). Wider-ranging critical collections include Phyllis Bennis and Michel Moushabeck, eds., *Beyond the Storm: A Gulf Crisis Reader* (New York: Olive Branch Press, 1991); and Cynthia Peters, ed., *Collateral Damage: The New World Order at Home and Abroad* (Boston: South End Press, 1992).

52. Ellen Goodman, *Boston Globe*, March 14, 1991.

53. Rowena Chapman, "The Great Pretender: Variations on the New Man Theme," in Chapman and Rutherford, *Male Order*, p. 235.

54. Michel Foucault, *The History of Sexuality*, vol. 1 (New York: Random House, 1978), p. 86.

55. Although there does seem to be some indication of an increasing openness to feminist approaches and discussions of gender in world politics, if the reception of feminism by Robert Keohane ("International Relations Theory: Contributions of a Feminist Standpoint," *Millennium* 18, 2 [1989]) is anything to go by, the prospects for change are not so good. Despite his proclaimed tolerance and liberal attitude toward other ways of knowing and understanding world politics, Keohane ends up attempting to discipline feminist thought within the narrow parameters of his empiricist "neoliberal institutionalism," which, quite in line with the new-world-order masculinity outlined in this chapter, "smokescreens a strategic orientation aimed at controlling the other" (Sylvester, *Feminist Theory and International Relations*, p. 63). For further critical comments on Keohane's doubled-edged reception of feminist theory, see Marysia Zalewski, "Feminist Standpoint Theory Meets International Relations Theory," *Fletcher Forum of World Affairs* 17, 2 (Summer 1993); and Cynthia Weber, "Good Girls, Little Girls and Bad Girls: Male Paranoia in Robert Keohane's Critique of Feminist IR," *Millennium* 23 (Summer 1994).

7

Gays in the Military: Texts and Subtexts

Carol Cohn

Female Caller: "The biggest tragedy would be having two men in dress [unintelligible] dancing in, you know, in the Marine Corps Ball. I'm serious, to see two men dancing at the Marine Corps Ball. I mean which one is gonna wear the dress?"[1]

In his presidential campaign, Bill Clinton announced that if elected to office, he would issue an executive order lifting the ban on gays in the military. He was, he did, and all hell broke loose. This intense resistance to acknowledging the historical and contemporary reality of gays in the military is often criticized as a homophobic response.[2] Surely this is part of the story, but the military nonetheless has always had many homosexual soldiers.[3] Many assume that allowing homosexuals in the military is a recent, radical departure from standard practice, but in fact it is the prohibition of homosexuals in the military that is a recent event: The U.S. armed forces have had policies prohibiting homosexuals from serving only since the beginning of World War II.

Prior to World War II, the military considered sodomy a criminal act (sodomy defined as anal, and sometimes oral, sex between men), and any man convicted of it, whether heterosexual or homosexual, could be imprisoned. But the military never officially screened, excluded, or discharged *homosexuals as a class of people* until the mobilization for World War II. That exclusion policy was a product of the expansion of the psychiatric profession's authority in the military.

At that time, the rationale was that the psychiatric screening of recruits for mental disorders [of which homosexual orientation was only one among many] would enhance the psychiatric profession's prestige, as well as be less costly to the government over the long term. That is, it was anticipated that such screening would reduce the patient load of veterans' hospitals after the war.[4]

It was also hoped that psychiatric screening would weed out soldiers who might break down in battle given the high number of mental casualties on the battlefield in World War I. Although attempts were made to exclude homosexuals from joining the military and to discover homosexuals already within the military, discharge of homosexuals was not automatic during this period. Homosexuality was viewed as a treatable illness. The psychiatrists' inclusion of homosexuality as a mental disorder introduced the idea of homosexuals *as a kind of person* unqualified for military service, thereby shifting the military's attention from punishing individual sexual acts viewed as criminal behavior to identifying and excluding a category of person viewed as inherently unfit.[5]

It was not until January 16, 1981, that the Department of Defense formally declared that "homosexuality is incompatible with military service."[6] And even with the prohibition, the armed forces turned a blind eye to openly homosexual soldiers when it served their purposes, especially during wartime. For example, in World War II, all the branches of the military had a hard time meeting their quotas for female recruits. Women were screened much less thoroughly than men and not subjected to the same questions about their sexuality. Even after formal regulations for screening out lesbians were finally put in place near the end of the war, many overt lesbians were accepted into the military.[7]

Accommodation to individual gays and lesbians in the military, then, is not unprecedented and does not itself seem problematic enough to have provoked such a powerful response. Instead, the congressional hearings sparked by Clinton's order and the public discussions that surrounded them suggest a different concern—not about gays in the military per se but about the cultural meaning of the military as an institution.[8] What is so upsetting and unacceptable is not homosexuals in the military but having people who are *openly* gay in the military—having the military appear as anything other than a strictly heterosexual institution.

Mixed public reaction to the military's appearing as anything other than a masculine, heterosexual institution is not simply a reflection of individual heterosexual men's feelings, whether those feelings are moral repugnance or a desire for privacy (as asserted by pro-ban forces) or homophobia and heterosexual soldiers' anxiety about their sexuality (as is sometimes asserted by the anti-ban forces).[9] To explain the public outcry on both sides of the issue, we need to focus on the way the military functions in our society as a central guarantor and producer of masculinity (see also Chapters 5 and 6). Pro-ban sentiment appears to represent anxiety about sexuality, but I think this anxiety is just as much, if not more, about *gender*, and more specifically, *male* anxiety about gender.

One striking factor that points to this conclusion is the relative absence of lesbians in the controversy. The specter that haunts Marine Corps balls and boot camp showers is not just any homosexual but a gay *man*. The arguments made at the hearings themselves make this point immediately evident. Military sociologist Charles Moskos, an opponent of lifting the ban, announced that he would focus on homosexual men because "data collected from American soldiers by Laura Miller and myself convincingly show that support for the gay ban is significantly higher among men than it is among women. . . . If we had an all female force we probably would not be having these hearings today."[10]

One apparently gender-neutral argument at the hearings actually had men as its subtext. "Military effectiveness" was the banner under which gays in the military were most frequently opposed; more specifically, we were told that the military's mission of providing national security would be compromised by the difficulty of maintaining unit cohesion if homosexuals were allowed to serve openly. Speaker after speaker warned that gays in the military would undermine good order, discipline, and morale, especially since most regarded it as self-evident that some heterosexual soldiers would beat up homosexuals. Marine colonel Fred Peck, in one of the more dramatic moments of the hearings, announced that he had a gay son (he had only just learned about his son's sexual orientation) and that although he loved his son, he did not think he should serve in the military. "I would be very fearful that his life would be in jeopardy from his own troops."[11] It stretches credulity to suggest that these speakers were worrying about heterosexual women beating up on lesbians in their unit.

Another issue raised repeatedly, namely homosexuals' higher rates of AIDS and HIV infection, was portrayed as a threat to the already overburdened military health care system; a threat to the health of other soldiers (since they might come into contact with each other's bloody wounds on the battlefield or receive transfusions from each other); and again, a threat to unit cohesion, as soldiers would reputedly fear going to each other's aid. Here, too, it is perfectly evident that the image of homosexuals is really an image of male homosexuals, since lesbians have the lowest HIV infection rate of any group in the country. Since the fastest spread of HIV infection is now among young heterosexual adults, if HIV were really the issue, current pro-ban advocates would actually be in favor of a military predominantly composed of lesbians.[12]

This chapter will largely focus on the response to the idea of openly gay men in the military. This is in part because the military's response to lesbians and its persecution of both straight and gay women as lesbians should be as much understood as a product of its misogyny as its homophobia (and thus needs its own analysis and discussion) and in part because I think the debate reveals that it actually is gay men whose specter haunts the minds of heterosexual military men.

I begin with a brief overview of the current framing of the policy debate about gays in the military with specific focus on the logical structure of the arguments. More specifically, I look at the way the debate is framed and the discourses largely absent from current debate that occasionally burst through and reveal another layer of meaning. I also look at the social construction of gender and sexuality and its relation to the military as an institution and at the central, if often unarticulated, role this relation plays in the debate.

Rights Versus Readiness

The debate about gays in the military has been framed in several different ways. The congressional hearings represent what might be considered the official story, that is, the carefully crafted arguments made by both proponents and opponents of the ban on gays in the military, arguments that each considers the most respectable and justifiable to the public. At this level, we hear a civil society, equal rights discourse (i.e., gays should not be denied the privilege of serving their country in ways they have already proven they are capable of, etc.) set in opposition to a discourse on military readiness and national security (see Chapter 5). As one general I spoke with said, "It is the concept of civil rights of the individual versus military necessity."[13]

At first these discourses seem incommensurate, talking at cross purposes: If you accept one, you deny the competing claims of the other. In the context of the role and value we place on the military, its national security discourse would seem to have priority. If it does take precedence, the only remaining question would appear to be whether gays *do* compromise military effectiveness. Indeed, opponents of the ban seldom challenge prevailing assumptions about what constitutes military effectiveness, devoting most of their efforts to proving that gays do *not* compromise this aspect of military life.

However, even at this first, public, official level of discourse, the reality is far more complex than simply two competing incommensurable discourses. We need to examine the arguments in more detail.

The military's argument goes as follows:

1. The military is separate and different from the rest of civil society.
2. The military's mission, to provide security for the country, is singular, and the needs that follow from it must take precedence over all else.
3. Therefore, the military must be an institution that does not grant the same individual rights to its members as does the rest of society.
4. And thus, it is inappropriate to ask the armed forces to be laboratories for social experimentation or engines of social change. Their

mission is national defense, not carrying out any of society's other goals and values.

The military thus claims that a civil rights discourse may be fine elsewhere in the society but is irrelevant here. The military is a world apart from the wider social world with requirements coming not from that world but from the military's purpose and mission. This perspective was frequently articulated in the congressional hearings:

> Civil rights do not apply to people in the service. Civil rights must be subordinated to the good of the whole.
> The military cannot and should not be concerned with individual rights. The question is what is best for national security, and not social policy.[14]

In this way, spokespeople opposed to gays in the military suggest that issues of importance to a civil society can have no meaning or relevance to the military if the military is to fulfill its mission of protecting that same society.

Civil rights for gays in the military would undermine combat readiness, military effectiveness, and, by extension, national security itself. This argument's logic and its rhetorical impact both direct and divert our attention—toward encoding a distinction between civil society and the military and away from questions about the military's role in civil society and the cultural assumptions about masculinity that inform that role.

Is the Military a Part of Civil Society?

The question in the heading requires redefinitions of what we consider "military" and "civil" in order to be entertained seriously because the two as currently defined seem mutually exclusive. Yet the separation between civil society and the military is in many ways a false one; the borders between them are far more fuzzy and permeable than portrayed in recent debates. The problem begins when we frame the question in terms of oppositions: Is the military separate from *or* a part of society? Is its primary, even its only, role to guarantee national security, *or* is it a reflection of society and a social laboratory? Within this framing, calling upon the military to formulate its policies in light of issues conceptualized as being in the realm of civil rights is seen by many as a perversion of a long-accepted separation and a threat to military effectiveness and autonomy.

But in a general sociological sense, the military has never been (and could never be) independent of social mores and values. In the United States, the public conception of and support for the military are based on the idea that the institution's function is not to uphold authoritarian regimes but to uphold the American way of life and American values, including equality of opportunity and tolerance. Public support for the military is largely based in the perception that the military should defend and uphold civil society's values.

The military has always been a reflection of society. The shape of the military and its place in the society always reflects societal organization at a general level—democratic instead of authoritarian, for example. And at a more particular level, individual military policies are always affected by the politics of the day.

As is amply evident in the history of African Americans and women in the military, public opinion and values are cited as justification for military policies and actions when they fit the institution's purpose. When they do not fit, they are ignored. Clearly, some decisions about the military have been made on the basis of using the military for explicitly social (rather than national security) ends—such as the integration of African Americans into the military after World War II. As a general who is influential in the policymaking community said to me, "Of course I let cultural mores drive policy."[15]

Although arguments to exclude gays from the military that are based on a rigid separation and opposition of military and civil priorities are neither logically nor empirically supportable, this in itself does not mean there are no conflicts of interest. The possibility that the needs of one can conflict with the needs of the other does exist, and the demands of society may lessen military effectiveness. For example, the political need to end the draft following the Vietnam War, combined with economic conditions, reduced training and manpower quality in the military in the late 1970s and early 1980s. The inescapable social embeddedness of the military sometimes does have military costs. But would it in this case?

What Are the Costs?

Suppose we do not accept the *separability*, the rigid borders between the military and society, but still accept the distinction between the two. In this case it is not clear that the goals of the military and of society are actually opposed to each other; it is not clear that meeting the claims of equal rights for gays will prevent meeting the claims of national security. Such is repeatedly asserted but is unproven. So we need to ask whether lifting the ban would have the costs that the ban's proponents claim. The answer is far from self-evident.

The assertion that gays in the military would degrade morale, discipline, and unit cohesion is an assumption based on expectations rooted in stereotypes and social attitudes. There are anecdotal, but *no empirical*, grounds to support this claim, and no one in or out of the military refers to research demonstrating that the presence of openly gay soldiers will degrade unit cohesion. The claim is based on the suppositions of current military leaders—all of whom have themselves been socialized by the military to believe that homosexuals are not fit for military service.[16]

The qualities that reputedly make gays unfit to serve, however, have little to do with them and everything to do with the heterosexual men with whom they serve. This shifting of the subject from gay soldiers to heterosexual ones is especially evident when we compare and contrast the debate about gays in the military with the debate about women in combat. The objections to women in combat can be divided into two categories: claims about women and their bodies, which supposedly make them less effective combatants than men; and claims about heterosexual men and their responses to having women in their units.

The claims about women's bodies all come down to the idea that women are incapable of doing the job (that is, are unfit for combat). They include assumptions about women's physical capacities (upper-body strength), pregnancy, single parenthood, menstruation, and their reputed need for greater privacy and more frequent showers. (The issue of upper-body strength has surprising staying power, considering that it is widely acknowledged to be easily resolved by having uniform job-related standards and testing for soldiers, male or female.) All of these are seen as problems that will not only prevent women from doing their jobs but will also, due to women's pregnancy-related nondeployability, impede units from carrying out their missions. Claims about women's bodies thus loosely correspond to the "readiness" issue.

The second set of arguments ignores the question of whether women are capable of doing the job and asserts instead that heterosexual men's responses to women in combat would degrade the *men's* ability to do their job: Men will be demoralized by seeing women injured or taken prisoner; men will go out of their way to protect women, doing things that will unnecessarily tax or endanger themselves; they will sexually harass women, which will undermine unit cohesion; and fraternization will undermine unit cohesion.

The subject of this second set of arguments—not what women bring into the military but how men in the military will respond to them—is similar to the position struck by supporters of a ban against gays in the military. Gay men's capacities to serve honorably and well are rarely seriously questioned. Instead, the threat to military effectiveness is seen to come from the difficulty of maintaining unit cohesion and morale *among heterosexual soldiers* should openly gay soldiers be allowed to serve. Gays are seen to cause the problem not because they are inadequate as soldiers but because heterosexual men do not want to serve with them. These are the more often claimed problems and, again, relate to unit cohesion and morale.

Central to the position against gays in the military is the idea that effectiveness in protecting national security depends upon unit cohesion, morale, and discipline, since soldiers' willingness to fight is seen to stem from their devotion to their unit. Opponents claim that the presence of gay men would undermine this devotion for a number of reasons:

- Sexual harassment and fraternization will undermine unit cohesion.
- Straight men will not take orders from gay officers because they do not respect gay men.
- Straight men's discomfort with openly gay men will lead them to commit acts of violence against men in their own units.
- The male bonding upon which unit cohesion depends will be impossible with gay men present.

It is not my purpose to address the validity of these particular arguments. I simply want to note the peculiarity that one group's problem is taken as reason to discriminate against another group. Although parallel arguments were made regarding other issues, American society did not find this an acceptable rationale for racial or sexual discrimination. Why is it deemed reasonable, then, in relation to sexuality?

Anti-ban forces, acknowledging the problems that might arise from the concerns and antipathies of straight soldiers, point to what the military learned when it integrated African Americans and women into the armed forces and suggest that similar antidiscrimination training for officers and enlisted personnel would go a long way toward overcoming whatever problems might exist. Senator Warner's response to this idea is typical: He objected that such training would burden already overburdened commanding officers and that the time they devoted to it would endanger readiness.[17] Looking at the structure of this argument, what is interesting is not so much the size of the burden but rather the question of what counts, what is even *seen* as problematic and time-consuming compared to what is ignored. The time and expense required for antidiscrimination training is seen as a problem. What is not seen or defined as a problem, or a readiness cost, is the inordinate amount of time and money spent investigating and discharging homosexuals; the cost of recruiting and training their replacements; and the time and money lost when highly trained gay soldiers decide to leave the military because of the burdens of secrecy and threat of exposure or because they know that the security clearances necessary to reach the top of their profession require investigations that could destroy their careers. (Although it is impossible to collect all the data that would allow these costs to be tallied, the cost of discharges, of "chasing down gays and running them out of the armed services," was estimated at a half-billion dollars for the 1980s.[18] And that figure, of course, does not include the costs associated with those who left "voluntarily" for fear of exposure.)

Finally, before we move on from the "claims about straight men's minds" category, there is one argument worth examining in more detail—the argument that unit cohesion will be destroyed, that the great intangible of high morale and esprit de corps will be impossible because the presence of gay men will make male bonding impossible. In this vision, esprit de corps, cohesion, and high morale are *equated* with male bonding; male bonding is seen as the indispensable key to making them all possible. And male bonding is assumed to be grievously threatened by the presence of gay men. Why? Surely, we could make the argument that gay men are even better than straight men at bonding with other men, and so they could be central to a fighting force. Although this may seem a flippant response, it actually reflects a different historical construction of masculinity. Randy Shilts points out: "In the Spartan armed forces, the most respected soldiers had an intimate male partner. ...The Greek Sacred Band of Thebes was 'one of the most fearsome, and thoroughly homosexual, corps of soldiers in the history of warfare....As the popular saying of the time went, 'An army of lovers can never be defeated.'"[19]

My point, however, is not that an army of lovers is better than an army of men who are straight; I want only to denaturalize the idea that for male bonding to occur, all soldiers need to be heterosexual.

Yet this is obviously a strongly held idea, deeply felt. But why? Why is the presence of gay men so disruptive to male bonding?

This leads to an even bigger question: Why is male bonding seen as such a self-evident good? In the public discourse, emphasis on male bonding is justified because it is seen as the key to unit cohesion. But is it really? Does cohesion depend on some mystical bonding activity that in some way depends on male hormones or male experience? Is there any reason for male bonding to be the glue that creates cohesiveness?

This male-bonding assertion is not explored. Although General Wm. Darryl Henderson testified in the Senate in favor of the gay ban, his well-respected book on unit cohesion emphasizes many different elements, including shared values, the ability to look up to officers, the belief that your leader has your interests at heart, and shared experience of adverse conditions.[20] Soldiers' accounts tend to emphasize bonds forged in adversity—be it in basic training or combat.[21] Whatever the complex combination and weighting of forces, male bonding is not reducible to heterosexual maleness. Major Rhonda Cornum, an army flight surgeon and POW in the Gulf War, when asked if women's presence prevented male bonding, addressed the question by saying, "Male-bonding is not gender specific."[22]

Yet this belief endures because although male bonding is neither a sufficient explanation for what makes it possible for men to fight nor the root of unit cohesion, men do care about it enormously. The preciousness of these bonds to the men who experience them gives rise to talk of "costs."

Civic Discourses, or a
Fight Based on Feelings?

I totally disagree with homosexuality as a normal lifestyle. It goes against my values not to mention God. I can't change or want to change any of them. But if you place one in my room, bunker, tent, or showers, I'd bash his head in.

I'd go AWOL. I don't want fags staring at me while I shower or dress or anything.

It's not right. It's sick, it's despicable, nauseating and I'll kill them.

Gays should be shot. Gays should all die.[23]

Whatever the merits and peculiarities of the military-readiness-discourse versus civil-rights-discourse framing of the debate, one thing is clear: Just underneath, there is a different sort of debate altogether, a debate not about institutions and their roles but about people's feelings—heterosexual male soldiers' "fear of intimate situations with someone of the same sex who is sexually attracted to them,"[24] their moral or religious objections to homosexuality, their anger about possibly being asked to accept gays in their midst, and their feelings about their military commitment and whether they want to reenlist. Gays name those feelings differently—homophobia, bigotry, or ignorance—but feelings they are nonetheless, especially about buddies and others in the unit. The issues of military readiness and soldiers' feelings are entangled: What makes gays so threatening to military readiness is not their abilities to be soldiers but straight soldiers' feelings about them. Feelings play such a predominant role in the debate that this might be read as a debate about feelings versus fairness, one in which cultural constructions of masculinity play a key role.

In our culture's gender hierarchies, the abstract, masculine ideal of fairness would typically be more highly valued than, and be expected to take precedence over, feelings, which are generally culturally coded as feminine. Yet in this case, feelings (straight military personnel's feelings) are transmuted into "military readiness," "unit cohesion," and "morale," masculinized terms that legitimate what men feel by transforming those feelings into abstract instrumentalities of military effectiveness.

The argument that gays cannot be in the military because they threaten morale and discipline is a good example. "Morale" and "discipline" are abstract, neutral-sounding terms, terms also coded as masculine and positively valenced in the military. In fact, they are an abstract overlay for prejudice, fear, sexual tension, and uncontrollable urges to commit acts of violence. It is easy to say, "Homosexuals in the military threaten morale and discipline." It is far harder to say, "We can't have gays in the military because of the prejudice, fear, sexual tension, uncontrollable urges to commit acts of violence on the part of heterosexual soldiers."[25]

But understanding that intense feelings underlie a debate cast in abstract terms still leaves much to be explained. For example, why the repeated emphasis on "openly avowed" homosexuals? Why are people so upset about gay men rather than lesbians? Why are men (both inside and outside the military) so much more opposed to gays in the military than women? We are left with a puzzle. Why is the opposition to openly gay men in the military so emotionally intense? Where does the enormous depth of feeling come from?

General Norman Schwarzkopf has said that "open homosexuality is the problem."[26] It appears that *visibility*, rather than the mere *presence* of gays, is the issue. This is evident in the congressional hearings with their many solemnly intoned warnings about an "openly avowed" or "declared" homosexual (with echoes of being an "avowed Communist" echoing through the chamber). The "openly avowed" seems to connote brazenness, impudence—as though open acknowledgment constitutes a challenge to heterosexuality. And daring to openly acknowledge one's homosexuality implies that it is not something to be ashamed of. There seems to be some outrage on the part of heterosexual soldiers that gays dare to act as though they have nothing to be ashamed of. The image invoked by the comments in the hearings about "avowed" homosexuals is not of people who just want to be honest about who they are; the underlying image seems to be of legions chanting, "We're queer, we're here; get used to it!"—with all of the in-your-face attitude this implies.

The issue is not homosexuality per se but people speaking of it. Why is this problematic? First, because by speaking of it, homosexuals simultaneously deny not only that homosexuality is shameful but that it is natural to be secretive and silent about what others may consider shameful. They deny the inferiority of their sexuality and identity and that they are incompatible with military service.

Visibility becomes even more clearly the issue in the compromise passed by Congress in November 1993, which amounts to a "don't ask, don't tell" policy. On the face of it, this position appears to be a way to protect gays: We won't throw you out by starting witch hunts; we won't interrogate you about your sexuality, so you can serve. As long as you KEEP IT QUIET.

But who is really being protected by this compromise? Not gays in the military. First, they must still fear being open about their identities. Second, the compromise does *not* rescind the 1981 statement that homosexuality is incompatible with military service; it leaves intact the formulation that gays do not belong in the military. Third, in practice, it offers gays no protection.

By February 1995, one year after the new policy was implemented, the Servicemembers Legal Defense Network (SLDN) had already documented over 340 violations of the policy. In addition, SLDN reports that the discharge rate for homosexuals has remained unchanged since the policy went into effect— about .04 percent of total military personnel, or 597, in 1994.[27]

Since the policy does nothing to protect gays, the question becomes, Who and what is being protected by the "compromise"? The debate's focus on the feelings of straight soldiers would suggest they benefit most in that they are spared the discomfort of knowing about their buddies' homosexuality. Far from being a compromise, the policy's subtext speaks for the discomforted heterosexual: "You homosexuals can be in the military as long as you don't force us to acknowledge that your sexuality is in the military. Your sexuality is not in any way to be recognized by the military; nor is it to be associated in any way with military life, since that would implicate us." The need to protect the presumption that military life excludes homosexuality is preeminent.

Conversely, what is protected is the appearance of the heterosexual masculinity of the institution itself. The heterosexual grounding of the official policy perspective is preserved. By silencing gays, the policy suppresses the *open* legitimation of sexual relations between men, which are deemed incompatible with military service if they are practiced within a gay identity. This last distinction (sex between men vs. gay sex) is crucial to understanding the character of male bonding in the military, for it sustains the heterosexual commitments of the military's otherwise homosocial and homoerotic arrangements.

Sexuality and the Military Man

In the United States, males' anxiety about homosocial emotional intimacy, homoerotic feelings, and homosexual behavior is heightened by the way our culture conceives of sexual categories and identities. As Robert Padgug (and later, queer theory) points out, we think of sexuality as an essence in an individual.[28] And in mainstream culture at least, we believe that each individual has one of two diametrically opposed essences—either hetero- or homosexual. As with all binary categories, each is defined not only as the opposite of the other but also as the negation of or absence of the other. "Heterosexual" does not mean predominantly heterosexual but means utterly without homosexual impulse or desire. Apparently, if you feel one kind of impulse, you cannot feel the other. If you *are* one, you cannot *be* the other.

In this construction, to "be" a heterosexual and to experience a homosexual desire or participate in a homosexual act becomes far more than the feeling or act in and of itself. It becomes a threat, a potential negation of one's heterosexual status; it seems to belie the entire edifice upon which one's identity is founded. In seventeenth-century colonial New England, if a man had sex with another man, he was condemned for having sexual relations outside the bond of marriage, but in a society that lacked the category of "homosexual," his basic identity was not in jeopardy.[29] In modern America, because of our conception of sexuality as being composed of binary essences and the equation of those essences with identities, a (dominantly heterosexual) man who has sex with another man must immediately question if he is a member of the other category—if he is "really" gay. Thus behavior is equated with identity.

This modern conception of sexuality plays out in the military in contradictory ways. On the one hand, the military embodies this idea of sexuality. Ideologically, it recognizes two different categories of sexuality, heterosexual and homosexual. Heterosexual is normal, moral, good, glorified, and homosexual is immoral, abnormal, and clearly subordinated.

Yet the reality of military life seems to undercut this neat bifurcation of sexual categories. For young recruits, entering the military traditionally has meant entering a world without women. Many young men who would have been unlikely to engage in sexual activities with other men in the civilian world do so in the military. Whereas for some men this is an opportunity to discover and explore their own homosexuality, for far more of them, having sex with other men is simply what young horny males do when there are no women around. Allan Berube, for example, writes about sailors coming into port and looking for women prostitutes. When no more women prostitutes were available on the streets, soldiers went with male transvestites without thinking anything of it. They were not considered gay; it was just simply what one did. The phenomenon of soldiers who think of themselves as heterosexuals engaging in homosexual behavior without losing their heterosexual status is common in the military. This reality is enshrined in such soldiers' sayings as "It's only queer when you're tied to the pier" and in the riddle "What's the difference between a straight Marine and a gay Marine?" Answer: "a six pack," "three beers," or "a shot."[30] The idea that the absence of women and getting drunk are both reasons that nominally heterosexual men might engage in homosexual behavior is generally accepted. The men who participate in this activity think of themselves as heterosexual without fear of "really being gay." The culture's binary conception of sexuality is thus sustained—not undercut—in the military through the practice of distinguishing between sexual identity and sexual practice, now codified in the "don't ask, don't tell" policy.

Men's desires to look at each other and sexual tensions between men already exist in the showers, the barracks, and other gathering places. Berube suggests that if you ascribe that tension to homosexuals, then you can pretend that if you get rid of the homos you will get rid of the sexual tensions. Thus, keeping homosexuals out of the military keeps the military safe for homoeroticism.[31] Or more precisely, keeping acknowledged homo-sexuals out of the military or at least keeping the appearance of no homo-sexuality in the military makes the military safe for the rampant homo-eroticism and homoerotic tension that already exists—from butt-grabbing to drag shows to hazing rituals to facultative homosexuality. With the exclusion of homosexual desire in the military, as embodied by the gay ban, all that homoerotic activity is simply what men do in the military. And because the military is defined as the apotheosis of heterosexual masculin-ity, such activity could not be gay. If the military includes gays, what assures military men that all that homoerotic activity doesn't mean that they are queer? And then what assures them that they are men?

The Military and Manhood

The power of the U.S. military to transform male sexuality is integral to its cultural identity, which has long promised to "make men out of boys."[32] Indeed, the military has traditionally offered lessons in masculinity as a part of basic training.[33] New (male) recruits are called "girls" and "ladies" to convey to them that they are nothing. This is a part of the process of mor-tification of the self, stripping them of all previous identity claims before rebuilding them into military men who fight enemies referred to as "girls" or "faggots."[34] Recruits learn to hate, fear, and destroy the feminine—in themselves and in others (see Chapters 4 and 5).[35] Moreover, by virtue of its primarily male-centered history, the military is the most homosocial and homoerotic environment that recruits may ever encounter: Large numbers of men engage in very intense and intimate experiences, live in close quar-ters with little privacy, and focus on the body in training. Some military rit-uals, including the navy's famous crossing-the-line, or shellback, ceremony have typically featured such elements as transvestitism, simulated fellatio, sadomasochistic role playing, and group nudity.[36] Given that recruits usu-ally are *young*, late-adolescent males who are confronting questions of self-definition, the situation would seem to foster erotic impulses at precisely a time when identity is in flux and experimentation occurs.

This sense of sexual vulnerability informed the policy debate masked as a discussion about the privacy rights of heterosexual soldiers. The image evoked repeatedly was of the straight soldiers forced to take showers with their gay comrades, their naked bodies subject to the lustful gaze of the gay.

The image itself is based on stereotypes of gay men. Implicit in the image of gay soldiers lusting after their buddies in the showers and "hitting on" adamantly heterosexual men are the following beliefs: Unlike straight men, gay men are defined by their sexual practices; sexual desire is the center of their identity, running their lives and determining their actions to such an extent that other considerations are close to irrelevant; gay men cannot or will not control their sexual and social behavior; gay men are predatory, driven to "convert" or seduce heterosexuals. In contrast, for most gay men the idea that one's thoughts are always on sex or that showers would be spent sizing up their straight brothers or even that they would find a bunch of straight, homophobic men attractive is ludicrous. When the Canadian government called upon (heterosexual) American psychologist Lois Shawer, an expert in bodily modesty, to assess whether the privacy rights of hetero-sexuals are violated by having to share quarters and facilities with homo-sexuals, she concluded that "homosexuals would not be likely to leer at heterosexuals or violate their modesty traditions."[37]

The introduction of the issue of privacy is all the more striking because although lack of privacy is uncomfortable, it is a fundamental characteris-tic of the military, and accommodation to it is an adjustment that all new recruits must make. This is so much the case that if the issue of privacy is raised in any context other than the gays-in-the-military debate, most sol-diers dismiss it as a trivial concern. (The issue has, of course, also been raised in the women-in-combat debate. When Major Rhonda Cornum was asked about the lack of privacy for women combatants during the Gulf War, her manner clearly communicated that she thought this an extremely trivial matter, and she just said, "Let 'em look."[38]) Nonetheless, speakers at the hearings uttered dire predictions about the large numbers of men who would leave the armed services if the gay ban were lifted.

A psychoanalytic analysis of why men get so upset about the (imagined) male homosexual gaze is that they are insecure about their own heterosex-uality. Fear and hatred of homosexuals is understood as being rooted in fear of incompletely repressed homosexual desires in oneself. The straight man is in terror of having a gay man come on to him not because he cannot fend off the advances but because such advances might mean that for some rea-son he appears to be gay. At the least, he would question the solidity of his heterosexuality.

Other feelings probably come into play as well. For many men, few insults are worse than being called queer; the gay man's implicit suggestion that the straight man might be interested would be experienced as an insult of the most grievous kind. Even worse, the idea that anyone might even wonder, might see the slightest hint of ambiguity in their sexual identity, must feel to some men like an incredible violation of their sense of self.

Although this psychoanalytic interpretation has some power and might well be an accurate analysis of some men's responses, it fails to capture the social meanings attached to privacy in relation to sexuality in our culture. Sexual practices are a private matter, but gay sexuality, unlike heterosexual sexuality, is taken to be practiced in public. Heterosexual sexuality, in this construction, gets displayed as a kind of model in the hearings, where the speakers repeatedly argued, "We wouldn't make women take showers or share quarters with men—so how can we ask soldiers to put up with a similar violation of their privacy?" (Of course, the fact that straight soldiers *already* share showers and quarters with closeted, and sometimes known, gay soldiers all the time without apparent damage is left out.)

This line was played like a trump card, as though once this analogy was made, no comeback was possible. In U.S. culture the image of people involuntarily being looked at by members of the opposite sex is disturbing. If you can transfer that sense of violation to heterosexual males sharing quarters with gays, the game is won.

But although the analogy may at first seem perfectly appropriate and reasonable, one aspect of it is glaringly incongruous—the comparison of straight male soldiers to women, the analogical positing of men in the women's position. In the military, this is simply not done.[39] Military men do not invoke women's experiences to explain or legitimate their own. They do not align their experiences with women's. It is close to inconceivable that they would use the argument "Women aren't expected to do it, so why should we?" in relation to any other activity. So we have to ask, What does the evocation of women in this argument reveal?

Returning to the fact that straight soldiers already share showers and quarters with gay soldiers, we need to ask why things would be so different if the ban were lifted. With the ban in place, the military is officially a heterosexual institution, and straight soldiers need not imagine anyone in the showers is gay. But if gays are no longer banned and if openly avowed homosexuals are integrated into the units, anyone in the showers might be gay—and straight soldiers would suddenly begin to imagine themselves as the objects of the male gaze—just as women are. It is not the absence of bodily privacy that is disturbing to male heterosexual soldiers but rather the imagining of themselves in the female subject position—being the object of the gaze, being desired, being powerless before the gaze, instead of being the gazer. Straight male soldiers do not want to be in that position and do not know what to do in it. Women have been treated that way for years and have learned to deal with it (although not without cost). But to straight men, being the object of the male gaze is utterly unacceptable; it is to be feminized.

The right argued for here is thus not the right of privacy but the right of heterosexual men not to be looked at (possibly with desire) by gay men whom they know to be gay. What they really cannot bear is being in the female subject position, the object of the gaze instead of the subject, the object of the fantasy instead of the one doing the fantasizing.

In this analysis (in contrast to the previous homophobia analysis), the problem is not that the imagined homosexual gaze turns straight male soldiers into gay men but that it turns them into women. Their gender, not their sexuality, is at stake.

No matter how definitely a man experiences himself as heterosexual, what it is to be a man is at stake here. Years of enacting and accomplishing masculinity arm men with a repertoire of ways to do the active gazing and desiring. But when they are put in the position of the recipient and have to find a way to respond, they are left in a realm where they have few resources in their behavioral repertoires, few known performance pieces that fit their gender (apart from beating the bastard up).

Conclusion

Although military leaders may articulate the question of gays in the military as one of morale, good order, and unit cohesion, such rationales do not even approach explanations for the intensity of emotion in the debate. To understand it, we need to look at the subtext, where issues about not only sexuality but gender emerge. The overarching concern is with maintaining the institution's heterosexual masculinity.

Gender is not a given but a situated accomplishment, a daily set of ways of being with different meanings in different contexts.[40] An important attraction of the military to many of its members is a guarantee of heterosexual masculinity. That guarantee is especially important because the military provides a situation of intense bonds between men, a much more homosocial and homoerotically charged environment than most men otherwise have the opportunity to be in. In that the military guarantees their manhood, men are allowed to participate in the intimacy of male bonding without being taken as sissies. In that context, the military's official heterosexual masculinity enables men to experience erotic, sexual, and emotional impulses that they would otherwise have to censor in themselves for fear of being seen (by others or themselves) as homosexual and therefore not real men. They are not only escaping a negative—imputations of homosexuality—but gaining a positive, the ability to be with other men in ways that transcend the limitations on male relationships that most men live under in civilian life.

So we have a paradoxical situation of an institution that constructs and upholds the most rigid stereotypes of hegemonic masculinity but at the same time provides a context that allows men to transcend some of these limits: the rigid constraints that typically prevent men from bonding with other men. These constraints break down in a controlled but nonetheless real way.

The foregoing is not the whole story behind the reaction to Clinton's plan to include gays in the military. It is important to recognize that massive campaigns of opposition were orchestrated by the military and right-wing political groups. However, the key to understanding the strident response is the fear that with gays officially in the military, the military can no longer be synonymous with manhood.

If gays are officially allowed in the military, it becomes impossible for the military to exert the same kind of masculinity-granting power; it also disrupts the chain of signification: military, real man, heterosexual. When African Americans fought for civil rights through ending racial segregation in the armed forces, leaders explicitly made the connection between the right to serve and *manhood*,[41] and being able to serve was seen as an acknowledgment of manhood. For some, opposition to gays in the military stems from resistance to acknowledging that gays are "real men."

A third issue involves the accepted concept of masculinity. If military masculinity still is our image of manhood, can manhood now expand to include homosexuals? The debate over gays in the military reached to the foundations of gender identity without, of course, making these issues explicit.

Notes

I have delivered versions of this chapter to various audiences, including the Workshop on Institutional Change and the U.S. Military at Cornell University and the 1994 ISA meeting in Washington, D.C. I am grateful to the many people who listened and offered insight and amplification. I also want to express my appreciation to Jane Parpart for a most useful conversation at a critical moment in this chapter's genesis and for her patience. My greatest debts are to Barry O'Neill and Mary Wyre; throughout the preparation of this final version I have benefited enormously from their insightful comments and support.

1. *Morning Edition*, National Public Radio, April 2, 1993. This quote comes from a call to a radio talk show in Jacksonville, North Carolina, where Camp Lejeune, the largest Marine Corps base in the East, is located.

2. In trying to understand what happened, we need to be aware of the politics behind the organization and timing of each side's mobilization. For example, the apparently spontaneous outpouring of outrage that greeted Clinton's January announcement was the product of months of extensive organizing by both the military and the religious right. These groups took Clinton's campaign promise far more seriously than did gay groups, for whom military service was not a front-burner issue.

3. Randy Shilts, *Conduct Unbecoming: Gays and Lesbians in the U.S. Military* (New York: St. Martin's Press, 1993), pp. 3–36.

4. *Defense Force Management: DOD's Policy on Homosexuality*, GAO/NSIAD-92-98, June 1992, p. 10.

5. For a more specific and extended account of the psychiatrist's role in the development of the post–World War II exclusion policy, see Allan Berube, *Coming Out Under Fire: The History of Gay Men and Women in World War Two* (New York: Plume, 1990), pp. 1–33.

6. *Defense Force Management*, p. 2. The full text of the statement reads: "Homosexuality is incompatible with military service. The presence in the military

environment of persons who engage in homosexual conduct or who, by their statements, demonstrate a propensity to engage in homosexual conduct, seriously impairs the accomplishment of the military mission. The presence of such members adversely affects the ability of the Military Services to maintain discipline, good order, and morale; to foster mutual trust and confidence among service members; to ensure the integrity of the system of rank and command; to facilitate assignment and worldwide deployment of service members who frequently must live and work under close conditions affording minimal privacy; to recruit and retain members of the Military Services; to maintain public acceptability of military service; and to prevent breaches of security."

7. Berube, *Coming Out Under Fire*, pp. 28–33. Most recently, according to the *Wall Street Journal*, soldiers who were known to be gay were deployed during the Gulf War and then subjected to discharge proceedings upon their return. Wade Lambert, "U.S. Moves to Discharge Some Gay Veterans of Gulf War," *Wall Street Journal*, July 30, 1991, p. B6. Also see Doug Grow, "Captain Did Her Duty, Despite Military's Mixed Messages," *Minneapolis Star Tribune*, March 16, 1993, p. 3B. For a general historical overview of the ways in which policies against gays are ignored in wartime see Shilts, *Conduct Unbecoming*, pp. 60–71, 725–734; and Randy Shilts, "What's Fair in Love and War," *Newsweek* 121, 5 (1993). During the Senate hearings of April 29, 1993, Senator Kennedy cited statistics showing that discharges for homosexuality go up in peacetime and down in wartime and pointed out that this directly contradicts the arguments of gay-ban proponents, since wartime is when cohesion is most critical. Senate Armed Services Committee Hearing, April 29, 1993.

8. House of Representatives Committee on Armed Services, *Assessment of the Plan to Lift the Ban on Homosexuals in the Military on H.A.S.C. 103-19*. 103rd Cong., 19th sess., July 21–23, 1993; House of Representatives Committee on Armed Services, *Policy Implications of Lifting the Ban on Homosexuals in the Military on H.A.S.C. 103-18*. 103rd Cong., 18th sess., May 4–5, 1993; Senate Committee on Armed Services, *Policy Concerning Homosexuality in the Armed Forces S. HRG. 103-845*. 103rd Cong., 2nd sess., March 29 and 31, 1993.

9. Throughout this chapter, I use the term "soldiers" to refer to enlisted personnel and noncommissioned officers in all branches of the military.

10. Senate Armed Services Committee Hearings, April 29, 1993.

11. Col. Frederick Peck USMC, Senate Armed Services Committed Hearings, May 11, 1993; Associated Press, "Gay Son Differs with His Marine Father on Perils of the Military," *Boston Globe*, May 13, 1993, p. A3.

12. Judith Stiehm makes the argument that the military's policies about gays are really based on gay men and ignore the realities of both lesbians and heterosexual women's reactions to them. She discusses two other arguments made at the hearings to illustrate her point. Judith Hicks Stiehm, "The Military Ban on Homosexuals and the Cyclops Effect," in Wilbur J. Scott and Sandra Carson Stanley, eds., *Gays and Lesbians in the Military* (New York: Aldine de Gruyter, 1994), pp. 149–162.

13. Personal communication, April 3, 1993.

14. Senate Armed Services Committee Hearings, March 31, 1993.

15. Personal communication, April 3, 1993.

16. Stiehm, "The Military Ban," p. 150.

17. Senator Warner, Senate Armed Services Committee Hearings, March 29, 1993.

18. Barry M. Goldwater, "The Gay Ban: Just Plain Un-American," *Washington Post*, June 10, 1993, p. A23. The problem is that only the costs of recruiting and training the personnel needed to replace those discharged for homosexuality can be estimated; no figures on amounts expended for investigations, out-processing, or court costs are available. (During fiscal years 1986–1990, Department of Defense investigative agencies conducted a total of 3,663 such investigations.) The General Accounting Office reports that in FY 1990, the costs of recruiting and initial training of replacement personnel were estimated at $28,226 for each enlisted person and $120,772 for each officer. *Defense Force Management*, p. 4. According to the Servicemembers Legal Defense Network, the cost of training replacements for the 597 men and women discharged in 1994 after the new policy was implemented was $17.5 million, and again, this figure does not include the costs of investigations and discharge hearings. Lawrence Korb and C. Dixon Osburn, "Asked, Told, Pursued," *New York Times*, March 19, 1995, sec. 4, p. 15.

19. Shilts, *Conduct Unbecoming*, p. 33.

20. Wm. Darryl Henderson, *Cohesion: The Human Element in Combat* (Washington, DC: National Defense University Press, 1985).

21. See, for example, J. Glenn Gray, *The Warriors* (New York: Harper Colophon Books, 1970).

22. Major Rhonda Cornum, comments at Quail Roost Conference, University of North Carolina at Chapel Hill, April 3, 1993.

23. Laura Miller, "Fighting for a Just Cause," in Scott and Stanley, *Gays and Lesbians in the Military*, pp. 79, 81. These are spoken and written comments by male servicemembers who participated in Miller's study.

24. Ibid., p. 75.

25. Allan Berube, *Fresh Air*, National Public Radio, March 30, 1993.

26. Eric Schmitt, "Compromise on Military Gay Ban Gaining Support Among Senators," *New York Times*, May 12, 1993, p. A1.

27. Korb and Osburn, "Asked, Told, Pursued," sec. 4, p. 15.

28. Robert Padgug, "Sexual Matters: On Conceptualizing Sexuality in History," *Radical History Review* 20 (Spring-Summer 1979), pp. 3–23.

29. John D'Emilio, "Capitalism and Gay Identity," in Ann Snitow, Christine Stansell, and Sharon Thompson, eds., *Powers of Desire: The Politics of Sexuality* (New York: Monthly Review Press, 1983), p. 104.

30. Steven Zeeland, *Sailors and Sexual Identity: Crossing the Line Between "Straight" and "Gay" in the U.S. Navy* (New York: Harrington Park Press, 1995), p. 14.

31. Berube, *Fresh Air*, March 30, 1993.

32. Randy Shilts cites several instances of gay men who joined the military explicitly because they hoped it would, as recruitment posters promised, "make a man" out of them. Shilts, *Conduct Unbecoming*, pp. 32, 115, 134.

33. For the classic explorations of the ways in which the U.S. military has defined heterosexual masculinity as central to its functioning, see the writings of Cynthia Enloe, including *Does Khaki Become You?* (Boston: South End Press, 1983); *Bananas, Beaches and Bases: Making Feminist Sense of International Politics* (Berkeley: University of California Press, 1989); "The Right to Fight: A Feminist

Catch-22," *Ms.*, July-August 1993, pp. 84–87; "Clinton Doctrine: The Masculine Mystique," *Progressive*, January 1994, pp. 24–26.

34. For an account of the use of gendered imagery in basic training, see C. J. Levy, "ARVN as Faggots: Inverted Warfare in Vietnam," in Michael S. Kimmel, ed., *Men's Lives* (New York: Macmillan, 1989). On the processes of breaking down and rebuilding the self that are part of the practices of total institutions, see Erving Goffman, *Asylums* (New York: Doubleday, 1961).

35. Levy, "ARVN as Faggots"; John A. Ballard and Aliecia J. McDowell, "Hate and Combat Behavior," *Armed Forces and Society* 17, 2 (Winter 1991), pp. 229–241.

36. Shilts, *Conduct Unbecoming*, pp. 400–402, 406; Zeeland, *Sailors and Sexual Identity*, pp. 143–145. The shellback ceremony marks the first time a sailor crosses the equator. The navy has revised its guidelines for this ceremony since the Tailhook incident.

37. Lois Shawer, *And the Flag Was Still There: Straight People, Gay People and Sexuality in the U.S. Military* (New York: Harrington Park Press, 1995), p. xiv. It is interesting that despite her track record of research on the issue, neither the Senate nor the House called on her to testify.

38. Major Rhonda Cornum, April 3, 1993. Once people are in a context in which privacy is no longer possible, this attitude quickly becomes common.

39. The exception, of course, is in basic training, when it is done to new recruits before they become real men, real soldiers.

40. On the conception of "gender as a routine accomplishment embedded in everyday interaction," see Candace West and Don H. Zimmerman, "Doing Gender," *Gender and Society* 1, 2 (June 1987), pp. 125–151.

41. "I must emphasize that the current agitation for civil rights is no longer a mere expression of hope on the part of Negroes. On the one hand, it is a positive, resolute outrea[ch]ing for full manhood. On the other hand, it is an equally determined will to stop acquiescing in anything less. Negroes demand full, unqualified, first-class citizenship." A. Phillip Randolph in 1948 testimony before the Senate Armed Services Committee, cited in Bernard C. Nalty and Morris J. MacGregor, *Blacks in the Military: Essential Documents* (Wilmington, DE: Scholarly Resources, 1981), p. 237.

8

Something's Missing: Male Hysteria and the U.S. Invasion of Panama

Cynthia Weber

The best strategy for challenging the phallic authority of the penis is laughter.[1]

Analyzing the cause of the 1989 U.S. invasion of Panama, a White House adviser told the *New York Times* the president "felt that Noriega was thumbing his nose at him."[2] Read symptomatically, Manuel Noriega's political gesture toward Bush is exposed as hysterical. The substitution of the unconscious impulse for the signifier—penis for thumb and the Central American isthmus for nose—suggests a geopolitical anatomy of frustrated desires.[3] Furthermore, it prompts a series of questions: Why did Noriega expose himself to Bush? What accounts for Bush's response (a military invasion)? And does this scenario as a summary statement of the Bush administration's position toward Noriega offer any insights about male hysteria as a motif for political leadership in the "new world order"?

What follows is a symptomatic reading of geopolitical bodies (diplomatic and territorial) and body parts (sexual and strategic) that appear in the discourse surrounding the U.S. invasion of Panama. Among the bodies analyzed are those of Manuel Noriega and George Bush (diplomatic), Panama and the United States (territorial), and the Panama Canal (sexual as well as strategic body part).

This symptomatic reading of the invasion discourse draws upon the work of Luce Irigaray, particularly her books *Speculum of the Other Woman* and *This sex which is not one*, to make two theoretical moves.[4] The first move reads Noriega and Bush as hysterical males by examining them as isolated corporal signifiers and later relating them to the Panama Canal, their figural support. I suggest that both Noriega and Bush lacked phallic power, and this lack was related to a lack of a feminine object (in this case, the Panama Canal). Noriega lacked the Panama Canal because he was denied access to the canal by the Bush administration. Noriega's lack may be read as a discourse of externally imposed celibacy. Bush, in contrast, controlled the Panama Canal yet also lacked the canal. Bush's lack derived from his position as the leader of a state that was a declining hegemonic power in international affairs. Bush lacked the canal, then, because he and his state were nearly impotent. Both Noriega and Bush attempted to compensate for their lack by excessively miming masculinity in the invasion discourse.[5] The effect of their discursive practices was to uncode the male bodies of Noriega and Bush as men.

The second theoretical move concerns feminization rather than emasculation. Thanks to their emasculation (uncoding as men), Noriega and Bush were open to feminization (recoding as women). For Noriega, feminization both preceded the U.S. invasion of Panama and continued during and after the invasion.[6] I focus primarily on Bush, though, because it was the Bush administration's discursive invasion strategy of encirclement rather than penetration that led to the feminization of Bush.

More important in terms of international relations theory generally and theories of state sovereignty and intervention specifically, the Bush administration's strategy of encirclement invited a deconstruction of two dichotomies upon which the invasion discourse relied. These dichotomies were domestic politics/international politics and the complementary engendering of domestic politics as feminine and international politics as masculine, resulting in a domestic = feminine/international = masculine dichotomy.[7]

The invasion discourse disrupts the logic whereby sovereign nation-states and their ultimate affirmation of manhood—intervention—are masculinely engendered. Rather than regarding posthegemonic (postphallic) states simply as old, nearly impotent masculine bodies, this reading suggests they might instead be interpreted as transvestites because in what is regarded as the masculine sphere of politics (international space), posthegemonic states rely upon simulated feminine modes of conduct.[8]

Irigaray's focus on miming, mimicry, or mimesis invites an analogical reading of the invasion discourse. This strategy of reading deliberately employs the metaphorical imagery found in Irigaray's work for two reasons. First, attending to the mimetic performance of engendered language enables one to refuse to position oneself either within or beyond symbolic and cultural codes of phallocentrism that value male terms over female terms. In this context, miming—like laughter—allows me to perform a parody of phallic authority. Following from this, one is positioned to bring gender dichotomies into question. Second, as Margaret Whitford explained,

"The tactic of mimesis can be seen as a kind of deliberate hysteria, designed to illuminate the interests which are at stake in metaphors."[9]

Although this reading embodies profane treatments of "honorable" institutions (such as the presidency) and humorous analyses of "dishonorable" acts (rape and a bloody military intervention), the political implications of this reading should not be overlooked. By attending to these aspects of the U.S. discourse on the Panama invasion, I focus on a neglected feature of what enables such atrocities to occur and of their effects on institutions, events, and engendered representations of subjectivity. It is not my intention to deflect attention from other political implications of the invasion discourse; rather, in accordance with feminist readings of politics, I attempt to explode the notion of politics.[10]

This reading of the invasion discourse equates deauthorization (the death of the author) with the hystericization of male subjectivity.[11] It deliberately engages the invasion discourse with humor. As Mikhail Bakhtin noted, "Laughter liberates not only from external censorship but first of all from the great interior censor."[12] Laughter defamiliarizes discourses and events for readers, giving readers license to disobey common expectations about what meanings a text ought to generate. Attention is drawn to subtexts and double meanings embedded in texts. By "liberating" the interpretation of a text from the sole domain of its author's intentions, texts are remotivated with plural interpretations.

Male Hysteria,
or Nose Thumbing and Sign Posting

The hysteric . . . cannot assume his/her own discourse; everything is referred for validation to the "you."[13]

Whereas the statement "I am" expresses subjectivity, the question "Am I?" denotes hysteria. Hysteria has been defined as "a response in symptomatic form—that is, one made through a substitution of corporeal signifiers for unconscious impulses—to a sexual demand or urge that the subject cannot accommodate."[14] Lack and excess are the two complementary motifs of hysteria. Hysteria appears as the excessive miming of masculinity (which psychoanalytic discourse equates with subjectivity) that "stands in" for a lack of phallic power (inability to make meaning). In the case of female hysteria, this lack of phallic power follows from an anatomical lack of a visible penis.

Irigaray reminded us that hysteria is not an exclusively female pathology.[15] Yet male hysteria takes a different form than female hysteria. Whereas female hysteria illustrates the coding of women as men, "what male hysteria shows us is not so much the coding of men as women, as the uncoding of men as men."[16] Male hysteria is the emasculation of men (uncoding of men as men) rather than the feminization of men (coding of men as women).

One expression of emasculation is the exposure of the phallus. Exposure combines excessive display with a lack of phallic power. Exposing the penis (excess) demonstrates the absence of phallic power (lack). Thus male hysterics, like female hysterics, excessively mime masculinity to compensate for a lack of phallic power; however, they do so not because they lack a penis but because their penis is exposed.

Noriega's nose thumbing at Bush, then, artfully combines excess and lack in the form of male hysteria. Referring to this gesture as the summary statement of why the U.S. invaded Panama, the interviewed White House adviser hinted at a pervasive hysterical backdrop. Indeed, as they appear in the discourse concerning the invasion, both Noriega and Bush display hysterical symptoms.

To encounter Noriega is to encounter a symbolic excess of masculinity. Manuel Antonio Noriega's name—read as an acronym (M.A.N.), as a proper name ([Man]uel), or as a nickname ([Man]ny)—attests to his manliness.[17] So too did Noriega's possessions. Recounting the assets of Noriega's personal fortune, then deputy secretary of state Lawrence Eagleburger noted that Noriega had "three large pleasure yachts, the Macho I, Macho II, and Macho III—now that's a lot of macho."[18]

Bush's hysterical excess was displaced from his physical body to his geopolitical body, from George Bush the man onto George Bush the commander in chief of a posthegemonic state.[19] The military invasion of Panama marked the attempted masculine projection of his stately authority not only into the international sphere but also into the territory of another domestic space, more specifically into the "canal zone"—a femininely engendered passageway (vagina) through which male/international subjects reach maturity. As in psychoanalytic discourse, it was the phallus that was the masculine projection of authority internationally and the feminine ôholeö—the Panama Canal—that was its domestic and geopolitical underwriter.

In both of these cases, excess was tied to a lack of phallic power. For Noriega, phallic power was undercut by his lack of staying power. Shortly after the coup attempt of October 3, 1989, Noriega boasted, "Virility is proved by staying in [power]."[20] Noriega's staying power was to last a brief time after this. Noriega's difficulty with staying in was that he was left with nothing to stay in. He had no domestic space, no nation-state, no canal in which he could express his phallic power. Noriega became a man without access to a canal—a hysterical male who, in this case, could be read as a man with a useless phallus thanks to externally imposed celibacy.

Bush's lack (man)ifested itself differently. Rather than having no domestic space(s) in which to project his authority, he found that his projection of hegemonic authority was in decline. Like Noriega's excess, Bush's lack played on the thumb metaphor. Noriega was waving his thumb (penis) at Bush; Bush was attempting to revitalize his stately thumb (penis coded as hegemonic power). Touring Panama after the invasion, Representative Lee Hamilton observed that Panamanians would "come out and give us a thumbs up signal."[21] Apparently, the mission was a success.

Prior to the invasion, Bush's thumb did not speak so loudly in the region. To compensate for the impending impotence of declining hegemony, General Colin Powell, chair of the Joint Chiefs of Staff, offered a formal display of hegemonic power. Powell was "reported recently to have said that we have to put up a shingle outside our door saying 'superpower lives here.'"[22] Whereas Lacan argued that the phallus as the psychoanalytic standard of value functions as a signifier "only as veiled," Powell's countervailing strategy of announcing the obvious contradicted the message he "posted."[23] It was an act of exposure that was "the equivalent to announcing that the central postulate is in fact being called into question."[24] The announcement of hegemonic power unveiled the phallus and displayed the penis that could not stand on its own. This accounts for Senator Sam Nunn's insistence in the joint hearings on the invasion that American "legitimacy . . . is going to depend on . . . reduced American visibility."[25]

Speculum of the Other Country

Irigaray described the relationship between the sexes in psychoanalytic discourse as "specularized." The word "speculum" refers to both an "instrument for dilating cavities of [the] human body for inspection" and to a "mirror, usu. of polished metal."[26] Both the masculine and the feminine share aspects of the speculum. The masculine instrument or tool (the penis) penetrates the formless empty cavity (the vagina) of the feminine, and the feminine acts as a "faithful, polished mirror" that reproduces masculine subjectivity but not itself.[27] The mirror (feminine), symbolized by the speculum, depicts both the transformation of the mother into a ghost (specter) in the Lacanian mirror stage and the concavity of the mirror (speculum) that turns images upside down.[28]

Yet another meaning of speculum is a lens that focuses light on a hole. This understanding of speculum combines the masculine and feminine aspects of the term. Wrote Irigaray of the speculum, "It may, quite simply, be an instrument to *dilate* the lips, the orifices, the walls, so that the eye can penetrate the *interior*."[29] She went on to explain that man's eye is "understood as substitute for penis."[30] It is by separating the vulva (lips) and penetrating the vagina with his penis (eye) that man sees his subjectivity reflected back at him in the concave mirror (woman).

The masculine ability to penetrate and the feminine ability to reflect images correspond to a hierarchy of solids and fluids found in psychoanalytic theory. Visible forms (penis) are privileged over formless voids (vagina). Irigaray traced this hierarchical relationship of solids over fluids to physics, in which matter was privileged long before a theory of fluids was expounded.[31] Irigaray's observation that gender is coded in terms of solids and fluids led to her account of the potentially turbulent role the feminine may play in psychoanalytic discourse. The feminine as mirror reflects masculine subjectivity only if it is placid, unclouded, and fixed. Irigaray noted that in psychoanalytic discourse it is necessary to have a fixed feminine object. Otherwise, "the erection of the subject might thereby be disconcerted and risk losing its elevation and penetration. For what would there be to rise up from and exercise his power over? And in?"[32]

When the feminine ceases to function as a reflective pool, masculine subjectivity is in crisis. Wrote Irigaray, "Perhaps for the time being the serene contemplation of empire must be abandoned in favor of taming those forces which, once unleashed, might explode the very concept of empire."[33]

The Panama Canal

Geopolitical bodies in international relations may be described in terms of gender. A sovereign nation-state, for example, is said to have a feminine domestic side and a masculine international side. "Domestic" refers to the private sphere of state relations that gives a particular state a unique national character.[34] "International" refers to the projection of this domestic identity into the public sphere of relations among states. In international relations theory, as in Irigaray's account of psychoanalytic theory, the feminine (domestic) makes the masculine (international) possible. For without a clearly identified domestic sphere, a nation-state would have no voice to project into the international sphere.

Panama and the United States can be described as engendered geopolitical bodies. For each state, it was a domestic citizenry and territory (the feminine) that provided the basis for international authority (the masculine). When these geopolitical bodies were conjoined with the bodies of their respective heads of state, what were highlighted were the sources of hysteria for Noriega and Bush. What comes into focus is the particular geopolitical lack each leader compensated for through a discourse of excess.

Each leader in a different way lacked the feminine object that would affirm his masculine subjectivity. For Noriega, the feminine was a domestic space (a nation-state) that he could claim as his own so that Panama under his leadership would have a legitimate voice in international affairs. For Bush, the feminine object was an international space in which to project hegemonic authority. This space was also Panama. But in the Bush administration discourse, Panama did not compensate for Bush's lack of a domestic space; rather, Panama helped Bush compensate for his lack of the "vision thing," for it was in the Canal Zone that U.S. hegemonic authority was reflected. These two very different ways of understanding Panama as lack were combined in the discourse on the invasion through the Bush administration's attempt to project its authority internationally by withholding the feminine object from Noriega.

This feminine object showed up in the Bush administration discourse as both an anatomical and a geopolitical body. These bodies had in common the fact that they were victims of attempted rape by the Noriega administration. In his speech to the American public outlining the justifications for intervention in Panama, Bush explicitly stated that all the fighting was about sexual abuse. Panamanian "forces under his [Noriega's] command shot and killed an unarmed American serviceman; wounded another; arrested and brutally beat a third American serviceman; and then brutally interrogated his wife, threatening her with sexual abuse. That was enough."[35]

The anatomic body of the American serviceperson's wife implies another body that, according to the Bush administration, Noriega sexually abused. This feminine geopolitical body was the Panama Canal. Noriega's discourse inscribed the canal in terms similar to those used by Irigaray to describe how the feminine appears in psychoanalytic discourse. A few months before the invasion Noriega commented, "Panama [is] like a mirror in which all of America . . . see themselves."[36] The locus of Panama's reflective power was the Panama Canal. State sovereignty was symbolized by various nation-states' flagged ships floating in this man-made passageway that spawned a nation-state.[37]

Noriega's rape of the canal seemed to be imminent to the Bush administration. The invasion occurred just eleven days before the administration of the canal was scheduled to be handed over to a Panamanian commission.[38] Panamanian administrative control of the canal troubled the United States because of Noriega's leadership style. In the Bush administration discourse, Noriega signified a disruptive force that threatened to stir the still waters of the canal. Discussing the invasion, General Kelly remarked about Noriega, "He knows how to swim in that environment down there."[39] Another Bush administration official refers to Noriega's government and style of rule as "Noriega's (Tit)anic."[40]

A Bush administration official noted, "We must recognize . . . that Panama's ability to responsibly pursue its own interest —and hence the long-term future of the canal—cannot be assured in the context of political instability." He went on to stress that democracy is "an essential element of political stability on the isthmus." The "firm" position of the Bush administration was that "securing the long-term future of democracy in Panama and of the canal" were two elements that were "indissolubly linked." "Noriega's continuation in power is a threat. . . . And . . . it will be the canal's users who ultimately must face the burden of bearing the costs."[41]

Democracy is valued, then, for its stabilizing influence —for its ability to calm formless feminine fluids so they may serve masculine purposes. Until a democratic environment could be established in Panama—until the Endara government could be seated—the United States had to retain administrative control of the canal. So long as Noriega governed Panama, he endangered the U.S. "broad national interest" of maintaining "a safe, efficient, and neutral Panama Canal."[42] "Broad" in this context may refer to both the scope of U.S. interests and to a vernacular expression of the feminine component of U.S. interests.

Both interpretations are suggested by what became the epitome of the Bush presidency: "Read my lips." A symptomatic interpretation of this phrase replaces "lips" for "vulva." Bush's "lips," then, refer to the canal, "my" is his assertion of ownership of the canal, and "read" denotes the autistic character of the feminine.[43] So long as his lips (the Panama Canal) could be read but could not speak, Panamanian stability was ensured. But like General Powell's sign posting, Bush's challenge to his audience ("Read my lips") was as disempowering as it was empowering. Bush's lips at once claimed the Panama Canal as a reflective pool of U.S. hegemonic power and displayed the feminization of the American president. Read as a sign of female reproductive ability more generally, Bush's lips silently announced that the president had egg on his face.

In the Bush administration discourse, a distinction was drawn between preserving Panamanian sovereignty and removing Noriega from power. What this suggests is that the Bush administration did not want to become the only user of the canal. Rather, the ôneutralityö of the canal had to be ensured so that the United States and Panama could be among the canal's users. The achievement of this goal entailed separating the disruptive masculine subject (Noriega) from his feminine object (the canal). By denying Noriega his feminine object, the United States effectively denied Noriega's masculine subjectivity. And as a head of state without a state, Noriega was no longer a threat to U.S. hegemony in the region. A joke by a senator at the joint congressional hearings on events in Panama explicitly linked masculine subjectivity with the feminine object. When a man testifying before the committee announced, "I was confirmed in June," a senator added, "No pun intended."[44] Read as the proper name of a woman rather than as a month, "June" signifies the body in which masculine subjectivity is achieved. It is not so much the pun as it is the pun's structure that is of interest here. Notice that it was the U.S. senator who substituted the unconscious impulse (confirmation of male subjectivity in a female body) for the corporal signifier (June read as a woman's body), thereby revealing the hysterical subtext of the hearings.[45]

Speculum turned to spectacle when the United States invaded Panama to capture Noriega. And spectacle turned to farce while Noriega was eluding the U.S. military. Even so, this moment of the invasion served the U.S. ôbroadö national interest. William Bennett, the president's director of national drug-control policy, said of Noriega at this juncture, "He's not running drugs; he's not running Panama; he's just running."[46] The transformation of Noriega from solids to fluids guaranteed that Noriega would no longer pose a threat to the canal. Indeed, as the papal nuncio remarked, Noriega was politically castrated. "The entire nation thinks [Noriega is] a man endowed with powers he doesn't have. I found him a man who, without a pistol [penis], could be handled by anyone."[47]

Specularized Policy

Military intervention joins the affirmation of state sovereignty with violence. In international relations theory, intervention is defined as the violation of one state's sovereignty by an uninvited intruder.[48] It is rape on an international scale. A recent panel at the American Political Science Association meetings conveyed the masculine inscription of intervention and its relationship to a feminine object. The panel was entitled "Dilemma of Protracted [specularized?] Intervention," and the primary titles of the papers are "Getting In," "Staying In," and "Getting Out."[49]

Given this, the Bush administration's strategy of denying Noriega his feminine object (a nation-state and the canal) through the act of military intervention is consistent with the account of Bush as a hysterical male. If Bush embodied the United States during a refractory period that signaled the impending impotence of the United States (hegemonic decline), then the U.S. invasion of Panama exemplifies the excessive miming of masculinity. But this begs the question: Does a nearly impotent commander in chief have the capacity to "get in?" Put differently, is a declining hegemon able to project its masculine subjectivity internationally through an act of military intervention?

The answer to these questions appears to be both yes and no. A U.S. military operation clearly took place in Panama. However, it replaced penetration with encirclement as its modus operandi. Instead of internationally projecting U.S. hegemonic power into the domestic affairs of Panama, the United States domesticated Panama. The U.S. discourse on Panama effectively subsumed Panamanian domestic affairs within the scope of U.S. domestic policy. Territorially, these countries' domestic/international boundaries did not change; discursively, however, Panama was left with no domestic sphere distinct from that of the United States. The U.S. strategy of encirclement made the more common intervention tactic of penetration unnecessary. Thanks to this initial act of domestication, the invasion could be viewed as an internal act undertaken to consolidate one domestic space. Two factors made the U.S. domestication of Panamanian space possible. The first is historical. Panama's history as a sovereign nation-state cannot be separated from U.S. history. It was the U.S. desire for a canal in Central America in the early 1900s that led the United States to support a Panamanian claim of independence from Colombia. To this day, this initial act of genesis lingers in U.S.-Panamanian relations. For it is the United States that controls the vital circulatory systems of Panama—the Panama Canal and Panamanian currency (U.S. dollars).

Staged against a background of shared history is a second, more immediate factor—the U.S. discursive claim to Panama couched in terms of the "war on drugs." Although the Bush administration held that "this is a war as deadly and as dangerous as any fought with armies massed across borders," the administration rhetoric on drugs erased any distinctions between what was domestic and what was international.[50] According to that administration, drug trafficking "is a worldwide problem" that "threatens the security of nations."[51] "The drug issue knows no national borders."[52]

The administration's refusal of the domestic/international dichotomy made Noriega's drug-related indictments by two Florida grand juries less objectionable. Noriega was transformed from a head of state to a common domestic criminal. "The story these indictments tell is simple and chilling. It is the story of that same shameless excess in the criminal field that we have already seen in the political field."[53] Bringing Noriega to justice meant bringing Noriega to trial in the United States. The community of judgment in this case was a jury composed of U.S. citizens. "Justice" here refers to U.S. domestic justice and not international justice.

The Bush administration discourse on the invasion of Panama always found its point of reference in the U.S. citizenry. Unlike with the U.S. intervention of Grenada in 1983, the United States did not direct its justification for intervention in Panama to some international community. No organization analogous to the Organization of Eastern Caribbean States was created so that it could ask for U.S. military assistance. A regional or international request for intervention was unnecessary because the U.S. invasion of Panama was an internal matter. Only the U.S. citizenry needed to be consulted and, in the event of a military action, offered an explanation. Operation Just Cause, the administration's codename for the invasion, was just by U.S. domestic standards and was justified to the U.S. public.[54]

The U.S. invasion of Panama abides by a specularized logic both because it transforms a traditional account of intervention into its negative image and because the traditional locations of domestic and international policy appear upside down in the concave mirror of Panama. With respect to intervention, the Bush administration's domestication of Panama reinscribed the meaning of intervention in this case. President Bush asked, "What, in God's name, would we . . . call the international drug trade—and those who aid it and abet it—but intervention in our internal affairs?"[55] This notion is expanded upon elsewhere.

There are times when good principles force us to defend bad men. Some argue that this was the case with Noriega and Panama. They argue as if the principle of nonintervention required us to accept whatever Noriega did.

But nonintervention was never meant to protect individual criminals. It was never meant to promote intervention by drug traffickers in our societies against our families and children. It was never meant to prevent peaceful and diplomatic action by sovereign states in support of democracy. And it was never meant to leave the criminals free to savage the good and the good powerless to react.[56]

Additionally, the strategy of encirclement specularized the logic of the invasion by transposing domestic and international policy. The U.S. war on drugs encircled Noriega in a threefold sense—first by domesticating Panamanian policy, second by surrounding the Vatican embassy with rock and roll music, and third by encapsulating Noriega in a U.S. prison cell. Manuel Noriega—the head of state of an independent sovereign nation—became U.S. federal prisoner 41586. Looking at the discourse of the U.S. invasion of Panama, then, one finds foreign policy located in U.S. domestic space (Noriega in a U.S. prison) and domestic policy located in U.S. foreign space (the U.S. war on drugs fought in Panama).

This State Which Is Not One

If male hysteria refers to the uncoding of men as men (emasculation) rather than the coding of men as women (feminization), this reading of the U.S. invasion of Panama suggests both emasculation and feminization. That Noriega and Bush lacked phallic power and compensated for this lack with the excessive miming of masculinity indicates male hysteria. Yet it would be an oversight to stop analysis at this point. For in their moments of excess, the bodies of Noriega and Bush were femininely engendered. Recall, for example, Noriega's transformation from solids to fluids and Bush's display of female reproductive organs on his face. Furthermore, the name ôBushö announces the location of female genitalia. The most critical moment of feminization in the invasion discourse pertains to the Bush administration's strategy of encirclement. In this section, I focus on this move because it deconstructs masculine standards of "international" and "intervention."

For Bush and the United States, hysteria or the crisis in subjectivity was brought about by hegemonic decline. The Panama Canal functioned in Bush's discourse as the reflective pool that could mirror U.S. hegemonic subjectivity. Because the U.S. invasion of Panama secured the stability of the canal, one might conclude that the reflective function of the canal, and therefore U.S. hegemonic subjectivity, were rescued.

This conclusion overlooks the feminization of Bush and the United States. Specifically, it neglects to theorize the implications of an intervention strategy based on encirclement rather than penetration. As noted earlier, intervention in international relations theory is rape on an international scale. Rape commonly refers to an act committed by a male against a female or male. Considered from a psychoanalytic perspective, the U.S. invasion of Panama might be said to include two different scenarios of rape—the first by a woman of a man and the second by a male transvestite of a woman. These unusual sexual pairings of rape are suggested by penis envy and the threat of castration as they appear in psychoanalytic discourse.

The first rape scenario—by a female of a male—symbolizes the threat of castration. In psychoanalytic discourse, the threat of castration is not reserved for the Father, who is located on the side of the Law and the phallus. The woman too may pose this threat to a man, only differently. Whereas the Father's threat is to cut off his son's genitals, the woman's threat—owing to her presumed penis envy—is to refuse to relinquish the penis that has penetrated her. Should the woman whose body encircles the penis refuse to surrender it, the male would experience a sense of loss similar to that of being castrated. Encirclement or entrapment, then, are modalities of female rape of a male.

In the discourse of the U.S. invasion of Panama, it was the Panama Canal that threatened to encircle and symbolically castrate Noriega and Bush. Noriega never experienced this form of castration because the Bush administration denied him access to the canal and thus symbolically castrated him first. Bush also avoided castration by the canal—not because he was denied access to it but because even given access, he was incapable of penetration. In this regard, the canal's threat of castrating Bush served as an embarrassing reminder of Bush's lack of phallic power. For both Noriega and Bush, the threat of castration posed by the Panama Canal was never anything more than a threat.

Even though it was not actualized, this first rape scenario is important because it acts as an interpretive guide for the second rape scenario—by a male transvestite of a female. A transvestite male is a man acting or appearing as a woman. Although this transvestite is anatomically male, his actions are those of a female. The transvestite is both emasculated (a man uncoded as a man) and feminized (a man recoded as a woman).

In the U.S. invasion of Panama, the transvestite was Bush and the female was the Panama Canal. Bush was a transvestite in international politics because in the masculine arena of international politics, his actions as commander in chief were feminine. The U.S. invasion of Panama was a feminine act because it was carried out via a strategy of encirclement. This act of encirclement takes on interesting implications when examined psychoanalytically. As noted earlier, encirclement may be interpreted as both the threat of castration and as female rape. When encirclement as rape occurs against a female, the threat of castration is canceled because the female in psychoanalytic discourse is already castrated. The focus, then, is on female rape.

This act of female rape by Bush had two effects. First, it suggests that in the international arena where states project their masculine authority, the masculinely engendered United States was reengendered as feminine. The move from penetration to encirclement marked the uncoding of man as man as well as the recoding of man as woman. This first effect was emphasized by the second effect. Rather than miming masculinity directly (hysteria), Bush mimed masculinity in a way that was once removed. What Bush mimed was female rape, specifically his own threatened rape or encirclement by the Panama Canal. Thanks to the declining hegemon's inability to project its phallic power into international politics, Bush was able only to mime his own castration through the female model of rape. The U.S. invasion of Panama reminded Bush that he and his state had already been effectively castrated—they were impotent. They had already been rewritten as feminine. Because this reinscription of man as woman occurred in what should have been the international sphere, which is reserved for actions by male subjects, Bush appeared as a transvestite rather than as a woman.

Two final implications of the invasion are suggested by this reading. If, as Freud and Lacan argue, it is through the castration complex that subjects enter the symbolic order and become "civilized," then the castration of the former hegemon marked the end of one symbolic order and the beginning of a new order. During the invasion, the United States confronted its own castration, which it then mimed through its intervention strategy of encirclement. This encounter with its castration and feminization in international politics led the U.S. and Bush to reinscribe the symbolic order in terms that could accommodate the refigured United States. In this "new world order," two quite different models of "civilization" or "meaning" are at work. For Panama, the terms of the old international order are still meaningful. Although Noriega has been effectively castrated by the United States, Panama without Noriega appears in this order as simply "immature." It can reach maturity under the terms of the "old" world order when it receives possession of the Canal Zone at the turn of the century. The United States, in contrast, is mature but impotent. In its old age, it must go through a recivilizing process into a new world order in which its international interactions will be expressed by the body of a man acting as a woman. The posthegemonic state is a postphallic state because it grafts female modalities of action onto a male subject.

The final implication has to do with how theorists think about intervention and sovereign statehood. Intervention may still be rape and the bodies that perform that rape may still be male, but the performance of the rape mimes the female threat of castration. Given this and given that intervention practices are only meaningful in the international arena, this analysis suggests that the old dichotomy of domestic = feminine/international = masculine may not be appropriate in a posthegemonic world order.[57] Intervention practices by posthegemonic states reengender sovereign statehood. The intervention practices of the posthegemonic United States deconstruct the terms "masculine" and "international" in this dichotomy. For contained in the masculine, international realm are feminine processes of intervention. Similar to how Irigaray described women in psychoanalytic discourse, posthegemonic sovereign states engaged in intervention practices are both a state and a sex which is not one. Posthegemonic states are lesser, impaired states because they lack the ability to project phallic power internationally. Described in terms of sex, they are hysterical men. Furthermore, posthegemonic states are not just one but more than one. Their surplus, again, may be described in engendered terms. Internationally (or in what traditionally is regarded as the international realm), posthegemonic states are transvestites. With respect to intervention, posthegemonic states are cross-dressed men who abide by female modes of conduct.

Taking transvestitism subjectivity into account leads to a rethinking of sexual difference because transvestites—subjects who combine male and female terms—disrupt the logic whereby sexuality can be managed with dichotomies. This is so as much for some theories of psychoanalysis (those of Freud and Lacan, for example) as it is for theories of international relations.

Transvestite transgressions have the effect of destabilizing the subjectivity of singularly sexed bodies—both diplomatic and territorial.[58] Because the United States and its president do not represent stable, single-sexed subjects in this reading of the invasion discourse, they signify an erasure rather than a reinscription of gender dichotomies. It is a misreading to continue to describe these bodies as either males acting as women or women miming the actions of men because in a posthegemonic, postphallic world order the male/female dichotomy breaks down (see Chapters 6 and 9). This reading calls into question the practice in international relations theory of deploying a masculine/feminine dichotomy to write the domestic/international boundary. Transvestite subjectivity embodied in a state or a statesperson focuses attention on the artificial and arbitrary distinction between that which is male and that which is female and between that which is domestic and that which is international. In so doing, transvestite subjectivity suggests another series of possible inscriptions of gender that can be found in diplomatic practice but that have generally been neglected in international relations theory.

Returning to the title of this chapter, "Something's Missing," I conclude that what is missing from diplomatic practice is a stable, singularly engendered domestic subject—a masculine-only or feminine-only sovereign state—that can ground claims to legitimate international actions. Attending to how unconscious codes and presumed dichotomies hysterically mime this fundamental lack so that acts such as military intervention become possible is as important for international relations theory generally as it is for this specific reading of a foreign (domestic?) policy.

Notes

This chapter is a revised version of a piece that appeared under the same name in *Genders*. Presentations based on that paper were given at the Purdue University Women's Studies Brown Bag Series; the 1992 International Studies Association Meetings in Atlanta, March 31–April 4; the 1992 Midwest American Political Science Association Meetings in Chicago, April 4–7; and the Middlebury College Women's Lecture Series. I am grateful to many people who offered suggestions at those meetings. In addition, thanks to the editors of this volume as well as to Thomas Biersteker, Berenice Carroll, Barbara Hinckley, Alon Kantor, Lyn Kathlene, Ann Kibbey, Timothy Luke, Marianne Marchand, Tamar Mayer, Diane Rubenstein, William Stearns, David Sylvan, Gerard Toal, Michael Weinstein, and two anonymous referees for their comments and to Monica Monroe and Carol Pech for research assistance.

1. Elizabeth Grosz, *Jacques Lacan: A Feminist Introduction* (New York: Routledge, 1990), p. 187.
2. Brian Morton, "And Just Why Did We Invade Panama?" *Dissent* 37 (1990), pp. 148–150.
3. In Saussure's system of semiotics, a signifier is what joins the object with its acoustic image. In this example, the signifier "thumb" joins the mental image of the material object thumb with the sound produced by the pronunciation of the word thumb. For a discussion of semiotics, see Terry Eagleton, *Literary Theory: An Introduction* (Minneapolis: University of Minnesota Press, 1983); Vincent Descombes, *Modern French Theory*, trans. L. Scott-Box and J. M. Harding (Cambridge: Cambridge University Press, 1980); and Kaja Silverman, *The Subject of Semiotics* (New York: Oxford University Press, 1983). Regarding the substitution of a presidential nose for Central America, see Diane Rubenstein, "Oliver North and the Lying Nose," in Frederick Dolan and Thomas Dumm, eds., *Rhetorical Republic: Governing Representations in American Politics* (Amherst: University of Massachusetts Press, 1993), pp. 97–120.
4. Luce Irigaray, *Speculum of the Other Woman*, trans. Gillian C. Gill (Ithaca: Cornell University Press, 1985); and *This sex which is not one*, trans. Catherine Porter (Ithaca: Cornell University Press, 1985).
5. Irigaray uses the terms miming, mimicry, or mimesis to refer to the practice of positioning oneself in relation to masculinity so that, at least superficially, the subject appears to be masculine. Subjects located in this space can be either male or female. See Irigaray, *This sex*, p. 76.
Although Irigaray arrives at her characterization of hysteria through a focus on how females mime masculinity, nothing in her discussion of hysteria precludes males from having a similar relationship to masculine subjectivity. Of psychoanalytic representations of hysteria Irigaray wrote, "The hysteria scenario, that privileged dramatization of feminine sexuality, is condemned as so many 'bad' copies or gross

caricatures of a 'good,' and valuable and valid, relationship to origin. Hysteria . . . must be unmasked, interrupted, brought back to the reality of a repetition, a reproduction, a representation that is congruent to, consistent with, the original" (Irigaray, *Speculum*, p. 60). Transvestites who mime feminine positions have a similar relationship to origin—the phallus—as do female hysterics.

6. For example, Noriega's dependence on the United States prior to the invasion contributed to his feminization in the invasion discourse.

7. For accounts of how states are engendered in international relations theory, see Jean Bethke Elshtain, *Public Man, Private Woman: Women in Social and Political Thought* (Princeton: Princeton University Press, 1981); Jean Bethke Elshtain, *Women and War* (New York: Basic Books, 1987); Rebecca Grant and Kathleen Newland, eds., *Gender and International Relations* (Bloomington: Indiana University Press, 1991); V. Spike Peterson, ed., *Gendered States: Feminist (Re)Visions of International Relations Theory* (Boulder, CO: Lynne Rienner, 1992); and Anne Sisson Runyan and V. Spike Peterson, "The Radical Future of Realism: Feminist Subversions of IR Theory," *Alternatives* 16 (1991), pp. 67–106.

8. I am not the first to suggest that Bush can be read as a transvestite. See Diane Rubenstein, "This Is Not a President: Baudrillard, Bush and Enchanted Simulation," in Arthur Kroker and Marilouise Kroker, eds., *The Hysterical Male: New Feminist Theory* (New York: St. Martin's Press, 1991), pp. 253–265. Although this reading of Bush employs the term "transvestite" to refer to cross-dressed men, it should be pointed out that a transvestite could also be a cross-dressed woman— a woman in men's clothing. Cross-dressing by women often goes unnoticed because its transgressive function for the most part has been reinscribed by symbolic and cultural codes as not ôdeviantö but "normal." See Marjorie Garber, *Vested Interests: Cross-Dressing and Cultural Anxiety* (New York: Routledge, 1992).

9. Margaret Whitford, *Luce Irigaray: Philosophy in the Feminine* (London: Routledge, 1991), p. 71.

10. See, for example, Carol Cohn, "Sex and Death in the Rational World of Defense Intellectuals," *Signs* 12 (1987), pp. 687–718.

11. For works that read the president as a sign, see, for example, Michael Rogin, *Ronald Reagan, The Movie* (Berkeley: University of California Press, 1987); Anne Norton, "The President as Sign," presented at the 1985 American Political Science Association annual meeting, New Orleans; and Diane Rubenstein, "The Mirror of Reproduction: Baudrillard and Reagan's America," *Political Theory* 17, 4, pp. 582–606. For critical analyses of the president done through linguistic and symbolic categories, see Murray Edelman, *Constructing the Political Spectacle* (Chicago: University of Chicago Press, 1988); Roderick Hart, *The Sound of Leadership* (Chicago: University of Chicago Press, 1987); and Barbara Hinckley, *The Symbolic Presidency* (New York: Routledge, 1990).

12. Quoted in Edelman, *Constructing*, p. 128.

13. Whitford, *Luce Irigaray*, p. 35.

14. Thomas DiPiero, "The Patriarch Is Not (Just) a Man," *Camera Obscura* 25–26 (1991), pp. 101–124, esp. p. 104.

15. Irigaray, *This sex*, p. 46.

16. Lynne Kirby, "Male Hysteria and Early Cinema," *Camera Obscura* 17 (1988), pp. 115–131.

17. Because it is the Bush administration's encounter with Noriega that is of concern here, the English-language plays on Noriega's Spanish-language name are noteworthy. Had the acronym of Noriega's name spelled out *ômanö* in Spanish (hombre), it would not have announced Noriega's symbolic excess of masculinity so boldly to the English-reading Bush.

18. Lawrence Eagleburger, "The Case Against Panama's Noriega," *Current Policy* 1222 (August 31, 1989), pp. 1–6, esp. p. 3.

19. The U.S. status as hegemonic or posthegemonic is a matter of much debate in international relations. In this analysis, I regard the United States as posthegemonic because a symptomatic reading of the invasion discourse suggests this interpretation. See further on in the text. For more on the hegemony debate see, for example, Robert O. Keohane, *After Hegemony* (Princeton: Princeton University Press, 1984); Susan Strange, "The Persistent Myth of Lost Hegemonies," *International Organization* 4 (Autumn 1987), pp. 551–574; Paul Kennedy, *The Rise and Fall of the Great Powers* (New York: Random House, 1988); Joseph S. Nye, "The Misleading Metaphor of Decline," *Atlantic* (March 1990); and Isabelle Grunberg, "Exploring the 'Myth' of Hegemonic Stability," *International Organization* 4 (Autumn 1990), pp. 431–477.

20. *New York Times*, October 4, 1989.

21. "Rebuilding Broken Economy Will Strain Purse Strings," *Congressional Quarterly Weekly Report* 48 (January 6, 1990), pp. 43–44, esp. p. 43.

22. *London Times*, December 22, 1989.

23. Irigaray, *Speculum*.

24. Ibid., p. 27.

25. Senate Hearings, October 16 and 17 and December 22, 1989, "1989 Events in Panama: Joint Hearings Before the Committee on Armed Services and the Select Committee on Intelligence," p. 135. Senator Nunn's warning to veil the phallus was itself contradictory because it was made from a feminine location—the joint hearings on the invasion. The term "joint hearings" recalls Irigaray's characterization of feminine lips that must be read but must not speak. I thank an anonymous reviewer for bringing this to my attention.

26. *Oxford English Dictionary*, quoted in Toril Moi, *Sexual/Textual Politics: Feminist Literary Theory* (London: Methuen, 1985), p. 130.

27. Irigaray, *Speculum*, p. 136.

28. At the culmination of the Lacanian mirror stage, the child leaves the imaginary (in which the child views its body and the mother's body as one) and enters the symbolic order (in which the child sees itself as separate from the mother). Irigaray refers to this as an act of matricide. See Irigaray, *Speculum*, p. 144.

29. Ibid., p. 144; italics in original.

30. Ibid., p. 145.

31. Irigaray notes that the longtime neglect of fluids by physics is related to its neglect of gender. See "The 'Mechanics' of Fluids," in *This Sex*, pp. 106–118, esp. p. 106.

32. Irigaray, *Speculum*, p. 133.

33. Ibid., p. 136.

34. The engendering of domestic and international spaces is occasionally reversed. Domestic space coded as order may be engendered as masculine and

opposed to international space coded as feminine anarchy. My analysis follows the domestic = feminine/international = masculine engendering scheme because it is the most common in international relations theory. As the concluding section's discussion of transvestite states suggests, it is less important how international relations theorists engender domestic and international spaces than it is that domestic spaces are described by only one gender and international spaces by the opposite gender.

35. George Bush, "U.S. Military Action in Panama," in *American Foreign Policy Current Documents 1989* (Washington, DC: U.S. Department of State, 1990), p. 720.

36. Foreign Broadcast Information Service, May 9, 1989, pp. 40–41; brackets in original.

37. Recall that it was the U.S. wish to build a canal in Central America that led to the U.S.-supported independence movement of Upper Colombia (present-day Panama) against Colombia in the early 1900s.

38. *London Times*, December 21, 1989.

39. Senate Hearings, October 16 and 17 and December 22, 1989, "1989 Events in Panama," p. 140.

40. Lawrence Eagleburger, "The OAS and the Crisis in Panama," *Current Policy* 1205 (August 24, 1989), pp. 1–3, esp. p. 2.

41. Michael G. Kozak, "Panama Canal: The Strategic Dimension," *Current Policy* 1226 (November 2, 1989), pp. 1–3, esp. p. 2.

42. Ibid., p. 2. In this particular speech, this Bush administration official repeatedly referred to the U.S. "broad" national interest.

43. Irigaray argued that the feminine lips cannot speak in a phallocentric discourse, although the lips simultaneously invoke language and the feminine.

44. Senate Hearings, October 16 and 17 and December 22, 1989, "1989 Events in Panama," p. 137.

45. In the postinvasion discourse, "June" as a time/location serves as an embarrassing reminder that Bush's masculine subjectivity was unconfirmed. It was in June 1992 that Bush visited post-Noriega Panama only to be greeted by "menacing stares and defiant thumbs-down gestures," as well as by a possible assassination attempt. See *St. Croix Avis*, June 12, 1992, p. 35.

46. *London Times*, December 21, 1989.

47. *Newsweek*, January 15, 1990, p. 18. That Noriega sought sanctuary in the Vatican embassy may suggest that he attempted to compensate for his own lack of a phallus by turning to his phallic mother (the Catholic Church). Thanks to a member of the audience at my Midwest APSA panel for suggesting this interpretation.

48. For an analysis of the relationship between state sovereignty and intervention, see Cynthia Weber, *Simulating Sovereignty: Intervention, the State, and Symbolic Exchange* (Cambridge: Cambridge University Press, 1995).

49. 1991 American Political Science Association Preliminary Program.

50. George Bush, "Freedom and World Prosperity," *Current Policy* 1210 (September 27, 1989), pp. 1–3, esp. p. 2.

51. Eagleburger, "The OAS," p. 2.

52. John S. Wolf, "UN Program Coordination and Narcotics Control," *Current Policy* 1219 (October 17, 1989), pp. 1–2, esp. p. 2.

53. Eagleburger, "The Case," p. 2.

54. For a comparison of the U.S. invasions of Grenada and Panama, see Weber, *Simulating Sovereignty*.

55. Bush, "Freedom," p. 2.

56. Eagleburger, "The Case," p. 6.

57. Indeed, that the domestic = feminine/international = masculine dichotomy was ever meaningful is problematic, as are the dichotomies domestic/international and feminine/masculine.

58. The disruptive logic of a "deviant" sexuality has been addressed most recently by "queer theory." See the 1991 issue of *Differences* (3, 2) edited by Teresa de Lauretis. Writes de Lauretis, the work of queer theory is "intended to articulate the terms in which lesbian and gay sexualities may be understood and imaged as forms of resistance to cultural homogenization, counteracting dominant discourses with other constructions of the subject in cultureö and explores questions ôsuch as the respective and/or common grounding of current discourses and practices of homo-sexualities in relation to gender and to race, with their attendant differences of class or ethnic culture, generational, geographical, and socio-political locations. . . . 'Queer Theory' conveys a double emphasis—on the conceptual and speculative work involved in discourse production, and on the necessary critical work of deconstructing our own discourses and their constructed silences" (pp. iii–iv).

9

Sex, Power, and the Grail of Positive Collaboration

Ralph Pettman

Though not sports fans, my then-wife and I were once watching a soccer game on television when she suddenly said: "Why don't they give them all a ball? If they each had a ball then they wouldn't have to fight over that one."[1]

I immediately had an image of the men before me, each with a soccer ball of his own, dribbling and shooting goals to his heart's content and bothering others only on a reciprocal basis, the better to develop his ball-handling skills and his general awareness of movement itself. Soccer players do this at practice. They do it for fun. To do it in a match, however, would defeat the whole purpose of the game.

Nonetheless, the sudden image of so many players doing nothing but practicing made me wonder why people do anything else. Why do players try so hard to win? Why do people struggle so hard to prevail?

The teams were made up entirely of highly assertive males. This does not of course mean that males are more conflictual than females; conflict behavior is manifested by "women" as well as "men." However, men do enjoy greater preponderance than women in the world in politico-strategic, politico-economic, and politico-social terms. Could this be because conflict behavior, and the penchant to prevail that motivates it, is somehow more typical of men than women?

Using conflict to prevail entails using power of more than one sort, for example, brute force, physical dexterity, material wealth, or intellectual ingenuity. The exercise of such powers may require drawing on spiritual convictions, group loyalty, rhetorical resourcefulness, or (in the case of a gun-slinging standoff) physiological reflexes. In practice, power is not a noun; it's a verb. It's always about powering, about specific patterns of human practice that promote preponderance.

Most people some of the time and some people most of the time like powering. They like the feeling of preponderance. The soccer players we were watching wanted that feeling. Even the most kind and collaborative among us can find it affirmative.

As to the question of sex or gender specificity previously posed, it seems only to exacerbate long-standing confusions and obfuscations about the gendering of human attributes, the construction of gender itself, and the significance of sex-based dimorphism. This question is important, but it is not my main concern. I want to ask, What else feels affirmative? What practices of a nonconflictual kind might the struggle to prevail obscure or repress? And does human gendering have anything to do with this obscuring, repressing process?

Positivism and Masculinism

Before addressing this concern I want to ask some preliminary questions. How should one proceed with such an inquiry? What methodological approach should one take? What epistemological and ontological principles should one privilege?

Customary academic practice assumes the need to adopt an objectifying mind-set. Questions are posed in the analytic terms consonant with the canons of positivist social science with the expectation that this methodology can explain all phenomena. For example, words such as "Japan," "women," or "men" assume the possibility of creating concepts that both describe and explain "reality" at a more concise and therefore higher analytic order.

Without presuming closure to some important ongoing debates between modernists and postmodernists, I feel that this social scientific positivism is reductionist. Whatever its strengths, it fails to account for all of our experiences, and the reification it promotes is in no small part to blame. The consequence is inadequate, incomplete, and therefore potentially inappropriate, even potentially dangerous, policy implications and the suppression of other ways of thinking about and practicing world affairs that could conceivably be "better," that is, more peaceful, more just, less exploitative, and less alienating.

Take the issue of experience. This chapter began with a personal anecdote. This was not just an attempt to catch the reader's attention. I deliberately used a subjective experience in a piece of social analysis both as admissible evidence and as a legitimate research tool.

Personal anecdotes are epistemologically and ontologically interpretivist. Interpretivism is anathema to positivist social science, however. It subverts the claim that one can render a complete account of experience (including, of course, the gendering experience) from outside experience itself.[2]

One way to transcend the limits of positivism is to allow as admissible evidence and as a legitimate research tool accounts of other people's experiences, even fictional experiences. One such account is a short story by Ray Bradbury that describes a baseball game in the southern United States between a team of black (male) players and a team of white (male) ones. The two teams played very differently, at least to begin with. The whites played to win, whereas the blacks, though notably better than the whites, played more for the love of it.

As the blacks ran onto the field, their expressions did not say, "'Look at me run, look at me run!' No, not at all." Their faces said: "Lord, but it's sure nice to run. See the ground swell soft under me?" It is an entrancing scene. "There was no purpose to their running," Bradbury says, "but exhilaration and living."

The whites "worked at their running as they worked at everything. You felt embarrassed for them because they were alive too much in the wrong way. Always looking from the corners of their eyes to see if you were watching."[3]

Though the story is one of interracial conflict and an ultimately violent masculinist competition and though Bradbury uses some rather crude stereotyping to heighten the dramatic effect, the story does evoke two very different experiences of play. The feelings and the shared meanings that it documents can be described analytically. They cannot, however, be duplicated analytically. That is why a story like this is admissible evidence and a legitimate research tool. Without it we cannot account for all that happens when people play.

If documenting experience in objectifying ways did justice to that experience (if questionnaires or opinion polls, for example, fully explained human experience), then the positivist account of world affairs would suffice. We would not require firsthand accounts of any kind to help us understand how world affairs work. However, positivists' claims to provide an adequate account of how the world works are at best suspect, which is why I believe experiential narratives are also required to account for world affairs.

Objectifying analysis does more than delimit what can be used as evidence. It also creates a clear distinction between the objectified analysand and the objectifying analyzer. This distinction is used in turn to create a hierarchy between the two. There is no logical reason for this hierarchical distinction. This way of knowing and being was first systematically articulated by upper-class Europeans (mostly, though not exclusively, male) with scientific and industrial revolutions to run and with imperial interests to promote and protect.

The elitism of these analysts was reflected in their assumptions of superiority. Thus one finds a plethora of "objective" analyses by colonial authorities (mostly male) of their colonized subjects, analyses that not coincidentally involved the construction of dominance/subordinance relationships and the reinforcement and legitimation of already powerful elites.[4]

The domineering did not always need to be so direct. The elites' use of power could also be (and indeed often was) quite diffuse, involving discourses of identity and difference, for example, or authority and marginality.[5]

The (largely male-made) hierarchy of methodological dominance/subordinance led to the presumption that positivism could account for the meaning of all experience. The limits of such a presumption are clearly apparent, however, if we consider again the Bradbury story, where the imaginative involvement of the reader not only provides research information unavailable from objectifying analysis but has nothing to do with the dominance/subordinance dichotomy.

Nothing to do with dominance-subordinance? But don't writers dominate readers in the way they set up their narratives? Are readers not subordinate to writers in the way they must follow what is written to catch its gist? Again, without legislating a conclusion to an important contemporary debate (this time in literary theory), I believe there are two issues here. One has to do with artistry, and this is not something that dominates or subordinates. The other has to do with artifice and with techniques such as rhetoric and polemic.

Bradbury's story is not a polemic. It describes conflict in play and the high importance particular kinds of men place on prevailing. As an artist, he depicts, in the kind of interpretivistic/hermeneutic detail that positivists cannot, some men's efforts to win social approval by acting in a highly conflictual way and other sorts of men's ability to gain satisfaction from the exercise of their personal skills. The latter do not need to win—or rather, "not lose"—to experience affirmation of a nonconflictual sort, though these males later lapse into conflict mode.

This lapse is particularly interesting because it provides a nuanced account of racialized as well as genderized identities. The black male "hero" in Bradbury's story, though socially subordinate, rises to meet the challenge by the white "antihero." The hero's act of righteous and violent revenge, which constitutes the story's climax, not only asserts his culturally specified manhood (exaggerated by his superior physical strength and size) but also is a blow by a member of an oppressed race against a member of an oppressing one.

Sexing and Gendering

"Men" and "women" are radically contentious concepts. Many have striven throughout history to render them natural to the analytic ear. They are highly contrived, however, a fact that generations of feminist scholars have been at pains to point out.

In anthropological parlance, for example, "there is no such thing as the natural body." It is "inevitably cultural . . . [a] medium of thought and expression that enters into our most basic concerns."[6] Judith Butler makes the same point even more forcefully, arguing that "'sex' is . . . part of a regulatory practice that produces the bodies it governs," demarcates the bodies it "controls," and materializes sexual difference in order to consolidate what she calls the "heterosexual imperative." In her view sex is "not simply what one has, or a static description of what one is." Rather it is "one of the norms by which the 'one' becomes viable at all, that which qualifies a body for life within the domain of cultural intelligibility."[7]

The capacity of such regulatory practices to demarcate, differentiate, consolidate, and control is evident in the way we deal with human diversity. People are born as either male, female, both male and female (hermaphroditic), male and part female, or female and part male. These five "sexes" are cultural norms, however, and they determine the way bodies are treated in material terms. Sex is not a "bodily given on which the construct of gender is artificially imposed" but more of an "exclusionary matrix" that defines both "subjects" and "abjects" (the latter to be found "'inside' the subject as its . . . founding repudiation").[8]

Where the technology is available, those who are born in some discursively "abject" form are usually changed surgically or chemically at or soon after birth to conform to one of two predefined "subject" forms, that is, male or female. The preference for such subject forms is global, though it is policed with differing degrees of tolerance.

Why abject forms of sexuality should ever be considered aberrant, to be reviled (or revered), rendered invisible (or made objects of veneration), has nothing to do with human diversity. The results of species reproduction are shamelessly, prodigiously, riotously various. In Darwinian terms this is a distinct advantage.

Given the rapidly changing world in which we live—the increasingly polluted character of the environment, for example—we may need this very diversity as a species to survive. Hermaphrodites, currently an abject sex, in the future may prove superior to currently subject ones (superior in the sense of being better reproducers). Reducing the human roster of hermaphrodites could be singularly counterproductive, threatening survival fitness in evolutionary terms.

Sex, in other words, is a material process, the "matter" that is materialized, having "stabilize[d] over time to produce the effect of boundary, fixity, and surface we call matter."[9] Sex is always, in short, a matter of "sexing."

Gender is likewise a matter of "gendering." Usually construed as a cultural rather than a biological process, the term is used here to denote more than making cultural choices about sex. It denotes the regulatory norms used to materialize sex. These regulatory norms predate birth. In those cases where a fetus is aborted for being abject—for being female, for example, in a Chinese or Indian cultural context where the preference for male babies is currently marked—these norms can clearly be seen at work in practice as well as principle.

"Gender performativity cannot be theorized," Butler argues, "apart from the forcible and reiterative practice of regulatory sexual regimes." Gendering human beings, in other words, is a matter of sexing them (not, as is commonly supposed, the other way around). Gender is not just a social category imposed on a sexed body. It is used to determine the sex of that body itself and of the bodies that "fail to materialize," the bodies that in failing to materialize fortify those "bodies that matter." Sex is very much a cultural construction.[10]

The bimorphizing principles and practices that gendering typically represents are coded descriptions of social relationships, descriptions that are used to structure much more than social relationships. They structure human identity and constitute power hierarchies (where males are deemed superior to females, for example). They sex bodies, and they are used to perpetuate power relations through the sexing process.[11]

So comprehensive are gendering practices that all aspects of human society are affected by them. Some would say determined by them, though precisely what determines what is difficult to say not only because of the instability of the distinction between sex and gender (a consequence of the complexity and indeterminacy of human sexual diversity and of human regulative ideals) but also because of other dimensions of social experience such as ethnicity, age, and class.

World Politics as World Sexism

International politicians are not notably interested in these issues of gender principles. Like most politicians, they perpetuate in practice diverse forms of masculinism. This may not be conscious, but then most international politicians are assertive males who take for granted the global desirability of assertive masculinism. The states they make, the markets they help create, the ideologies they promulgate, for the most part systematically favor and further men, exploit and marginalize women, and render seemingly natural this presumptive furthering and favoring process.

Not only do men make states, for example, but they do so in sexist ways. The delimitation of territories, the centralization of governments, the promulgation of statewide nationalisms, all promote assertive and often violent forms of masculinity. Statemaking and warmaking are cognate activities, and warmaking has long been a way of defining and demonstrating a range of stereotypically masculinist traits. Similar observations could be made of global capitalists in the world market (the heroic entrepreneur doing battle for greater profit or market share), as it could of those who promulgate modernism (a messianic and masculinist mixture of materialism, rationalism, secularism, and individualism) (see Chapters 2 and 3).

The assertiveness of these practices suggests the possibility of less assertive or nonassertive alternatives. Their very particularity points to the prospect of international political practices that foster less aggressive types of masculinism. Their particularity even points to the prospect of antimasculinism (see Chapter 6).

The same suggestion arises when we consider the amount of cooperation as well as competition that statemaking (and wealthmaking and mindmaking) entail. Just as there is plenty of cooperation on a soccer field in the struggle by teammates to prevail over the rival team, statemaking (as well as wealthmaking and the making of the world's major ideologies) would not be possible without cooperation. Indeed, the more complex and extensive the cooperation, the more complex and extensive competition can be (a point not lost on the communally minded Japanese). In their bid to prevail, men deploy practices across a continuum of conflict that ranges from competition to cooperation. This makes it possible to conceive of cooperation as well as competition as the point of world political practice.

Could masculinism prevail on a cooperative basis alone? I would say not, since masculinism of any sort is about building and perpetuating a man's world where men rather than women prevail. Regardless of how cooperatively statemaking, wealthmaking, and mindmaking are pursued, they are first and foremost about (male) domination. This domination is always contested, and because it is always contested, cooperation alone is not possible.

Positive Collaboration

How can we transcend the competition and the cooperation for the purpose of competition that all current international affairs entail? We might begin, in a humanist, species-centric way, by considering ourselves as people first and as men or women (or whatever) second. In this way we could subsume sex and gender differences under a more synoptic category, that of humankind as a whole. Life choices and life chances might then be construed in terms of individual rights and the meeting of basic needs. The sex and gender characteristics of any particular individual could then be construed as having no—or very little—bearing on the nature of her or his moral entitlements.

This familiar liberal prescription, although it offers an attractive, albeit idealistic, alternative to the sociopolitical and socioeconomic practice of male domination, stems from an ideological tradition developed by and still most closely identified with well-off, white Western males.[12] Whereas it need not remain suspect indefinitely, the sociology of its heritage is a matter of legitimate concern to communalists, for example, and to Marxists and to nonliberal feminists (some of whom are communalists or Marxists as well).

This prescription also relies on the radical sublimation of a sense of sex and gender difference. Such a radical sublimation may not be possible even in principle. It may not even be desirable, which is one reason for the long-standing attempt to posit a form of feminism independent of masculinism and a sense of being female not conditioned by what masculinists do; to define the feminine, that is, without reference to the masculine at all.[13]

Whether we actually can escape the male/female spectrum by moving off the end of it, or rather by bringing our conception of what is female to such a focus that it excludes the male "other," is arguable. We can do it in theory, though such a focus could not, given the universal force of gendering practices, be sustained for very long—not at present at any rate. Such a form of feminism would be evanescent. It would exist without reference to masculinism, but its emancipatory appeal would not reach far.

Having a grail that may ever elude our grasp doesn't make that grail worthless. Quite the contrary. A grail that is impossible to attain may still be worth pursuing, particularly given what might be achieved in the process. In this case the grail is a conception of being female that permits a range of self-referential selves rather than one cast in opposition to various masculinities.

Such a conception entails one sense or many distinctive senses of being female, senses that are insubordinate and spiritually open-ended. Such senses have very practical political implications in that they posit female identities of a sort quite independent of any masculinist construction of self. Ideological independence of this sort makes political independence not only conceivable but imperative.

I am going over these familiar points not because I think they are reinforced by my recognition of them but to show by analogy with a well-known feminist argument that the attempt to escape another continuum, that is, the competition/cooperation one, may be worth pursuing.

If we focus our conception of cooperation so that it excludes competition altogether, we get positive collaboration. Positive collaboration is uncompetitive, empathetic cooperation. It is a self-affirming, socially constructive practice that has nothing to do with the conflict spectrum that nonempathetic cooperation and competition lie along. It has nothing to do, therefore, with any of the modes of masculinism, since they all entail competition and cooperation. It has nothing to do with any of the forms of feminism either (with the notable exception of the radical forms just mentioned), since feminists contest male hegemony, and they compete and cooperate with each other and with hegemonizing males in the process of doing so.

I know that collaboration is commonly used to mean "going along with" someone or something, as for example those who "collaborate" with an army of occupation. However I am not using the word in the negative sense. I am using it in the sense it is used in aikido,[14] that is, in a positive sense that differs altogether from competition or cooperation for the purpose of competition. I am using it to mean reciprocal self-realization, which is the egalitarian attempt to further the good of others while having others further one's own. Defining the meaning of "the good," by the way, is part of the same process.

Competition and cooperation engaged in for the purpose of competing are so familiar and so pervasive that we can fail to appreciate the difference between the spectrum these two concepts create and the kind of empathetic cooperation that eschews conflict altogether. It can be difficult to understand, in everyday terms, what moving off the end of the spectrum means, for it is neither a familiar place nor a familiar experience, particularly given the present-day prevalence of domineering masculinisms and the pervasiveness of the conflicts that masculinisms entail.

If people choose neither to compete nor to cooperate (in the ordinary instrumentalist sense), if they choose instead to try to provide for each other in an affirmative, nonconflictual way (like soccer players practicing with soccer balls), then we have positive collaboration. If statemakers choose to do this among themselves and if the world's wealthmakers and mindmakers choose to do the same, the sociopolitical consequences will be profound.

This begs the question of how needs should be defined, though arriving at a definition of "needs" is part of the collaborative process. Indeed, it would have to be a part of the process if the collaboration were to be affirmative and creative. This points the way to a politics that is capable of rescuing us from yet another false sense of escape.

Talk of positive collaboration is idealistic in the extreme. It smacks of the Golden Rule, to do unto others as you would have them do unto you. It smacks of even more than that, actually, since the benevolence of the Golden Rule is based on enlightened self-interest, and positive collaboration means more than enlightened self-interest. It means trying to understand the needs of others and trying to enhance their life choices and life chances while they do the same for you. It is radically altruistic and requires considerably more than self-interest.

Three well-known ways of categorizing world politics may help illustrate what I mean. If competition corresponds to the Hobbesian conception of world politics (as the war of each against all) and cooperation corresponds to the Grotian one (where competition is controlled by acting in concert), then positive collaboration corresponds to the Kantian conception of world affairs.[15]

The Hobbesian and the Grotian conceptions define each other. Competition and cooperation are cognate concepts. They define a spectrum of international practices that further or mitigate conflict. The Kantian conception is something else again. It denotes a cosmopolitan awareness, a way of being in the world that is without dominance or subordinance. It doesn't mean finding ways to deal with competition by using cooperation. It denotes individual global citizenship that is furthered by affirming one's peers.

Given the ubiquity and cost of male dominance, it seems untimely, diversionary, academic, even reactionary to ask why one would want to collaborate in the Kantian sense. What possible significance could positive collaboration have given the amount of gender-based repression, impoverishment, and alienation that goes on in the world—to say nothing of the repression, impoverishment, and alienation due to class, race, and ethnic or age-specific factors? Shouldn't we be tackling these problems head-on rather than spending a single minute expecting people to behave in enlightened, ideologically loaded, and unrealistic ways?

The short answer is yes. The longer answer is yes, but we also need to know how to create the conditions for the kind of world where problems like these are much less in evidence. In this chapter I am concerned with the longer answer not only because any attempt to approximate positive collaboration would have to entail antidiscrimination, including anti-sex-and-gender discrimination, but because such collaboration, although impossible to fully realize in principle, possesses enormous potential to radicalize politics in theory and practice.

Like the most radical forms of feminism, positive collaboration is an evanescent ideal. Again, like the most radical forms of feminism, the inspiring and liberating example the grail provides may be the point. It is not necessary to be a mystic to acknowledge the importance of human vision, that is, the power and importance of visualizing what is desirable for society (or societies) or the self (or selves). It is not necessary to surrender all one's critical faculties to appreciate positive collaboration as an aspiration.

Power and Powering

Positive collaboration would seem to involve a very different idea of power from the one normally used. Then again, defining the normal idea of power is not a simple matter. I began by referring to some of the different kinds of power used in competition. This was not a systematic appraisal of what power (and powering) involve; nor is this the place to attempt one. Power is notoriously difficult to define, and given the diversity of reasons people want to know about power—what it can do and where it comes from—it may simply not be possible, as Steven Lukes argues, to agree on a single definition.[16]

As indicated earlier, competition is clearly about power, about dominance/subordinance, about trying to prevail. Nonempathetic cooperation is also about power, that is, about how the efforts of the one can be magnified by joining, willingly or unwillingly, with others.

What about the kind of cooperation where there is no competition at all, however? This is the kind of cooperation envisaged in win-win soccer play where everybody has a ball. Is it meaningful to talk of power in this less-than-usual case, where cooperation has passed off the continuum of conflict altogether?

I think so, since players who engage in positive collaboration do achieve something. They feel extended. They feel empowered. We still need the concept of power to describe positive sorts of collaborative practice, but we are clearly talking about power of a very different kind.

But if we can talk about power of a kind that affirms those who collaborate and power of a kind that affirms those who compete (albeit cooperatively), how do we reconcile these two? Basically, we cannot. We are talking about radically different practices and radically different experiences; trying to translate the one into the other is pointless. The fact that we can discuss both using the concept of power only illustrates the portmanteau character of the concept itself.

Collaborative Empowerment

Is collaborative power (in the sense of the empathetic realization of our various selves) something we find in world affairs? Not at the moment. Competition and the cooperative endeavors that enhance competition are the staple fare of contemporary world politics. This is not to say, however, that what happens now always has to happen and that world politics need always stay the same.

A collaborative world, or rather an approximation of one (given the grail-like nature of such an aspiration), requires us to institute collaborative practices of a positive sort. The question arises: Who might best advise us as to these practices?

Here we return to gender difference. There is, first, nothing intrinsically male or female about positive collaboration. For very concrete and sexist reasons, however, positive collaborative practices are largely associated with femininity rather than masculinity. The experience of power as the experience of extended understanding is seen to be more a female than a male one, since it is females more often than males who are taught, in most societies, to sublimate or eschew the desire to compete.

Hence it is from those people socially constructed not only as female but also as feminine that we would expect to hear from most about power as a matter of collaborative self-realization. We do not, of course, because the male hegemonizers who do most of society's hearing in this regard turn to other males. This is one more way, in fact, in which they promote and protect their hegemony.

Gandhi, for example, a person who was socially constructed to be both male and masculine, was often asked to pronounce (via his life example and written works) on social hierarchies of dominance and subordinance, the power of nonviolence to transcend them, the democratic source of nonviolent action, and the spiritually affirmative effects such action can confer. The millions of those socially constructed as female and feminine—who are socially designated to be the "primary care takers of children"; whose lives are "frequently determined by the needs of others"; for whom "relationships are of primary importance";[17] and who have learned, often from bitter daily experience, about the denial, the desirability, and the worth of positive collaboration—are totally ignored.

I had to learn how to positively collaborate in my coparenting years. This form of collaboration, which I still practice as a student of aikido, is most marked by the sense that power over others is possible only at the expense of the power of positive collaboration. Dominating others, in other words, inhibits our capacity to respond to them empathetically. This in turn makes it impossible for us to get past our preconceptions about the inevitability of conflict.

"Truncated" by our desire for dominance or our desire for subordinance, we are "incapable" of "responding to the plight of others with the fullness of ourselves."[18] We are incapable of understanding what makes self-realization possible. We are rather sorry, albeit representative, examples of what it is possible to be as a human being.

Collaboration of the sort I am discussing is radically democratic. It sees dominance and subordinance as frustrating the realization of our individual and collective selves. A world where positive collaboration is the norm would be of necessity radically egalitarian. By the same token, it would be a world where people could be themselves even if this meant, as would most likely be the case, that they chose to emulate others. Again, this is a grail-like norm, but arguably one worth aspiring to even if the results remain forever approximate.

In discussing the possibility of an alternative approach to human interactions and power, I wish not only to introduce this approach but to highlight, by contrast, the throttlehold that assertive masculinists have (whether male or female) on ideas about how the world works and how that throttlehold (with all the preconceptions about what is real in world affairs, about objectivity, about rationalism, and so on) often preempts the possibility of personal or collective empowerment.[19]

Berenice Carroll, in her germinal article on the subject of power,[20] highlighted the limitations of a concept of power that dwells on those conventionally considered to be powerful. This "cult of power" is practiced, she argues, by all those preoccupied with finding out what the powerful need to know. It is practiced by those who would limit change to problem-solving, who would keep it small.[21] It is practiced most of all by those who construe the ostensibly powerless as incapable of alleviating their plight.

To illustrate what she calls the cult of power, Carroll identifies no less than nine kinds of power that the "weak" can exercise. She calls these disintegrative, inertial, innovative, legitimizing, expressive, explosive, resistant, collective, and migratory. Disintegrative power, for example, is the power large numbers of people possess to overload legal systems, defy "law and order," withhold labor, and generally wear down the social, economic, and political superstructures of those who seek predominance. Migratory power denotes the capacity people have to move away from those who would control them and to relocate where they feel better rewarded or more free.

Is pointing out the power of the "weak" just another way to blame victims for their plight? I do not believe so. I am not saying that the poor, the exploited, and the oppressed have no excuse for not radically revising the conditions under which they live. After all, as Machiavelli somewhere remarks, there is nothing more difficult, more uncertain of outcome, than the institution of a new order of things. However, I do believe there is more to the concept of power than is commonly assumed.

It is an interesting and informative exercise to read the concept of the balance of power in terms of a balance of Carrollian competencies. Rather than considering the matter in terms of a balance among statemakers seeking to dominate all or part of the international state system, Carroll prompts us to discuss the balance between those marginalized by contemporary state-, wealth- and mindmaking practices and those who do the marginalizing. The disintegrative power of masses of people to erode structures of dominance through crime, apathy, and alcoholism is counterbalanced by the capacity of top dogs to imprison and punish, segregate and bribe. If disintegrative power eventually stymied the Soviet statemakers, for example, what else might it render inoperative?

The failure of the conventional reading of the balance of power to understand this "two worlds" view, preoccupied as the conventional reading is with states, warmaking, and diplomacy, could yet lead to its undoing. "People power," in the two-worlds view, could yet prevail.[22]

Carroll is still talking about hierarchies of dominance/subordinance, however. Her world is still defined by competition and cooperation on the continuum of conflict. Thus I now think Carroll's approach does not go far enough. Though it is an important and long-neglected contribution to our understanding of the "cult of power," it is trapped in that same discourse.

To set this discourse in a larger context we have to talk, I believe, about positive collaboration. We have to do so in the most radical of terms, namely those of reciprocal regard. Those who do not reciprocate can then be seen for what they are, that is, promoters and protectors of this world as the best of all those conceivable.

I do not believe this world is the best to which we can aspire. The question is, then, the relevance of the ideal I have just outlined. Is it a meaningful alternative to conflict? What bearing might it have on world affairs today?

I believe it is both meaningful and relevant. The benefits of competition and cooperation are limited by the conflict mentality common to them both. Yet we live in a world of nuclear and other security dilemmas, desperately uneven development, an impending ecocrisis, and male hegemonizing, and all these areas would seem to call for the radical revision of current practices. Under these circumstances, not to attempt positive collaboration is simply asking for trouble.

We obviously are not going to achieve this egalitarian kind of reciprocity on a world scale overnight. We can never achieve it, actually. But it is important to know that such collaborative practices (carried out in any number of spiritually evolved ways) are part of the human repertoire. Knowing this, we can seek out those many women and a few men who already have the needed knowledge and experience. Indeed, their knowledge might prove to be the most valuable resource of our species.

Notes

1. Raymond Aron, by the way, has likened world politics to a soccer game without a clearly defined playing field, shared rules, or a neutral referee. Aron's use of the soccer game metaphor is consistent with his European realism and differs from its use here. See his *Peace and War: A Theory of International Relations* (New York: Doubleday, 1966), p. 8.

2. Mark Neufeld, "Interpretation and the 'Science' of International Relations," *Review of International Studies* 19 (1993), pp. 39–61. The paradox inherent in critiquing rationalism by rational means is resolved, I think, by trying to understand the ideological character of rationalism itself (something I had to do daily when teaching in Japan). This ideology can also be exposed by repudiating rationalism's exclusive claim to be able to approximate "the truth." I am, in part, a rationalist. I think its claims to be able to approximate "the truth" to be pretty good, though I have come to appreciate of late some of the limits of rationalism. I would like to transcend them, though not by romantic disavowal. I'd like to find other ways of using the mind, ways repressed in the Enlightenment "experiment with reason." What other ways of using the mind should be "brought back in"? Intuition, perhaps, offers an answer, though it would need to be scrutinized in a careful, ongoing, rationalistic way to avoid such politico-social perversions as Nazism, for example, with its celebration of *Blut-Gefühl* (thinking with the blood). We could also bring back experience in its autobiographical or fictional forms, always assuming the need to scrutinize such disclosure rationalistically as well.

3. "The Big Black and White Game," in Ray Bradbury, *The Golden Apples of the Sun* (London: Grafton Books, 1977), pp. 79–80.

4. See, for example, Edward Said, *Orientalism* (New York: Pantheon, 1978); Mrinalini Sinha, *Colonial Masculinities* (Manchester: Manchester University Press, 1995).

5. Documented in detail by Michel Foucault. See *Power/Knowledge* (New York: Pantheon, 1980), p. 140. See also James Clifford, *The Predicament of Culture* (Cambridge: Harvard University Press, 1988), despite Clifford's preference for talk about nativism rather than sexism (or classism).

6. Nigel Barley, *Native Land* (Harmondsworth: Penguin, 1990), p. 61.

7. Judith Butler, *Bodies That Matter: On the Discursive Limits of "Sex"* (New York: Routledge, 1993), pp. 1–2.

8. Ibid., pp. 2–3. That this is merely the tip of a very large analytic iceberg is demonstrated by Michel Foucault in his book *The History of Sexuality* (Harmondsworth: Penguin, 1990). In pointing out the socially constructed character of sex as well as gender, I emphatically do not want to suggest that there is a non-gendered, asexual humanist approach, unsullied by masculinism, that is to be preferred. This would be "backlash" preemption at its very worst. It would be an attempt to establish a postfeminist high ground before feminism, in whatever form, has had a chance to demonstrate the ideologically loaded nature of what is happening in the lowlands. To the contrary, I am trying to show that pervasive hetero-masculinist gendering principles are so pervasive that they are able to determine both sexing and gendering as politico-social practices. That they are not all pervasive is Butler's point about the emergence of "collective disidentifications" capable of reconceptualizing "which bodies matter, and which bodies are yet to emerge as critical matters of concern." See Butler, *Bodies That Matter*, p. 4.

9. Butler, *Bodies That Matter*, p. 9.

10. Ibid., pp. 15–16.

11. Kathleen Jones, "The Trouble with Authority," *Differences* 3, 1 (1991), p. 117.

12. See here Catherine Hall, *White, Male and Middle Class: Explorations in Feminism and History* (Cambridge: Polity Press, 1992).

13. See the work of French feminists such as Hélène Cixous, Luce Irigaray, and Julia Kristeva as cited, for example, in Maggie Humm, *Feminisms: A Reader* (New York: Harvester Wheatsheaf, 1992). Also see Butler *(Bodies That Matter)*, who argues (p. 29) that "the question never has been whether or not there ought to be speaking about women. This speaking will occur, and for feminist reasons, it must." Surely it is possible, she concludes "both to use the term . . . tactically even as one is, as it were, used and positioned by it, and also to subject the term to a critique which interrogates the exclusionary operations and differential power-relations that construct and delimit feminist invocations of 'women.'"

14. Aikido is a Japanese martial art of relatively recent origin. It is an art of reconciliation, not counterattack, and the most radical schools foster, as an explicit training method, the deliberate use of positive collaboration.

15. The Hobbesian model of the state system is the "realist" one in which war predominates and statemakers act (because the state system is formally ungoverned) as if each were the potential enemy of all. The Grotian model, equally "realistic," in fact, but usually called "idealist," focuses on the extent to which statemakers must and do cooperate in order to create some semblance of order (anarchy, that is, rather than chaos) in their system on a day-to-day basis. The Kantian model, also equally "realistic" but usually called "utopian," describes one way in which the state system might evolve, in this case into a cosmopolitan world society in which

states are only one, and potentially not the most important, of its political foci and in which the individual is a world citizen first and a member of some other community second.

16. S. Lukes, "Introduction," in Lukes, ed., *Power* (London: Basil Blackwell, 1986).

17. M. Riordan, "Non-violence, the Ethic of Care and the Question of Love," paper presented at the ISA conference, Washington, D.C., April 1990, p. 2.

18. Riordan, "Non-violence," p. 3.

19. J. Ann Tickner, "Hans Morgenthau's Principles of Political Realism: A Feminist Reformulation," *Millennium* 17, 3 (Winter 1988), pp. 429–440, reworked as "Man, the State, and War: Gendered Perspectives on National Security," in her *Gender in International Relations: Feminist Perspectives on Achieving Global Security* (New York: Columbia University Press, 1992).

20. B. Carroll, "Peace Research: The Cult of Power," *Journal of Conflict Resolution* 16, 4 (1972), pp. 604–607.

21. Ibid. See page 600, where she argues, "We need to consider very seriously the possibility that the radicals are right: that peace—even negative peace—is ultimately not possible in the prevailing nation-state system of international relations and that a commitment to peace requires a commitment to revolutionary social change. We must consider seriously the possibility that war is inherent not in human nature, but in the power system of dominance in human relations which Galtung calls the feudal system, Kate Millett calls 'sexual politics,' Marxist radicals call 'corporate capitalism' and peace researchers sometimes call 'the threat system.'"

22. R. Walker, *One World/Many Worlds: Struggles for a Just World Peace* (Boulder, CO: Lynne Rienner, 1988).

10

"Masculinity," "Femininity," and "International Relations": Or Who Goes to the "Moon" with Bonaparte and the Adder?

Christine Sylvester

I

Can there be "masculinity," "femininity," and "international relations?" Are they possible—separately and conjoined?

No, of course not. Fluff they are:

One reason the rhetoric of hegemonic versions of masculinity is so compelling is that it rests on an apparent certainty that "a man is a man" everywhere, and everywhere this means the same thing. . . . [And yet] notions of maleness, designations of manhood, and attributions of masculinity have no essential referent, nor even a finite range of referents.[1]

As feminists have revealed in the last decade, every public power arrangement has depended on the control of femininity as an idea.[2]

Professionalized IR discourse, whether as abstract strategic doctrine advertising itself as realism brought up to date, or as most alternatives that would take us "beyond realism," is one of the most dubious of many dubious sciences.[3]

So there is no gender *in* or *and* international relations?

Of course there is.

States chockablock full of men. Wars and barrels of men's guns. Historically, always men secretaries-general of the UN have all the "good offices." Diplomacy is "the mediation of men estranged from an infinite yet abstracted power which they themselves have constructed."[4] Columbus sails the ocean blue and Colombia sends men into beyond international spaces. The National Gallery of Australia pays $1.3 million to hang an American man—Jackson Pollock—on its walls, and three-piece-suited Japanese bankers pay to gain the European aesthetic of Vincent Van Gogh. It's the post–Cold War. And strategic and defense studies centers persevere.

Meanwhile, carriers of, assignees to, the feminine are relied upon. They have the backlot assignments. They curate (sometimes). They type (always). They tie the shoelaces and stir the stews. They carry the wood and the water and the weapons to guerrillas in the bush ("The boys only gave us orders," say a group of women ex-combatants in Zimbabwe's independence war). Hedley Bull, neorealist guerrilla of professional IR, calls our attention to nuns in international relations by saying of his science-minded IR colleagues: "They are committing themselves to a course that keeps them . . . as remote from the substance of politics as inmates of a Victorian nunnery were from the study of sex."[5] Right. American nuns are shot dead by "freedom fighters" in Central America, after being raped. The remote ones are fit for insults. Stage center, men joyfully reenact the allied landing at Normandy in World War II, parachuting again in their dusty, too-small uniforms. Recreation mania: The Gettysburg battle is rehearsed every July, regular as jockey shorts; and of course, men go to the moon and then pat themselves on the back twenty-five years later for being clever enough to go to the moon.

What if it's true, as Cynthia Enloe argues, that "we can make sense of men's gendered reactions only if we take women's experiences seriously?"[6]

"I came home from school one day—I must have been about fourteen—so excited about the news that the Americans had landed on the moon that I blurted it out to my grandmother in Shona. Her response was swift. She grabbed me by the ear and started to beat me until I retracted my words. I had used a language permitted only in women's spaces; the phrase *kuenda kumwedzi* (to go to the moon) is used to talk about menstruation. Later, as I sat, still sobbing, she turned on the radio and heard the news. She turned to me and said: 'I hear that Americans have gone to the moon. If they are men, how could they? And if they *have* gone to the moon—so what? Women have gone to the moon every month—so it is nothing new.' "[7]

II

Reality, it seems, is not what it used to be in International Relations.[8]

(AND SONS): . . . To paraphrase R.E.M. . . .
FATHERS: What?
(AND SONS): My point precisely. Michael Stipe of R.E.M. sings that it is the end
of the world—*as we know it.*[9]

III

The intricacies. The delicacies. The identities given and transgressed. An international relations field weeded over and overweening.

Hold your hand under your chin and stare out glinty-eyed. Then set it straight. Straighten it out. Show them the way.

Oh dear, but it comes on again, this urge to deny IR and simply go mooning . . .

A is for Adder
by FRS
The adder's
a smooth fella, heavy
at the tail-end, bright
canary'd black. Folie de jeunesse, God
when younger
threw him down among the clay.
And now
waistcoated as a pansy, rare,
he boogies there; again and again attempts
the cursive codes that rattle
the ground elder stalks, whisper
what he knows and cannot know . . . [10]

IV

IR is serious. Gender is ponderous stuff. MASCULINITY is surely as heroic as fem~in~in~ity is sweet-scented and frivolous—the stuff of a warm spring afternoon of punting, clothes all semidrenched, the lady reclining, the gentleman manning the ship of Oxford's little byways. "Waistcoated."

V

No worries, mate. No problems.

VI

It is no longer productive, say some, to tie the feminist ship to the lodestar of gender (just to the right of the moon). We can still ask "how we think, or do not think, or avoid thinking about gender,"[11] which has always been my favorite definition of the enterprise named "feminist theory." But now, rather than outline the dimensions of masculinity and femininity in a pre-given international relations, or any other field, one steps back to notice the inlines of that which is spoken of as gender or as the field, as one might notice the inlines of homelessness in our discourses about policy "problems" facing contemporary societies: "Homelessness is ... circumscribed by and takes its form from being a shelter problem, an income problem, a deinsti-tutionalization problem, a welfare problem, a race problem and the like."[12]

Gender takes its form from being "no problems, mate"—a class, race, homeless problem—every problem except gender. One notices gender inlines when tracing feminist aesthetics. The art of the sexed body and the gendered individual was always too cozily fleshed in feminist and com-monsense understandings. For some, there must be wrentings because the way folks talk about biology, the way we link it to social expectations about appearance and behavior, gives outline to sex as the material reality that births gender. We see that women can have babies. We see women in the kitchens. There is an inevitability to it all.

Nature, you know. Anatomy.

But mightn't male bodies now carry fetuses and deliver through cesarean sections? And for as long as one can remember, has not the female "sex" materialized within Shona-speaking culture, been the one going to the moon—not the "sex" we associate with a particular historical feat? And then there are those nuns in IR, the ones cross-dressed as scientists, the ones Bull bellowed about. With their help, can we conduct a telephone or per-son-to-person survey and note the "sex" of the respondent by the sound of the voice on the box, by the anatomical appearance at the stoop?

No. *"Folie de jeunesse."*

Is there no natural or even necessarily commonsensical link between "male" and "masculinity" and "female" and "femininity?" Is there just nothing there to outline?

We may speak of these linkages. Indeed, gender maps onto bodies and sometimes takes them over, albeit "if gender is constructed, it is not neces-sarily constructed by an 'I' or a 'we.'"[13] But is it fixed there as timeless, uni-versal, and stable? What in the world would "sex" tell us about the sup-posed "gender" of our survey respondent? And what would the survey tell us about our cultural obsessions with getting sex and gender right—in research and in daily life? Where do "we" simply choose to ignore or deny what Judith Butler calls "manipulable artifices" in our quest to control for the right variable, the variable that outlines men and women?

It seems we are having difficulty finding outlineable whole persons. "Sex" and "gender" seem real, are made to feel real, and can really matter in one's life. But are they materialized or phantasmic subject statuses? Are they assignments, stories, narratives, memories, notes on the power of discourse, residual effects of listening? Bumper stickers? While proclaiming and differentiating, gender announcements coherently admonish us to "dress for success" (even though we are women). They advertise us: "Women Are Born Leaders. You're Following One Now." They get us off the hook: "Boys will be boys"; "Women For Peace." And they admonish others: "Pass the ERA." The combinations, though, are really the most interesting: Those who dress for success and think the ERA is a good idea go drinking with the boys-will-be-boys and happen to be women who may not really exist. Where is the masculine vis-à-vis the feminine in mobile and interparticulated identities?

Butler asks us to consider the performativity of "sex" and "gender." She says that "the materiality of sex is constructed through a ritualized repetition of norms."[14] Sex is a regulatory ideal. It materially makes the bodies that it governs. It is reiterative and citational and, in those senses, sex "performs." Andy Warhol, for example, performs Marilyn Monroe, and the sex is blondied, bossomed, langorous. The body is built, and the bodies of observers materialize as wannabes, as refusals, as queens, as camp, as abject "plain women." The girling of girls. It only seems to be theatrical. But there are other performances about. Orlando performs as man and then as woman. We dollie up and are women. We butch and become men. We try to paint a portrait of Margaret Thatcher and end up with Man with Beehive Hairdo. Queer that there's a better woman in *Crying Game* than I'll ever be.

Burn, Paris, burn—if you're able, if you're not weighed down by the man in the moon yelling, "Git home, girl!" or "Pansy!" If you haven't just been raped in the anatomy by someone performing material sex for real—not seeing the discursive limits, you see. (The Butler but: "Why is it that what is constructed is understood as an artificial and dispensable character?"[15])

Gender is performance too.

We already knew that.

We knew that "gender performativity cannot be theorized apart from the forcible and reiterative practice of regulatory sexual regimes."[16] But did we know that the very limits of socially constructed gender performances lie "at those boundaries of bodily life where abjected or delegitimated bodies fail to count as 'bodies'"?[17]

Absolutely right, say some of the feminisms of IR, the ones that like to inline rather than outline "femininity," "masculinity," and "gender" as against "international relations." Gender may be a big, fat, bogus adder. But the academic field of IR, the field that outlines international relations, performs bodies that it takes as already produced (statesmen), already fully embodied (soldiers). It is puppeteer—again and again rattling from behind the screen what the God elders used to be, again and again ignoring the rare pansies stalking the end of that world. Again and again it produces legitimate and abjected bodies through narratives of who may or may not belong, act, trade, negotiate, war, peace, aid, nurse, feed, terrorize, go to the moon. It is ventriloquist. It "whispers what he knows." Does it also whisper what he "cannot know"? That is the question in the mouth of feminist IR. For the inliners do not hold the fort. The outliners do. Or is it that we share an adder's gender trouble?

The Cursive Codes That Rattle

The Vietnam War and its veterans became the springboard for a general remasculinization of American culture that is evidenced in the popularity of figures like Ronald Reagan, Oliver North, and J.R. Ewing, men who . . . favor images of strength and firmness with an independence that smacks of Rambo and confirms their faith in a separate culture based on a mythos of masculinity.[18]

IR already knew this.

IR has been in the business of masculinizing and remasculinizing certain relations for seventy-five or so years. Or so say the feminists. We talk a lot about IR's now strutting, now limpid, but always stalking, masculinity. Open up a feminist IR book. It's there.

A woman who presumes to theorize about militarism is frequently dismissed, as if she had wandered uninvited into the men's locker room.[19]

The public student of history and politics, inhabiting the sphere of official public/academic discourse, being taught the ways of the political world as the "realists" (Machiavelli, Hobbes, Bismarck, Clausewitz) understood it, and the private dreamer, mother, novel reader, and Beatles buff parted company.[20]

International politics has always been a gendered activity in the modern state system. Since foreign and military policy-making has been largely conducted by men, the discipline that analyzes these activities is bound to be primarily about men and masculinity.[21]

Across three debates in the field, there is a recurring sense that "men" have coherent homes in IR and "women" are suited for other places from which they may venture forth to visit international relations, only in order to provide support services for "men's" politics.[22]

But what are "we" saying, precisely?

Are we arguing that it is important to outline men and women and their places in IR, the way Eduard Manet outlined some painted people in black, making the bodies, impossibly, conform to boundaries affixed to a canvas by boundary-smearing oils? Are we?

Yes, yes, answer some—with or without qualification.

Cynthia Enloe says yes unequivocally. Look, she says, we have to see women in international relations because international relations and the field of IR rely on women's ways of upholding and maintaining the global order in their capacities as sex workers, soldiers, mothers, yellow-ribbon tie-on-ers, patriots, and a whole host of other always uncited actions. If anything, she insists, IR has underestimated the amount of power it takes to make a world spin.[23] It has underestimated the gendered homebases so crucial to the waging of war and postwar, the making of international trade, the making of the European Community. She says straight out, no mucking around, that "it has taken power to deprive women of land titles and leave them little choice but to sexually service soldiers and banana workers. It has taken power to keep women out of their countries' diplomatic corps and out of the upper reaches of the World Bank."[24] She says, straight edge: "To operate in the international arena, governments seek other governments' recognition of their sovereignty; but they also depend on ideas about masculinized dignity and feminized sacrifice to sustain that sense of autonomous nationhood."[25]

Touché gender.

Others equivocate a bit but ultimately want to show us the men and women in international relations, femininity and masculinity, and where the world should go topsy with gender. Ann Tickner begins:

As a scholar and teacher of international relations, I have frequently asked myself the following questions: Why are there so few women in my discipline? If I teach the field as it is conventionally defined, why are there so few readings by women to assign to my students? Why is the subject matter of my discipline so distant from women's lived experiences?[26]

Clearly, women exist and they are collectively everywhere getting a raw deal, in no small part because "masculinity and politics have a long and close association."[27] Sharing a thought presented as universal to all feminists, Tickner posits "gender equality as a social goal."[28] To gain "equality" one must outline the aspirants for it and the philosophies they wish to make equal. And she does that. She also alludes to inliner feminists, obliquely, as people "who argue that a unified representation of women across class, racial, and cultural lines is an impossibility."[29] (Ahem. They also query "women," "sex," and "gender"). The outlines of women and men, masculinity and femininity, rarely snuff out.

In outliner analysis, one gets the Frederic Jamesonian sense that "anxieties about privacy seem to have diminished, in a situation in which its tendential erosion or even abolition has come to stand for nothing less than the end of civil society itself."[30] *As we know it*, that is. The end of masculinized civil society as we know it with its citizensandstates all wrapped up with being something called men.[31] The fictionalization of civil society at the end:

> I knew about Egypt because Bonaparte had been there. His Egyptian campaign, doomed but brave, where he had remained immune from the plague and the fever and ridden miles in the dust without a drop of water.
> "How could it be," the priest had said, "if he isn't protected by God?"[32]

God protects Napoleon. Women protect the privates. Men protect women. But women are ravaged as a war-fighting strategy in the Bosnian War tragedy of privacy diminished, eroded, abolished, politicized. The sturdy truss is breached. The protections of gender place come rotted. One small step for man. One giant step for mankind to moonshine on what used to be thought of as private spots, because privacy has less meaning in a postmodern world.

Jameson goes on: "It is as though we were training ourselves, in advance, for the stereotypical dystopian rigors of overpopulation in a world in which no one has a room of her own any more, or secrets anybody else cares about in the first place."[33] Or cares to respect. That's the point. The mooning fades. The secrets are out. The personal is political. The international is personal. The personal is international.[34] The political is personal. The woman is in the moon and the moon is in the man and Ichabod Crane rides tonight.

Some women are thus both "out" and "in" international relations. Yes, but does anyone care about the secrets or are "we" one group among many in a world overpopulated by rooms of no one's own? Do we actually need to draw the outlines hard to see in roomless places that still seem to be our abjected fate?

No, no, some others say. We are not doing the dastardly binary thing of snapshooting women with a wide-angle lens that picks up inherited gender, men, and masculinity. Gender is that construction, remember. It's a hegemonic discourse. We can change constructed discourses, dismantle hierarchies, reveal roving identities that resist colonization, if we make the texts and discourses, promises and punishments, lies and lines and lives, of gender more visible. If we can see that mothers and soldiers are pieces of rather than antipodes within constructed narratives of valiant care.[35] If we see that the "U.S.-Mexican border *es una herida abierta* where the Third World grates against the first and bleeds. And before a scab forms it hemorrhages again, the lifeblood of two worlds merging to form a third country—a border culture."[36] If we can see that "Nehanda carries her bag of words in a pouch that lies tied around her waist. She wears some along her arms. Words and bones ... She travels to the faraway place where her body turns to smoke."[37] At such places "we" can't go home again. There we must squint to find "women" in and around beef, the dog, mothers of courage (and her queens), cricket bats, spaceships, Rambos and Bonapartes and Prince.

• • •

"If only I knew how," he said. "We could have saved ourselves the digging."[38]

Yes, and boogied around.

• • •

I plunge in.

How 'bout them security discourses, eh? Women all homesided and men all sweatily protective in the international. Dilemmas to the left of us, to the right of us. Missiles at the ready. Man the mooncraft and flash one.

Look! Girlies over there . . .

Greenham Women. Gender all sloshed into the wrong places, so that gender (barely) counts as it should even though it seems to be counting for everything. Upsidaisy. Who got homesided with cruise missiles at Greenham and who got all sweatily protective of insecurity in order to gain a little sleep-eye in one's life? Who dilemmaed security dilemmas by letting women in here—the more women the less security in militarized masculinity? (God, why can't we militarize them too?) Who showed that the more one prepares for nuclear war the less secure the preparers are from infidels at their gates? Who had the words and who had the bones? "Protean tricksters,"[39] those Greenham women. Coyotes baying in the night.

"EVACUATE THEM."

("Bonaparte's own storeroom," said the cook. The space from the ground to the dome of the canvas was racked with rough wooden cages about a foot square with tiny corridors running in between, hardly the width of a man. In each cage there were two or three birds, beaks and claws cut off, staring through the slats with dumb identical eyes. I am no coward and I've seen plenty of convenient mutilation on our farms but I was not prepared for the silence. Not even a rustle. They could have been dead, should have been dead, but for the eyes. The cook turned to go. "Your job is to clear them out and wring their necks."[40])

"Yes, well. Yes Sir!" (Yes, after tea I'll get right down to it, Sir. All those nice tea sets on the fences now, you know, and me and the boys of Charlie could just, you know, edge over there. Just tip the itsy little divide. Have a chat with the, you know, ladies, a little cake maybe . . .)

"NO WORRIES," SIR. (I'm a smooth fellow.)

"The Ground Elder Stalks"

Ah, but you're still talking about women, maid, as though there could be some kind of odd femininity and some predictable masculinity and some place of international relations already understood—and some place where each of these conjoins.

Am I? Or is this a partial eclipse of gender, this "women" at Greenham—place forbidden, where the line of privacy, of "women's" autonomy from IR (despite heteronomy with international relations) is violated, where chimeric security is unraveled, where hierarchy is cratered.

DO NOT STEP TOO CLOSE. MIND THE BEAKS!

"Canary'd black" they be.

VII

Let's take it further. Let's stand in-line and look for out-lines. What happens when we get to Jack Kennedy's masculine White House? What happens in general to maids knitted into the realm of the abject within the realm of high political power? What happens in "those 'unliveable,' 'uninhabitable' zones of social life which are nevertheless densely populated by those who do not enjoy the status of the subject?"[41] Places where handmade handmaids serve subjects in ways we fail to notice. As if there were secrets. Are they really there? That is . . . you see I can't see. Who?

I'm talking about the usual "women" in the corridors of "men's" power. The backlot types scurrying around the West and East Wings, the ones, noted in Richard Reeves's recent biography of Kennedy, like Kennedy's secretary, Evelyn Lincoln, who "walked in and whispered to him."[42]

Ostensibly, they have no discursive codes in IR—neither of gender nor of anything else. But of course their gender is there, abjected, all the time.

> The roulette table. The gaming table. The fortune tellers. The fabulous three-breasted woman. The singing ape. The double-speed dominoes and the tarot. She was not there. She was nowhere.[43]

They have power to circumscribe the domain of the subjects they serve through their whispers and their reservoirs of unconditional loyalty. They are privy to reports, meetings, minutes, and the occasional hatbox:

> Of Mrs. Lincoln, his secretary, the President said that if he called to inform her that he had just cut off Jackie's head and wanted to get rid of it, the devoted secretary would appear immediately with a hatbox of appropriate size.[44]

Workaday outsiders are in foreign policy offices with their "sex" but are constituted by insiders as phantoms with hatboxes. Are they "women"? Always?

Arthur Schlesinger had sat in a corner throughout the meeting, too junior to vote on small surrogate wars. To many of the others, his professor's status was measured by the fact that his office was in the East Wing of the White House. "With the women," Rusk noted.[45]

Abject ones in the service of Men. They are "thrown down among the clay" with the adders. That's why we never read a re-creation of the Cuban missile crisis from the situated standpoint of John McCone's wife. She experienced, and perhaps even influenced, the course of Cuban missile crisis events when her new CIA-heading husband bombarded the president with the famous honeymoon cables from their marriage suite in France. Who? Schlesinger, by contrast, lives on in our memories, purged soon enough of East Wingedness.

So you see. Toujours Masculinity.

How thorough, though, is the removal of "women" from and the instantiation of "men" in the halls of power? That is the point. Try hard and there are still textual weaknesses about cool Jack's White House. There are women everywhere. There are numerous moments when the slop of "women" is not fully washed out of Reeves's hard-on text ("He was showing Stevenson the aerial photographs when his wife walked into the sitting room. Jacqueline Kennedy liked Stevenson as much as her husband disliked him, so there was some cheek-kissing before she left"[46]). Moments when the whispers under moonlight refuse the smudged oils of gender that hand-in-hand IR.

After it was over, Kennedy called Tiffany's, the New York jeweler. . . . Silver it was for Kennedy's men, and for two women, Jacqueline Kennedy and Evelyn Lincoln.[47]

Wait a minute.

The Executive Committee of men. The Cuban missile crisis. Of men. Against other men. The tales of rehabilitated "feminized men." The hints of power "women." The awards and rewards. Maybe there would have been an invasion of Cuba had "women" been at the helm. Maybe there would not have been a "crisis" dancing in anyone's eyes. Maybe one verse of "Moon River," sung liltingly, could have swayed those "heavy at the tail-end." Maybe there is no difference in "women's" perceptions from those officially recorded by the "men." Maybe such buried "women" have long ago disidentified with women.

You see, some citations are missing. And in their absence we can dream of many moons over Cape Cod Bay. We feminists can dream of identity places reinstated not as "femininity," not as "masculinity," but as the boogying adder who rattles the ground that the moon stalks—now crescent, now full, now forgetting to come up this evening at all. Autonomous and relational without being assigned the dirty dishes after the others transcend. Freed of being "only" with the women. Skeptical of cool Jacks. Associating with those whose masculinity does not stand like a suit of armor:

> He's a curious man; a shrug of the shoulders and a wink and that's him. He's never thought it odd that his daughter cross-dresses for a living and sells second-hand purses on the side. But then, he's never thought it odd that his daughter was born with webbed feet. "There are stranger things," he said. And I suppose there are.[48]

And there's more.

We can study "strange" relations of webbed internationals yet to be sighted, sited, and cited. We can refuse purses of protection that falsely make us "immune from the plague and the fever" as though we only ever "sat in a corner throughout the meeting"—throughout the great meetings of IR.

VIII

So don't whisper to me of "masculinity," "femininity," and "international relations." They are far from rare. Get out. Go to the moon. And take that fella adder with you because if you don't, Bonaparte will ignore the whispers, since "his face is always pleading with us to prove him right."[49] Even though A is for Abracadabra.

Notes

I am grateful to the Department of International Relations at the Research School of Pacific and Asian Studies–Australian National University for the visiting fellowship under which I wrote this chapter. To some special people special thanks: Rob Walker, Kate Manzo, and David Campbell for a chilly Australian afternoon of moon talk; the very best muse, Fiona Sampson; and, not least of all, Roland Bleiker.

1. Andrea Cornwall and Nancy Lindisfarne, "Introduction," in Cornwall and Lindisfarne, eds., *Dislocating Masculinity: Comparative Ethnographies* (New York: Routledge, 1994), pp. 3, 10.

2. Cynthia Enloe, *The Morning After: Sexual Politics at the End of the Cold War* (Berkeley: University of California Press, 1993), pp. 173–174.

3. Jean Bethke Elshtain, *Women and War* (New York: Basic Books, 1987), p. 91.

4. James Der Derian, *On Diplomacy: A Genealogy of Western Estrangement* (Oxford: Oxford University Press, 1987), p. 199.

5. Hedley Bull, "International Theory: The Case for a Classical Approach," in Klaus Knorr and James N. Rosenau, eds., *Contending Approaches to International Politics* (Princeton: Princeton University Press, 1969), p. 26.

6. Enloe, *The Morning After*, p. 21.

7. Chinjerai Shire, "Men Don't Go to the Moon: Language, Space and Masculinities in Zimbabwe," in Cornwall and Lindisfarne, eds., *Dislocating Masculinity*, p. 158.

8. Jim George, *Discourses of Global Politics: A Critical (Re)Introduction to International Relations* (Boulder, CO: Lynne Rienner, 1994), p. 1.

9. James Der Derian, "Fathers (and Sons), Mother Courage (and Her Children), and the Dog, the Cave, and the Beef," in James Rosenau, ed., *Global Voices: Dialogues in International Relations* (Boulder, CO: Westview Press, 1993), p. 90.

10. Fiona Sampson, "A Is for Adder," in *Picasso's Men* (Newbury: Phoenix Press, 1993), p. 9.

11. Jane Flax, "Postmodernism and Gender Relations in Feminist Theory," *Signs* 12, 4 (1987), p. 622.

12. Fred Riggs, quoted by Emory Roe, "Against Power: For the Politics of Complexity," *Transitions* no. 62, p. 96.

13. Judith Butler, *Bodies That Matter: On the Discursive Limits of "Sex"* (New York: Routledge, 1993), p. 7.

14. Ibid., p. x.

15. Ibid., p. xi.

16. Ibid., p. 15.

17. Ibid.

18. Susan Jeffords, *The Remasculinization of America: Gender and the Vietnam War* (Bloomington: Indiana University Press, 1989), p. 169.

19. Enloe, *The Morning After*, p. 39.

20. Elshtain, *Women and War*, p. 31.

21. J. Ann Tickner, *Gender in International Relations: Feminist Perspectives on Achieving Global Security* (New York: Columbia University Press, 1992), p. 5.

22. Christine Sylvester, *Feminist Theory and International Relations in a Postmodern Era* (Cambridge: Cambridge University Press, 1994), p. 4.

23. Cynthia Enloe, *Bananas, Beaches and Bases: Making Feminist Sense of International Relations* (London: Pandora, 1989), p. 197.

24. Ibid., pp. 197–198.

25. Ibid., p. 197.

26. Tickner, *Gender in International Relations*, p. ix.

27. Ibid., p. 6.

28. Ibid., p. 8.

29. Ibid., p. 16.

30. Frederic Jameson, *The Geopolitical Aesthetic: Cinema and Space in the World System* (Bloomington: Indiana University Press, 1992), p. 11.

31. See Christine Sylvester, "Homeless in International Relations? 'Women's' Place in Canonical Texts and in Feminist Reimaginings," in Marjorie Ringrose and Adam Lerner, eds., *Reimagining the Nation* (London: Open University Press, 1993).

32. Jeanette Winterson, *The Passion* (London: Penguin Books, 1987), p. 18.

33. Jameson, *The Geopolitical Aesthetic*, p. 11.

34. See discussion in Enloe, *Bananas, Beaches and Bases*, especially chapter 9.

35. Elshtain, *Women and War*, pp. 221–225.

36. Gloria Anzaldúa, *Borderlands/La Frontera: The New Mestiza* (San Francisco: Aunt Lute Books, 1987), p. 3.

37. Yvonne Vera, *Nehanda* (Harare: Baobob Books, 1993), p. 2.

38. Winterson, *Passion*, p. 19 (totally out of context).

39. Donna Haraway, "The Biopolitics of Postmodern Bodies: Constitutions of Self in Immune System Discourse," in *Simians, Cyborgs, and Women: The Reinvention of Nature* (New York: Routledge), p. 208.

40. Winterson, *Passion*, pp. 5–6.

41. Butler, *Bodies That Matter*, p. 3.

42. Richard Reeves, *President Kennedy: Profile of Power* (New York: Simon and Schuster, 1993), p. 117.

43. Winterson, *Passion*, p. 60.

44. Reeves, *President Kennedy*, p. 104.

45. Ibid., p. 82.

46. Ibid., p. 375.

47. Ibid., p. 426.

48. Winterson, *Passion*, p. 61.

49. Ibid., p. 25.

Conclusion: New Thoughts and New Directions for the "Man" Question in International Relations

Jane Parpart

Uncle Sam, born in the war of 1812, is badly in need of a makeover to capture the mood of 1996. It is time to invent Auntie Sam. For the country is going through a period of feminisation. . . . One of the most basic distinctions in human experience—that between men and women—is in America getting blurrier and blurrier.[1]

There has been a loser in women's march to equality and that is the man in the blue-collar uniform. Many of the gains that the West has made through enhancing the economic position of women will be tarnished if the male labourer is pushed to the margins. Once known as the salt of the earth, at the moment his troubles are making countries lose their savour.[2] Saddam thumbs his nose; Barzani strolls to power.

Did Saddam Hussein care? He did not. This week his aircraft and air-defence men in both Iran's no-fly zones were busy provoking the United States to resume the missile attacks of a week before.[3]

Saddam Hussein is still thumbing his nose at the United States, and according to the *Economist*, the United States is going through a period of feminization. It seems Saddam still knows how to act like a "man," but the leaders of the U.S. superpower are caving in to feminine pressures and adopting feminine ways. Political leaders and Olympic athletes in the United States are crying in public, spilling out their private lives, and even dressing like women. Meanwhile, women celebrities are puffing on cigars, moving into the boardrooms, and generally threatening male privilege. Male bastions such as the Citadel Military Academy are being forced to open their doors to female recruits. In Europe and North America, women are moving into the new jobs of the knowledge economy while male blue-collar workers are refusing to do this "women's work" and becoming the new unemployed—footloose, angry, and increasingly a threat to society.

What are we to make of this? Are the only "real men" left living in the developing countries? Are North American and European men becoming feminized "sissies," forced to choose between adopting feminine traits or losing their jobs and becoming social pariahs? Are men really going to be tomorrow's second sex? Will they turn to violence rather than give up their patriarchal "birthrights"? Why does the *Economist* care given that it is a magazine aimed at the elite male-dominated world of international finance and politics, rarely concerned with the fate of blue-collar males? Why is the failure of working-class males to adapt to global restructuring being heralded as a threat to society (and male hegemony)? What do these articles tell us about the centrality of international politics, economics, and the military to the making and maintaining of male privilege?

These are serious questions—questions that bring us straight to the issues addressed in this book. They require new thinking about the social construction of gender in international relations and its role in defining and maintaining rights, responsibilities, and power (or lack of power) to those seen as male and/or female.[4] Yet international relations in both theory and practice, indeed the profession itself, has generally presented itself as an impartial enterprise devoted to the science of high politics among states— to making both wars and peace and to forging international agreements and resolving disagreements. The pillars of IR—realism and neorealism—and even the more recent third debate have been presented as ungendered analyses of "real life." Steeped in the gender assumptions of nineteenth- and twentieth-century Western cultures, the profession has regarded the public arena of international relations as quintessentially and "naturally" male. Women were supposed to reside in the private realm, where statesmen and warriors could seek temporary respite and comfort before returning once again to the "real world" of international politics and business.[5]

Now, however, we are being told that women are taking over. According to the *Economist*, "real men" are being voted out of office or driven from their jobs. Women are flooding into the previously male-dominated public realm, upsetting the gender order, threatening the family, and disrupting social harmony in the nation-state as well as in the international arena. The unspoken solution—that women should return to the hearth and home— lurks in the background. Politicians call for the return of family values with the mother as guardian of the home. The *Economist* points approvingly to the Japanese, who don't have these problems because their labor market favors male employees, and laments, "The *trouble* [my emphasis] is that the West is unlikely to copy such a system. . . . Women are not likely to stride back to the past," even if politicians and business leaders would like them to.[6]

But is the presence of women in the economic and political realms really the issue? Are they really taking over? Feminist analyses reveal a very different picture. Women are moving into the workplace and politics, but rarely in positions of power. And those who achieve higher positions often do so because they know how to act like men. Most women continue to operate on the margins and in the lower echelons of male-dominated institutions at both the national and the international levels.[7] Moreover, although there are undoubtedly more women in these arenas than in the past, they are hardly a new phenomenon. As Cynthia Enloe so persuasively argues, women have always played a crucial role in international politics. They have been the helpmates, the servants, the girl Fridays, and the comfort women who made male domination of the international arena possible. Wars could not have been fought, political and economic activity would have ground to a halt, without women's participation and support both at home and in the workplace.[8] Why, then, are women increasingly seen as threats to male hegemony and to masculinity itself when, in the past, this kind of female participation was accepted and even required? Why the hysterical backlash when objectively not that much has changed?

Clearly, Enloe's call for a feminist analysis of international politics must be heeded if we are to explain these contradictions. An impressive array of feminist scholars (largely women, but some men as well) in IR and related fields have searched for ways to explain gender hierarchies and assumptions in the theory and practice of international relations. Liberal feminists, finding few women in the field of IR or the business of running states and militaries, have searched for statistics and arguments to convince sympathetic male colleagues that women can and should play an important role in the male world of international relations.[9]

The limited success of this strategy has pushed some feminists toward new questions and answers. Radical feminists have emphasized the interconnection between private and public spheres in international politics and the need to connect the politics of daily life with larger political events and power structures. Standpoint theorists have drawn attention to the experiences and voices of women.[10] Scholars drawing on socialist feminist perspectives have placed women's subordination and male privilege in the context of international political economies, reminded us of the close connection between control over resources and gender subordination, and focused on the social construction of gender and its role in defining and maintaining gender roles and hierarchies.[11] Black and Third World feminists, as well as some postmodernist feminists, have warned against the tendency to conflate the concerns and experiences of Western women with women everywhere, calling instead for attention to difference as well as commonalities. Some have focused on the way dichotomous thinking has defined maleness in opposition to femaleness, thus (re)presenting male superiority as natural and inevitable.[12] Others, preoccupied with the postmodern attack on stable subjectivities, have sought to destabilize gender dichotomies and to think about how to construct a world where women and men can share power and "be many things at once."[13]

Although manhood and masculinities play a role in these analyses, they are rarely central. Indeed, too often men are characterized as an undifferentiated group with neither history nor divisions, uniformly committed to the subordination and exploitation of womankind. Yet as Cynthia Enloe points out in *Bananas, Beaches and Bases: Making Feminist Sense of International Relations*, "Understanding the international workings of masculinity is important to making feminist sense of international politics."[14] Without abandoning their commitment to feminist perspectives and gender equity, the authors in this collection have taken up Enloe's challenge and turned their gaze not just to men but to the construction of maleness and masculinities in the international arena. This has turned out to be a very interesting and productive undertaking, for as Charlotte Hooper pointed out in Chapter 2, "the very masculinism of international politics makes it a particularly fertile ground for the study of men and masculinities."

True to the feminist insight that the personal is political, the authors in this collection have sought to connect the high politics of international relations with the business of daily life. The military emerges as one of the primary sites for the social and cultural production of masculinities, with profound implications for gender roles and relations in communities, households, and bedrooms. As Craig Murphy illustrated in describing his childhood as a military brat in the U.S. Army, military notions of masculinity dominated his life at home and in the community. As a boy who would one day be a man-warrior, he was expected to carry out the masculine role of protector (over women, children, and the weak—i.e., not "real men") while his warrior-father went to battle. To question this role, to resist its prescriptions, was to challenge the core beliefs of one of the most powerful institutions defining manliness and manhood, and clearly to put one's own potential legitimacy as a man at risk as well. Indeed, there was little room for women or men in military families to challenge these gender assumptions and hierarchies. Carol Cohn highlighted the U.S. military's role as producer and guarantor of masculinity in U.S. society, particularly among young adult males. Challenging the "official" arguments against permitting openly homosexual males in the military, she pointed to the more crucial problem, namely that such acceptance would undermine the military's role as a place where male warriors and boys who would be warriors could explore the often quite homoerotic world of masculine identities, sexualities, and feelings without fear of losing their status as "real men."

International politics and the study of international relations intersect with the personal in important ways as well. The metaphors of high politics reverberate with images of hypermasculine men ready to "do battle with their enemies." As Ralph Pettman reminded us, the masculinized images of politics and sports set standards of behavior for "manliness" (and "womanliness")—with profound implications for gender relations at home and at work.[15] International politics presents a world where men "naturally" hold power and women are "naturally" subordinate. These metaphors and assumptions reinforce the association between manliness/maleness/masculinity and power at all levels of society and thus contribute to the ongoing struggle to maintain gender hierarchies. Indeed, as Steve Smith and Craig Murphy pointed out, challenging this assumption within the highly masculinized field of IR can attract the ire of more conservative colleagues and no doubt explains the reluctance of many sympathetic IR specialists to openly side with feminist critiques.

The assertion that international politics and relations is a "man's affair" of course presupposes a single, biologically based, and largely Anglo-American vision of masculinity.[16] Whereas most of the chapters in the book are situated within this cultural context, no single agreed standard of masculinity comes to the fore. Indeed, one is struck by the variety and richness of definitions of manhood and masculinity that emerge. Steve Niva described a series of shifts in the dominant/hegemonic conceptions of masculinity in the United States. The defeat in Vietnam undermined the long-held myth of the American frontiersman-warrior only to fuel a remasculinization of America in the Ramboized rhetoric of Reagan and Bush. Panama and the Gulf War thus played a central role in the reassertion and redefinition of American masculinity. To Cynthia Weber, the hypermasculine posturing during the Panama invasion signaled not strength but male hysteria over the loss of American hegemonic power. Perhaps these cracks in U.S. hegemony explain the shift to a new definition of (superior) manhood described by Niva. This new "tough but tender" version of hegemonic masculinity ridicules the "insensitive" hypermasculinity of Saddam Hussein and Manuel Noriega, celebrating instead the "new" American man who is morally responsive, sensitive to the needs of women and children, and yet able to kick butt when needed.

The possibility that there is one, biologically based, predictable set of characteristics that define a "real man" dissolves in this complexity. Male associations with power, especially over women, youth, and subordinate males, are widespread (both historically and in the present), but definitions of masculinity(ies) obviously vary over time and place.[17] The historical context, the economic, political, and cultural/social factors at play at any given time, clearly have profound implications for the way manhood and masculinities are understood and maintained. As Spike Peterson and Jacqui True reminded us, new times require new ways of thinking about gender relations and manhood/masculinity(ies). I would argue that "old times" require (re)analysis as well, for definitions of manhood and masculinity(ies) have surely varied in the past. Indeed, colonialism and imperialism profoundly shaped the emergence of a hegemonic version of Euramerican manhood, which benefited from being compared with colonial images of soft and effeminate or warriorlike but technically "backward" colonial males. This was not simply a one-way process, however, with Western definitions erasing precolonial traditions of masculinity and manliness. Rather, interactions and contestations over the nature of manliness and male power evolved over time and in various cultures, often becoming a point of contention in nationalist struggles and in efforts to free postcolonial states from Western hegemony.[18] Jongwoo Han and Lily Ling, for example, argue that in Korea, the male elite has countered "the West's feminization of Asia into denigrated Western womanhood" by emphasizing "the authoritarian leadership of the Confusian husband-patriarch [i.e., the Korean ruling elite] bolstered by a feminized society indoctrinated into subservient Confusion womanhood."[19] Thus gendered Confucian value systems have provided a means for legitimating male power and privilege and strengthening patriarchal authority. Much more needs to be known about these gendered contests over meaning and power, both internationally and across time and place, before we can generalize about the male experience.

Despite the admitted need for more comparative, historical research, some themes have surfaced in the book that may be relevant to broader considerations of masculinity, power, and international relations. All the chapters support Robert Connell's belief in a hierarchy of masculinities.[20] Whereas most people associated with masculinity (i.e., manliness and males) have some power over others, particularly women and children, not all versions of masculinity have equal power and legitimacy in society. Some men and their definitions of manliness and masculinity and gender relations have more power or hegemony than others. Hegemonic masculinity is generally defined and practiced by men (and some women) who occupy positions of power and influence in society. Not surprisingly, hegemonic males and their visions of masculinity predominate in the world of international affairs. As Cohn, Niva, and Murphy revealed, the military plays a crucial role in reinforcing this hegemonic vision in the United States. Jan Pettman and others suggest this is also true in many other societies.[21]

The international arena is also a place where competing hegemonic interpretations of male power and manliness struggle for predominance. As we have seen, the military confrontations in the Gulf and Panama were struggles over contending versions of masculinity as well as battles over land. As Luke Ashworth and Larry Swatuk pointed out, competition between realist and neorealist theories of international relations has often been couched in masculinist terms, each side arguing that they represent "real" masculine values and practices. Thus international politics, war, and peacemaking are particularly revealing sites for understanding the construction of and competition among different hegemonic masculinities.

However, the international political and military arena is also an important site of integration and mediation between hegemonic and subordinate masculinities. Whereas military and political institutions generally buttress and reflect the concerns of hegemonic masculinity in a given society, neither institution is entirely run by elite males. The U.S. military is particularly interesting in this regard. Although the officer corps is generally well educated, most military recruits in the United States have less than a high school education. The military is a place where subordinate males can be part of the hegemonic masculinist vision. In the barracks and on the battlefield, men from all levels of society work, play, and even die together. Although on some levels military hierarchies replicate the hierarchy of hegemonic and subordinate masculinities, at the same time, the military provides opportunities for collaboration, offering even the lowliest recruit the chance to be part of the hegemonic masculinist world. This may explain the military's obsession with male bonding, mentioned by Carol Cohn, and its fear of undermining its "hypermasculinist" image. The widespread enthusiasm for Bush's attack on Panama and the Gulf suggests a similar process whereby high politics becomes an arena where working-class men in the United States can feel part of the dominant discourse about what it means to be a man in a world power. This may explain why political leaders find war, and metaphors of war and the military, so useful for mobilizing public sympathy and support. Is this why Bush and Dole, the military heroes, thought they would have an easy time beating draft-dodger Bill Clinton? Perhaps the drama of imperial conquest played a similar role in Britain in the nineteenth and early twentieth centuries.[22] The current intensification of military power in Asia and Africa suggests this process may be at work around the globe. This is a subject that deserves much more attention.

The close association between men and power, in all its endless variations, may be discouraging for those who dream of a more egalitarian world, but the complex, interactive, and fluid nature of masculinity(ies) offers some hope to a number of the authors of this book. The contradictions and cracks in Craig Murphy's hypermasculine military childhood pushed him into a very different conception of manliness and manhood. They led him away from militarism toward the mediator's role and now to a belief in the need to understand (and change) the gendered character of international affairs. Ralph Pettman explored the possibility of a world where assertive "male" notions of competition are replaced by more positive collaboration. To achieve this, he argued, those groups (largely male) who are addicted to competition need to draw on the more collaborative ethos of many women (and some men). Rejecting the notion that men are inherently competitive and women are inherently collaborative, he believes new synthetic gendered visions are possible and, indeed, desirable. Christine Sylvester posited a similar possibility. The international arena, she argued, is already more complexly gendered than one might think, and we know too little about the actual influence of the many women inhabiting the "corridors of power." Meanwhile, she calls on feminists to dream of a world not where identity places are reinstated as "femininity" or "masculinity" but where those who are biologically female do not have to take on a "male" persona in order to participate in the game of international power. More to the point, perhaps we can dream of a world where international relations are constructed from more collaborative, inclusive practices than the masculinized metaphors of battle and power.

Even as we dream of this world, it is important to recognize the tenacity and power of gender dichotomies and their association with male power. Whereas manliness and masculinity(ies) have many variants and, as we have seen, competition between these variants can be brutal and intense, it is important to note how often contending versions of masculinity rely on the dichotomy between masculinity/manliness and femininity/femaleness to assert their superiority. Coding a particular form of masculinity as feminine or womanlike is still the best way to undermine its authority and power. Maintaining the "natural" association between manhood and power is, as Cynthia Enloe reminds us, a constant struggle. Above all it requires keeping women in their place. Although men may compete with each other and various masculinities may struggle for ascendancy, all men lose if the close association between maleness/masculinity (in any form) and power is broken. Even the "tough but tender" masculinity described by Niva leaves male power intact. Indeed, one could argue that it allows masculinity to absorb feminist challenges without questioning the association between manliness and power. The struggle to maintain this association in the international arena is only dimly understood. Much more comparative and historically informed research is needed. This book is simply a beginning.

There can be no doubt that the field of IR and its institutions, at the levels of both of practice and theory, have contributed to the naturalization of male predominance in matters of international politics, finance, and war. It should come as no surprise that the *Economist* is so worried about Auntie Sam and those women taking "male" jobs in the new global economy. For anything that undermines the "natural" association between masculinity/maleness and political and economic power is a threat to male preeminence in all arenas, including the international. Perhaps this is also why we need to find out more about the gendered character of international relations, in all its many variations, and why we hope this book will encourage much more broadly based, comparative, and historically informed investigations into male power, masculinity(ies), and international relations.

Notes

1. *Economist,* September 14–20, 1996, p. 32.
2. *Economist,* September 28–October 4, 1996, p. 26.
3. *Economist,* September 14–20, 1996, p. 42.

4. For more on the social construction of gender, see V. Spike Peterson, ed., *Gendered States: Feminist (Re)Visions of International Relations Theory* (Boulder, CO.: Lynne Rienner, 1992); Jeff Hearn, *Men in the Public Eye* (London: Routledge, 1992).

5. J. Ann Tickner, *Gender in International Relations: Feminist Perspectives on Achieving Global Security* (New York: Columbia University Press, 1992).

6. *Economist*, September 28–October 4, 1996, p. 26.

7. Marianne Marchand and Anne Sisson Runyan, eds., *Gender and Global Restructuring* (forthcoming); Lourdes Beneria and Shelley Feldman, eds., *Unequal Burden: Economic Crises, Persistent Poverty, and Women's Work* (Boulder, CO: Westview Press, 1992).

8. Cynthia Enloe, *Bananas, Beaches and Bases: Making Feminist Sense of International Politics* (Berkeley: University of California Press, 1989); Cynthia Enloe, *The Morning After: Sexual Politics at the End of the Cold War* (Berkeley: University of California Press, 1993).

9. Sandra Whitworth, *Feminism and International Relations: Towards a Political Economy of Gender in Interstate and Non-Governmental Institutions* (London: Macmillan, 1994), pp. 12–16; Mona Harrington, "What Exactly Is Wrong with the Liberal State as an Agent of Change?" in Peterson, *Gendered States*, pp. 93–114.

10. Marysia Zalewski, "Feminist Standpoint Theory Meets International Relations Theory," *Fletcher Forum* (Summer 1993), pp. 13–32; Christine Sylvester, *Feminist Theory and International Relations in a Postmodern Era* (Cambridge: Cambridge University Press, 1994), pp. 42–52; Nancy Hirschmann, *Rethinking Obligation: A Feminist Method for Political Theory* (Ithaca: Cornell University Press, 1992); Jean B. Elshtain, *Public Man, Private Woman: Woman in Social and Political Thought* (Princeton: Princeton University Press, 1981).

11. Nellie Wong, "Socialist Feminism: Our Bridge to Freedom," in Chandra Mohanty, Ann Russo, Lourdes Torres, eds., *Third World Women and the Politics of Feminism* (Bloomington: Indiana University Press, 1991), pp. 288–296; Beneria and Feldman, *Unequal Burden*.

12. Mohanty, Russo, and Torres, *Third World Women*; Sylvester, *Feminist Theory*, pp. 52–63.

13. Sylvester, *Feminist Theory*, p. 213. Sylvester adopts a combination of standpoint feminism and postmodernist feminism as the bases for her analysis.

14. Enloe, *Bananas, Beaches and Bases*, p. 200.

15. See John Nauright and Timothy J.L. Chandler, *Making Men: Rugby and Masculine Identity* (London: Frank Cass, 1996); and Michael Messner, "Men Studying Masculinity: Some Epistemological Issues in Sport Sociology," *Sociology of Sport Journal* 7 (1990), pp. 136–153.

16. J. Ann Tickner, "Hans Morgenthau's Principles of Political Realism: A Feminist Reformulation," and Sarah Brown, "Feminism, and International Relations of Gender Inequality," *Millennium* 17, 3 (1988), pp. 429–440, 461–475; Craig Murphy, "Seeing Women, Recognizing Gender, Recasting International Relations," *International Organizations* 50, 3 (Summer 1996), pp. 513–538.

17. See Hearn, *Men in the Public Eye*; Michael Roper and John Tosh, eds., *Manful Assertions: Masculinities in Britain Since 1800* (London: Routledge, 1991); Catherine Hall, *White, Male, and Middle Class: Explorations in Feminism and*

History (New York: Routledge, 1992); Robert Nye, *Masculinity and Male Codes of Honor in Modern France* (New York: Oxford University Press, 1993); R. W. Connell, "The Big Picture: Masculinities in Recent World History," *Theory and Society* 22 (1993), pp. 597–623.

18. Mrinalini Sinha, *Colonial Masculinity: The "Manly Englishman" and the "Effeminate Bengali" in the Late Nineteenth Century* (Manchester: Manchester University Press, 1995); Ashis Nandy, *The Intimate Enemy: Loss and Recovery of Self Under Colonialism* (Delhi: Oxford University Press, 1983); Andrea Cornwall and Nancy Lindisfarne, eds., *Dislocating Masculinity: Comparative Ethnographies* (London: Routledge, 1994).

19. Jongwoo Han and Lily Ling, "Masculine State, Feminine Society: A Feminist-Postcolonial Interpretation of East Asia's Capitalist Developmental State" (mimeo, 1995), p. 22.

20. Robert Connell, *Masculinities* (Berkeley: University of California Press, 1995); Andrea Cornwall and Nancy Lindisfarne, "Gender, Power and Anthropology," in Cornwall and Lindisfarne, *Dislocating Masculinity*.

21. Jan Jindy Pettman, *Worlding Women: A Feminist International Politics* (London: Routledge, 1996), pp. 87–106. See also Lily Ling, "Feminist IR: From Critique to Reconstruction," (mimeo, 1996); Enloe, *The Morning After* and *Bananas, Beaches and Bases;* and Jean Elshtain, *Women and War* (New York: Basic Books, 1987).

22. Sinha, *Colonial Masculinity;* Peter Murphy, ed., *Fictions of Masculinity: Crossing Cultures, Crossing Sexualities* (New York: New York University Press, 1994).

About the Editors
and Contributors

Lucian M. Ashworth is a lecturer in politics at the University of Limerick in the Republic of Ireland. His current research projects include a book on the British liberal tradition in IR and a coedited collection (with David Long) on David Mitrany's political economy.

Carol Cohn teaches in the Women's Studies Program and Sociology Department at Bowdoin College. Her research focuses on the ways in which gender as a symbolic system shapes national security debates and policies. Her publications include "Sex and Death in the Rational World of Defense Intellectuals" (*Signs* [Spring 1987]) and "Wars, Wimps and Women: Talking Gender and Thinking War" (in Miriam Cooke and Angela Woollacott, eds., *Gendering War Talk* [1993]).

Charlotte Hooper is completing her doctoral studies in international politics at the University of Bristol. As an associate lecturer at the University of the West of England and visiting lecturer at the University of Bristol, she has taught gender politics, gender and social policy, international relations, and international political economy. Her current research interests include gender and culture in the theory of international relations; her doctoral dissertation explores multiple masculinities and their relevance to global politics.

Craig N. Murphy is M. Margaret Ball Professor of international relations at Wellesley College. He works on international organizations, North-South relations, and international relations theory. His most recent publications include *International Organization and Industrial Change: Global Governance Since 1850* (1994) and "Seeing Women, Recognizing Gender, Recasting International Relations" (*International Organization* [1996]). Murphy coedits *Global Governance,* the journal of the Academic Council on the U.N. System and the U.N. University, and a Cambridge University Press series on international political economy.

Steve Niva is a doctoral candidate in political science at Columbia University. He is currently working on a dissertation that explores the social construction of state sovereignty in the Middle East.

Jane Parpart is professor of international development studies, history, and women's studies at Dalhousie University. She has published widely on issues of women, gender, and labor in Africa as well as on gender and development theory and practice. She is co-editor of *Patriarchy and Class: African Women in the Home and Workforce* (Westview Press, 1988), and with Marianne Marchand, of *Feminism/Postmodernism/Development* (1995).

V. Spike Peterson is an associate professor at the University of Arizona in the Department of Political Science and affiliated with women's studies, comparative cultural and literary studies, and international studies. She is editor of and contributor to *Gendered States: Feminist (Re)Visions of International Relations Theory* (1992) and, with Anne Sisson Runyon, coauthor of *Global Gender Issues* (1993). She has published widely on feminist IR theory and written analyses of states, political identities, and globalization. She is currently working on a book provisionally titled *Gender and Globalization: Beyond Sovereign States/Men*.

Ralph Pettman is a graduate of the University of Adelaide and the University of London. Pettman has taught and researched international relations theory and international political economy in Australia, the United States, and Japan. He has also worked outside academia, primarily as director of a national program on teaching for human rights in Australian primary and secondary schools. He currently holds the position of Founding Chair of International Relations at the Victoria University of Wellington.

Steve Smith is professor of international politics at the University of Wales, Aberystwyth. He has also taught at the University of East Anglia and the State University of New York. He has published mainly in the area of international relations theory, and his most recent books are (edited with Ken Booth and Marysia Zalewski) *International Theory: Postivism and Beyond* (1996) and (edited with Ken Booth) *International Relations Theory Today* (1995). He is editor of the Cambridge University Press series Studies in International Relations.

Larry A. Swatuk is lecturer in the department of political and administrative studies, University of Botswana, and research associate, Centre for International and Security Studies, York University, Toronto, Canada. His publications include *Between Choice in a Hard Place: Contending Theories of International Relations* (1991). His latest book is a coedited collection (with David Black) of essays entitled *Bridging the Rift: The New South Africa in Africa* (1997).

Christine Sylvester has recently moved from Northern Arizona University to the National Centre for Development Studies of the Research School of Pacific and Asian Studies, Australian National University. Her research on feminist international relations and the political economy of gender and development in Zimbabwe continues.

Jacqui True is a doctoral candidate in the Department of Political Science at York University, Toronto, Canada. She is also affiliated with the Centre for International and Security Studies there. Her most recent publication is a comprehensive review of feminist international relations in *Theories of International Relations* (1996). She is currently doing dissertation research on gender and political-economic transformations in post-Communist East-Central Europe.

Cynthia Weber is associate professor of political science at Purdue University. She is the author of *Simulating Sovereignty: Interventions, the State, and Symbolic Exchange* (1995) and the coeditor (with Thomas Biersteker) of *State Sovereignty as Social Construct* (1996). Currently she is completing a book-length feminist analysis of U.S. hegemony. Her chapter in this volume will be a chapter in that work.

Marysia Zalewski is lecturer of international politics at the University of Wales, Aberystwyth. She is coeditor (with Ken Booth and Steve Smith) of *International Theory: Positivism and Beyond* (1996). Her work on international relations and feminist theory has appeared in several journals, including *Millennium*, *International Affairs*, and the *Fletcher Forum*.

Index